Still on all fours, I went up the bunker steps and stuck my head out to look around. I'll never forget my first impression of what had previously been one of the showplace camps in Vietnam. The entire American hill appeared to be engulfed in flame. The rock building that had been our mess hall and club was completely destroyed, and a fire raged in the ruins. Mortar rounds and grenades were exploding all over the hill, and tracers laced through the air.

I saw a crouched figure move through the smoke toward the entrance to the TOC. I thought it was one of our troops from the security platoon and yelled at him to get under cover before he got himself killed. "Hey! Over here!"

The still-crouching figure heard me and made an odd sort of grunt, which sounded rather like a startled pig. As he turned to face me, I saw the unmistakable outline of an AK-47 silhouetted for just an instant against the fiery background. . . .

By Leigh Wade
Published by Ivy Books:

TAN PHU: Special Forces Team A-23 in Combat
THE PROTECTED WILL NEVER KNOW
ASSAULT ON DAK PEK: A Special Forces A-Team in
    Combat, 1970

ASSAULT ON DAK PEK

A Special Forces A-Team in Combat, 1970

Leigh Wade

IVY BOOKS • NEW YORK

An Ivy Book
Published by The Ballantine Publishing Group
Copyright © 1998 by Leigh Wade

http://www.randomhouse.com

Library of Congress Catalog Card Number: 98-92559

ISBN 0-8041-1836-1

Manufactured in the United States of America

First Edition: October 1998

10 9 8 7 6 5 4 3 2 1

This book is dedicated to
William E. Spencer
Killed in Action, RVN

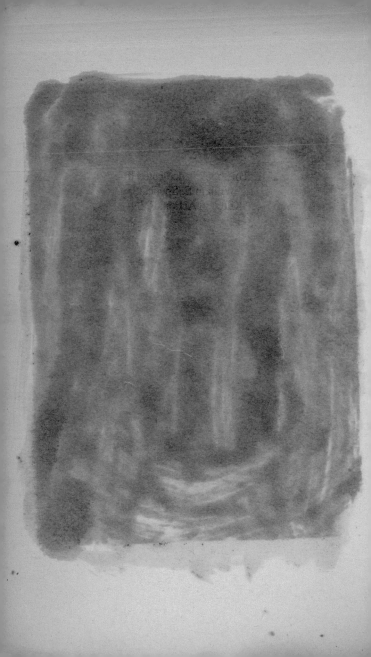

After the Second World War, France began fighting the Communists in Indochina. The French army had little support back home, and after the military disaster at Dien Bien Phu, the French conceded defeat and pulled back to their last colony, Algeria. In Algeria, history repeated itself, and the French army began fighting another no-win war with little support from the civilians back in Mother France. An abortive coup, led by various commanders of French parachute units, was put down. At his trial for treason, Major Saint Marc, former commander of the 1st Battalion, Parachute, French Foreign Legion, said this:

> We were given a simple mission: Defeat the adversary and get into motion some form of political equality. We put into this task all our faith, all our enthusiasm, all our youth. All we encountered in return was indifference, the incomprehension of many, the insults of others. Many of us lost our lives. And then one day . . . they told us we should start thinking about leaving . . . we wept.

II Corps Tactical Zone, 1964–1971

U.S. Army Special Forces Camps in II CTZ, Vietnam, 1964–1971

1-An Khe (An Tuc)
2-An Lac
3-Ban Me Thuot
4-Ben Het
5-Bong Son
6-Bu Prang
7-Buon Blech
8-Buon Ea Yang
9-Buon Brieng
10-Cung Son
11-Dak Pek
12-Dak Saeng
13-Dak Sut
14-Dak To
15-Dong Ba Thin
16-Dong Tre
17-Duc Co
18-Duc Lap
19-Ha Tay

20-Kannack
21-Kontum
22-Lac Thien
23-Mai Linh
24-Mang Buk
25-Nha Trang
26-Nhon Co
27-Phey Srunh
28-Phu Tuc
29-Plei Djereng
30-Plei Do Lim
31-Plei Me
32-Plei Mrong
33-Pleiku
34-Polei Kleng
35-Tieu Atar
36-Trang Phuc (Ban Don)
37-Vinh Thanh

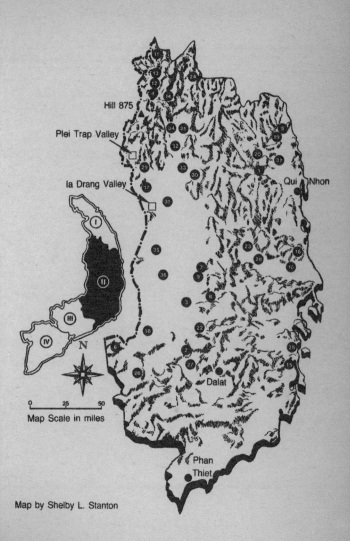

Hill 875

Plei Trap Valley

Ia Drang Valley

Qui Nhon

Dalat

Phan Thiet

N

0   25   50
Map Scale in miles

Map by Shelby L. Stanton

Chapter 1

Fort Bragg hadn't changed much while I'd been gone. It was March of 1967 and actually already spring in North Carolina, but I'd spent three years in the tropics of Southeast Asia, and the season felt more like winter to me. I was driving a new 427 Corvette that I'd purchased for myself while on furlough in Tucson. The damned thing didn't get very good gas mileage, but it sure would go fast. I'd driven from Arizona to North Carolina with only one short stop to sleep, and made pretty good time.

I had assignment orders for one of the newly activated Special Forces Groups, the Sixth, and signed in to Company B that evening after the troops had been released for the day. After drawing my bedding from the supply room, I found my barracks and bunk, stuffed my duffel bag and B4 bag in the wall lockers, then went looking for a telephone.

I'd heard that my old buddy Bill Martin was back at Bragg, and that he was newly married and living off post somewhere. "Hey, you old sumbitch, come on over right now," Bill told me as soon as I got in touch with him. "Want to show you my new house and introduce you to my wife. I have a new daughter too!" So I jumped back in my car and drove over to Spring Lake to see him.

I suppose I should have known better.

Once at his house, we had a few drinks. We told each other all our new war stories. Four years earlier Bill and I had been on an A-team together in Vietnam at a place called Tan Phu. When we got back to Bragg, I'd transferred to the 1st Group on Okinawa and Bill had stayed with the 5th. He'd rotated to Vietnam with the unit, and was assigned to another A-team camp.

Bill told me that one night they'd been overrun, and the American team had activated their escape and evasion plan. Bill ripped half his clothes off going out through their wire, and spent the next couple of days and nights hiding out from the enemy with his bare ass sticking out of torn jungle fatigues.

We were both on a cognac kick in those days, and Bill opened a brand-new bottle. We had a few more drinks to celebrate our mutual survival to date.

Bill's new wife was nice, and the baby didn't cry much. Bill was a cadre in Training Group, he told me. He was on the combat-swimmer committee and had a pretty flexible schedule.

We had a few more drinks.

I looked at my watch and saw that it was already ten o'clock. "Maybe I'd better be getting back to the barracks," I said. "I don't want to start off in my new unit with a DWI."

"Hey, don't be running off," Bill said. "I got a spare bed. We got a lot of catching up to do." I agreed, and we had a few more drinks.

At two A.M. we decided we should probably call it a night. His wife had disappeared several hours earlier, and the bottle of cognac was empty anyway. I asked Bill if he had an alarm clock he could loan me, as I needed to get back to the company area in time to get my uniform on. "Don't worry," he said, "I have to get up tomorrow and go in early too. I'll wake you up in plenty of time. I got the alarm set for 0430."

When I opened my tired, red eyes the next morning, the sun was shining through the window and birds were chirping outside. With a wave of panic I looked at my watch. I had twenty minutes to make it back to the company area before the morning formation.

"Bill, get up, we're late!" I yelled at him through his bedroom door.

"Oh God," I heard him mumble, "we did it again, didn't we?"

If it hadn't been for the heavy morning traffic, I still might have made it in time. Roaring into the company parking lot and leaping from the car, I ran toward the barracks. The brandy hangover caused my head to throb at each footfall. I needed a haircut, was unshaven, still wearing the civilian clothes I'd had on since leaving Tucson several days earlier, and in general looked and felt like hell. The troops were already in formation, and I had to walk around them to get to the barracks. I heard several snickers.

The company sergeant major was holding the formation, and he turned to me with a disgusted look as I went slinking past. "You don't happen to be our new man, Staff Sergeant Wade, do you?"

I had to admit that it was, in fact, I.

"About one fucking minute later and you would have been officially reported AWOL. Get in your uniform—if you have one, that is," he added sarcastically. "Get your nasty ass cleaned up, and report to me in my office as soon as formation is over with!"

That's how my tour with the 6th Group started. And it didn't get much better.

The Army was sort of schizo back in the 1960s. On one hand, we had a light infantry war raging over in Asia. On the other hand, we had a major presence in Europe that was preparing to fight a tank war which would utilize heavy, armored infantry. And finally we had the spit-and-polish army back in the good old U.S. which still acted like none of that was going on, and which spent most of its time performing all those beloved, peacetime, garrison-type duties such as police calls, polishing brass, whitewashing rocks, and all of that crap.

There were three groups of men in the Army back then. You had the guys who tried to stay in Europe as much as possible, those who preferred being stationed in Asia, and those who just wanted to stay home in America.

Once the war got going good in Vietnam, it became apparent to me that there were two other divisions. In one group were the guys who understood that combat was what being in the military was really all about, and who spent a lot of time in the war zone, no matter where it might be. And then there were the men who preferred that other Army, the phony one.

I was never too enthusiastic about the spit-and-polish, peacetime Army, even before the war started. Oh, I knew how to soldier, and could be a pretty sharp troop when I had to, but that stuff always seemed pretty absurd. Now, after having spent the better part of the last four years in Vietnam, I discovered that I was having a very difficult time fitting myself back into the routines of garrison duty.

In fact, I guess you could safely say that I really wasn't a very happy camper during those few months in 1967 I spent back in the U.S. Most of my old friends, such as Martin, were in other Groups, and I seldom saw them. Carl Hargus had recently returned to Bragg from Vietnam also, but was in the 7th Group. Carl told me he'd fallen in love while on furlough back home, and that he planned to get married soon.

It seemed like all my old drinking and carousing buddies were getting married. Even Gunboat Smith, the quintessential bachelor NCO, had come back to Bragg from a tour on Okinawa with a young, Okinawan wife—I emphasize the "young" part. A few days after Gunboat got back, the three of us decided to go to a local drive-in restaurant to get something to eat. We were in Gunboat's car, and he and I sat in front so we could talk. Mariko, his wife, sat in the back. After Gunboat and I had ordered, the carhop looked in the backseat. "And what will your little daughter have, sir?" she asked.

In those days, with the permission from his company commander, a single NCO could live off post in civilian quarters. You weren't authorized to draw extra money for quarters so the added expense came out of your own pocket. And unless you were married and "officially" living off post, you also had to maintain your bunk, and your foot and wall lockers, in the barracks because "officially" you still lived there. About a month after I joined 6th Group, I moved into a house off post with three other junior NCOs, and life got a little better, but not much.

The 6th Group's geographical area of responsibility in the sixties included the Near East, Pakistan, India, Afghanistan, and Nepal. Guys were studying languages like Arabic and Hindi-Urdu. I volunteered for as much field duty as I could get because while out in the woods, playing war, I felt like a real soldier again, and was also less likely to get into trouble.

In May of that year I was selected to attend the hush-hush, Special Atomic Demolition Munitions course known as SADM. It was so classified, and so much emphasis was placed on security, that I'm afraid to say much about it even today. The training lasted several weeks and included a field exercise that involved jumping "the device" into a "denied area" at night, sneaking over to a preselected target and emplacing it.

The SADM course was the most interesting training I had while with the 6th Group. I carried a note attached to my medical records after that which stated I was not to be given a general anesthetic unless my commanding officer was present. I suppose someone was afraid I might start talking and give away secrets.

That June, I heard through the grapevine, which was always how one found out about such things, that volunteers were being accepted to fill a levy for duty in Thailand with the 46th Special Forces Company, a relatively new outfit that had been in Thailand for a year by then, and looked like it might remain there for a while.

Lieutenant Colonel Bartelt was in command of the unit and had a good reputation with just about everyone as a top-notch officer. Bartelt had been in Special Forces since the old 77th days, and was one of those guys who loved Asia. I immediately put in my paperwork. I guess the 6th Group was glad to get rid of me, because a week or so later I got transfer orders and started a three-month premission training cycle for Thailand.

A premission training cycle always consisted of more or less the same stuff. Half of each day was spent in Thai language training. I had already taken the spoken Thai language course at the Defense Language Institute in Monterey, California, so that part was just a refresher for me. The afternoons were spent studying the culture, economics, and military situation of the country. We also reviewed and sharpened our military skills by cross-training in all the various specialties found in Special Forces A-teams.

Not long after the training began, I found out that some of us on the levy had already been selected to fill certain positions once we got to Thailand. For security reasons we were not told what we would be doing, but by comparing notes and finding out the sort of backgrounds we all had, we figured out pretty much what to expect.

One of the guys in my bunch was Master Sergeant Wally Sargent. A couple of years earlier, while we'd both been with Project Sigma in Vietnam, Wally had helped save my life during a particularly hairy exfiltration by McGuire rig.

I met another man, a staff sergeant named Bill Spencer, who soon became one of my best friends. Bill, a light-weapons specialist, was just back from a year's tour in Nam with Project Delta and had spent a lot of time on recon teams. Bill had a pretty, blond wife and a new, infant son.

The captain who would be in charge of us once we got to Thailand was a hard-charger named William "Wild Bill" Walker. Captain Walker had also just returned from Vietnam. He'd come back to a busted marriage and was anxious to return overseas. Walker and I got to talking, and I found out that he'd been the executive officer on the A-team that relieved us at Camp Vinh Thanh back in '65. Just a few months after our detachment left, he told me, there had been a big battle and he'd taken an AK-47 round through the face.

I also met Willie Chong at this time. Willie, another weapons man, had spent numerous tours in Vietnam while with the 1st Group on Okinawa.

The training went by quickly and seemed pretty routine to me. By this time I was getting to be an old hand, had already spent some time in Thailand, and had been through several pre-mission cycles. We performed numerous parachute operations as part of the training, and we culminated the three-month cycle with a two-week field exercise.

The exercise started with a night jump into a swamp in Florida. We then spent several nights moving overland to our target. After reconning the target for a couple of days, and reporting the intelligence info back by radio, we received a message in-structing us to perform a raid on it and blow everything up. After the raid, we were directed to go into escape and evasion mode, and move ten or fifteen miles to an exfiltration LZ where we would be picked up by chopper.

By the time the premission training was over, it was late sum-mer. We would all be shipping out of Travis AFB in California. I took another couple of weeks of furlough, threw all my worldly possessions in the trunk of the Corvette, and headed back toward the West Coast.

I stopped in Tucson again, had a great time, and before I knew it, it was time to catch a flight to California. I signed over the title of my car to my father, so he could sell it for me. The 'Vette had only eight thousand miles on it and I kind of hated to leave it, but getting back over to Asia was more important to me than any material possession I could think of.

My sister was living in San Francisco at the time, and I vis-ited with her and her husband for a couple of days before sign-ing in at the replacement depot in Oakland. Although almost broke by the time I got there, I spent an interesting couple of days hiking up and down the San Francisco hills, hanging around North Beach and watching the hippies. The famous "Summer of Love" was in full swing, so there were plenty of flower children in evidence.

As my sister and brother-in-law have often reminded me, I was acting slightly weird in those days. The last night I spent with them in San Francisco, I scraped together enough money to buy a gallon of cheap California red wine. Then I drank it all. The next morning my sister told me that about two-thirds of the way through the bottle I had begun mumbling incoherently to myself in Thai interspersed with occasional bursts of maniacal laughter. My hosts did not appear to be particularly unhappy to see me go.

The repo depot was mostly full of draftees who were getting ready to ship out to Nam. They were some sad-faced, sullen, scared men, let me tell you. By contrast, our bunch of Special Forces guys heading to Thailand was happy as hell and could hardly wait to get over there.

A huge, open warehouse was filled with at least a thousand cots, and the Vietnam-bound troops were kept there under tight rein, almost as if in prison, while they waited for their flights to the war zone. Evidently, many of the men on orders for Vietnam went into a last-minute panic and tried to desert.

The people in charge of the replacement depot knew they wouldn't have any trouble getting us Thailand-bound guys on a plane, and after drawing some advance pay, we spent most of the two days there hanging around joints in downtown Oakland.

The senior NCO in charge of our jolly band was Command Sergeant Major Fred Davis. Davis had fought with Darby's Rangers in WWII. During one of their raids, Fred had been captured by the Germans and held as a POW. He'd managed to escape, though, and make it back to friendly lines. During the Korean War, Fred served with the Airborne Ranger companies, and by 1967 he'd pulled several combat tours with Special Forces in Vietnam.

It would be an understatement to say that CSM Davis was completely unflappable, and just the man to play mother hen to a hundred or so crazed, wild, fun-seeking Special Forces NCOs. We managed to have a lot of fun those two days and nights while we waited for our airplane. No one got hurt, killed, or thrown in jail . . . and no hippies were murdered.

Davis got us all rounded back up to get on the bus, which took us from Oakland to Travis AFB. Our plane was on time, and about twenty-four hours later we landed in Bangkok.

Chapter 2

After the usual exciting, occasionally terrifying, ninety-mile bus ride from the airport in Bangkok up to the 46th Company headquarters in Lopburi, we were let off in front of temporary quarters at Fort Narai. It was late afternoon by the time we got there, and after listening to a short orientation briefing, we were turned loose until the next morning. Anxious to check out the area, everyone hurriedly changed into civilian clothes. Having been at Lopburi once with the 1st Group, I already knew where all the really interesting sights were, and several guys who were new to Thailand attached themselves to me so I could act as tour guide.

Although almost evening, it was still blistering hot. I took a deep breath, inhaling the exotic fragrances of the Orient. I'd been gone from Asia for six months, and it felt very good to be back. We boarded one of the crowded Thai buses and headed down the dusty street toward the downtown area. We passed Monkey Circle, then the train station.

"Where are we going?" one of the guys asked.

"I want to show you this place called the Wing-Ping," I told him.

Wing-Ping was a large, famous whorehouse. It nestled up against part of the ancient wall that had once surrounded Lopburi. There were tables and chairs in a pleasant courtyard where you could have a few drinks while you looked over the large selection of available "hostesses." I recognized several of the girls from my previous visits there and was glad to see that a couple of years' wear and tear hadn't affected them much.

My buddies and I took a table and I checked out the other customers. As usual, there were equal numbers of American and Thai Special Forces soldiers, along with a few Thai civilian tourists who were killing some time while waiting for their trains to arrive at the nearby station.

We all ordered Mekong whiskey and soda. The sun had set and someone turned on the colored lights strung overhead. Thai dance music played on the Wing-Ping sound system, and the girls were glad to dance with you if you wanted. I kicked back in my chair and looked around at my buddies with a grin. "Well, what do you think about it so far?" I asked.

"No wonder you were so anxious to get back over here," one of them told me, speaking around the head of the girl sitting in his lap. "C'mon, sweetie," he said, standing up and pulling the giggling girl toward the dance floor, "show me how to do that there Thai *ramwong*."

The next morning, suffering blistering hangovers, we began a day of in-processing. We had to go through Finance, then through Personnel, and finally Supply. At noon we broke for lunch and everyone knocked down a couple of beers to see if that would dull the pain any. The beer just made us more sleepy and grumpy.

All that afternoon we sat through one interminable briefing

after another. We learned that 46th Company had established three B-detachments, each in different parts of the country. Detachment B-4610 was three hundred miles north of us at Nam Pung Dam, which was close to the Laotian border and near the American air base at Nakhon Phanon. Detachment B-4620 was at Camp Nong Takoo near the Cambodian border, and detachment B-4630 was way down south at Trang, which was near the Malaysian border. The headquarters and signal company were stationed at Lopburi, along with a reinforced A-detachment which was preparing to begin various special training missions.

The briefing rooms were hot and uncomfortable. Most of the information we got was boring, stuff that everyone already knew. You have to remember that in those days we had men in Special Forces who had already been in three wars. Some of them had begun their military careers during WWII, operating in occupied Europe with the OSS, and others had been kicking around different parts of Asia for twenty years.

The last briefing we got was from a couple of young, counterintelligence guys who had come up from Bangkok just to give it. They obviously had presented the briefing many times, usually to other impressionable young troops, and had their routine down pat. In order to illustrate how we should be careful not to fall into a situation of entrapment, which might lead to our being blackmailed for classified information, they related the following anecdote.

An American GI had picked up a beautiful girl in a Bangkok bar and then taken her to his hotel room. He was unmarried and unattached, and couldn't see how that could compromise him in any way. Once back in the room, they turned out the lights and had just climbed into bed when the girl suddenly said she had to use the bathroom. When she returned, the lights were still out, and as soon as the unlucky soldier wrapped his arms around her naked body, the lights came on and three guys were standing there taking pictures. "And when the soldier looked at his female companion," the young CI agent told us, obviously savoring this punch line, "he discovered that he was no longer holding a woman, but a twelve-year-old boy!"

This was where the audience was supposed to "ohh and aww," but we'd all heard this same story a hundred times before. There was no reaction at all for ten or twenty seconds, then one of the older NCOs, one of those European-born displaced persons who'd been recruited into Special Forces in the early fifties, spoke up.

"Veelll," the sergeant drawled in his thick accent, "get to de part vare he fucks him."

The next day we got sorted out into several different A-teams. My new detachment, A-4609, was to move to an undisclosed location in a few weeks, or maybe months, but in the meantime we would be working with the men on team A-4641, who were preparing to teach Ranger and long-range recon courses right there in Lopburi. Many of the men on A-4641, such as David Disharoon, Dick Breon, Jerry Temple, Jack Long, Bob Bolton, and Bert Moore, were guys I knew from previous assignments.

We had a good bunch on A-4609 too. As I mentioned earlier the detachment commander was Captain Bill Walker. A young first lieutenant by the name of Cheston came aboard as executive officer. Master Sergeant Wally Sargent (paygrade E-8) was team daddy, and Sergeant First Class Thomas Belcher (E-7), who had served a year in Vietnam with the 173rd, was our intel sergeant.

In the weapons slots we had staff sergeants (E-6) Willie Chong and Bill Spencer, both of whom had extensive, prior combat experience in Vietnam. Another old hand, James Jamerson, held the position of senior medic, and his assistant was a young sergeant (E-5), fresh out of Special Forces medical training, by the name of Bill Carpenter. The engineer/demo slots were filled by two other hard-charging young NCOs, Bill Spurgeon and Don Bowes. Although at that time still a young guy with little time in the

Army, Spurgeon was one of those men with "lifer" written all over him.

Sharing the duties of commo sergeant with me was Perry Parks. Perry had spent some time in Europe with regular Army units before joining Special Forces. We'd gotten to know each other while in premission training back at Bragg and were already good friends. We were both staff sergeants, but Perry had some time-in-grade on me, so he got to be the radio supervisor. It was fine with me, because it meant he would get to take all the ass-chewings for both of us.

Our detachment stayed at Lopburi for about six weeks, helping A-4641 while we wondered exactly what our coming assignment would be. Usually, if something was classified and being kept under wraps it meant that it could be pretty exciting. You never knew, though. Sometimes those "special deals" never panned out at all and you'd end up being reorganized and transferred someplace else.

Space was limited in the barracks at Fort Narai and NCOs were encouraged to live off post if they desired. Parks, Spencer, and I shared a three-bedroom house owned by a local Thai, a judge. Our next-door neighbors were Bob Bolton, Phil Devlin, and Gary Queen. Life was sweet.

About two weeks after we got to the 46th, Spencer came in and informed Parks and me that he'd discovered we could extend our current, one-year tours if we wanted, so the next morning the three of us marched into Personnel and signed the extension requests for an additional year and a half, which were immediately granted. The catch was that at the same time, we had to request another year's tour in Vietnam, which would begin as soon as our duty in Thailand was finished. I gladly signed on, because to me, even Nam was a better alternative than Fort Bragg.

It was soon fall, and the Christmas season was approaching. Our detachment still hadn't heard anything concrete about the new assignment. We'd just returned from a month up north, helping the guys on A-4641 with the field training portion of a long-range recon course, and were ready for some excitement. I hadn't been to Bangkok since returning to Thailand, and after the time I'd just spent trudging through the jungle with a Thai recon team, I was ready for a blowout. We'd been given four days off between training cycles, so I took an entire month's pay and exchanged it for baht, the local currency. Spencer and Parks did likewise, and we were soon in a taxi heading for the big city. We called that "making a low-level leaflet drop."

Wherever Special Forces are stationed, they soon find local joints that become the "official" hangouts. In Bangkok, in the mid-sixties, the hotel everyone stayed at was the Opera, and the bar where you could always find a friend was the Three Sisters. We used to raise a lot of hell, get pretty raunchy and rowdy when we were on a tear, but Special Forces were also known to be big spenders. Our adopted hangouts were always willing to put up with the animal acts that were the norm in those wild days.

The Three Sisters bar was Bangkok's counterpart to the Sporting Bar in Saigon. If you wanted to know who else was in town, what hotel they were at, whom they were shacked up with, and so on, all you had to do was wander into either joint and ask one of the girls.

Occasionally one of the counterintelligence types would show up and attempt to pump us for info to find out if we were divulging classified data, but nothing of great military significance was ever discussed there. Anyway, outsiders were immediately recognized as such, and soon got the idea that they probably should find a new place to drink.

I recently read a crack made by the famous literary critic Edmund Wilson. "I always give the whores as little as possible," he joked, "because I don't think that prostitution should be encouraged." In Special Forces we took the opposite position. One of the popular jokes making the rounds was about the guy who came back from Bangkok and announced that he had paid a girl a hundred dollars for a "short-time."

"A hundred dollars!" his buddy says. "Hell, she only charged me two bucks."

"Yeah," the first guy answers, "but I don't hang around with cheap whores!"

Actually, an anthropologist could probably write an interesting doctoral dissertation on the social and sexual mores of our tight-knit group. Although occasionally one of the girls would live with one of the guys for a while, eventually all the girls floated around among us. The bar name, Three Sisters, was oddly appropriate. There appeared to be a sisterly relationship between the girls who worked there, and also between them and us. After a while the situation began to seem a bit incestuous.

While the Three Sisters was just your normal, sleazy joint, there was another place, a rather high-class nightclub called The Balcony, where we also sometimes went at night. The Balcony was a popular place with international tourists, and it featured a live band. The Balcony was so called because it was built on two levels, with a kind of mezzanine upstairs where patrons could sit, peer over the railing, and watch the festivities below. Special Forces troops pulled so many stunts in The Balcony—such as rappeling down to the dance floor—that we soon became almost part of the nightly act the tourists came to see.

While I was in town that time, the big story making the rounds was about one of our wilder, meaner NCOs, a man known to have a short temper. He'd just had a run-in with a long-haired Peace Corps volunteer who by some misfortune happened to be staying at the Opera Hotel. Words had been exchanged between them—the NCO being called a warmongering fascist, and the Peace Corps volunteer being called a faggot-peace-freak-commie—and in the ensuing, short exchange of fists the Peace Corps guy had been knocked cold.

Just to add insult to injury, the NCO had then taken out his pocketknife and, while the Peace Corps volunteer lay unconscious, cut off his hair. The next day the Peace Corps volunteer had gone sniveling and complaining to the U.S. Embassy, and the NCO was summarily transferred back to Fort Bragg. That NCO was one of our most experienced men, had been in-country only about two days at the time of the incident, and we all figured the embassy pukes had given him a raw deal. Some people just don't have any sense of humor at all. . . .

Finally, after several false starts, detachment A-4609 got the warning order to prepare for movement. We were going to a town named Hua Hin, which was on the coast, south of Bangkok. We were told that we'd be working with the Thai Border Police, and some special outfit call the Police Aerial Reinforcement Unit (PARU). On the way there from Lopburi we stopped at Bangkok, and the officers were given another briefing. Before we left Bangkok to finish the trip to Hua Hin, we were told to change into our new uniform—civilian clothes.

Chapter 3

This was the beginning of what was undoubtedly the best assignment I ever had in the Army. For one thing, we were under operational control (OPCON) of the U.S. Embassy in Bangkok, with our Special Forces headquarters in Lopburi only maintaining administrative control. Our civilian bosses down in Lopburi turned out to be Harry "the Hat" Munck (lieutenant colonel, Army Special Forces, newly retired) and Al Friend (sergeant major, Army Special Forces, newly retired). In those days, we weren't even allowed to utter the term "CIA," but we all knew whom Harry and Al had recently gone to work for.

Once our detachment got down to Hua Hin and began putting together the various courses we were to teach, we changed out of the civilian clothes and into a blue denim outfit that the Thai Border Police furnished us. Except for parachute wings, we wore no insignia or rank indicators. For headgear we wore black baseball caps with Thai police and American parachute wings.

None of that was done to really fool anyone. It was common knowledge that we were an American Special Forces detachment. Partly we wanted simply to maintain a low profile while in the area. Hua Hin was a popular beach resort, and the beautiful beach was filled with tourists from all over the world. Another reason we wore no rank or insignia was that we were instructing Thai senior NCOs and officers. It would be an insult for a Thai officer to have to sit in class and be instructed by an American junior NCO, but as long as we wore no rank, we could all pretend that we were civilian instructors.

Being old soldiers themselves, Harry and Al knew the score, and immediately put into effect the order that no other members of the U.S military could come to Hua Hin without prior approval of the embassy. That was a very smart move, because otherwise we would have found ourselves conducting an endless string of dog-and-pony shows for touring American officers who would use the excuse of "inspecting training" to come to our beach resort on TDY—that is, drawing per diem pay—for a few days of paid vacation.

The Thai Border Police was an interesting unit. At that time, Thailand was surrounded by Communist or pro-Communist countries, and was being infiltrated by bands of Communist terrorists (CT). At the same time, the Thais had an agreement with their neighbors that army troops could not operate within something like ten kilometers of each other's borders. To get around that, the Thais simply equipped and trained their Border Police as light airborne infantry. So although still officially police, the Border Police soon became one of the best military units the Thais had.

The Police Aerial Reinforcement Unit (PARU) was a small seven-hundred-man unit consisting of the elite of the elite. Members of the unit had occasionally conducted clandestine operations against the Communists in Laos. Their mission was along Ranger/Commando/LRP lines.

Sometime during the early history of the Border Police, they had done something that favorably impressed the king of Thailand, and it was common knowledge that the Border Police and PARU were a couple of his favorite military units.

Each year, the king and his family spent several weeks in Hua Hin, the royal visit usually coinciding with the annual Border Police birthday party, which he often attended. The first year we were at Hua Hin, our detachment attended one of these parties with the royal family. All Thais, including the king, like a good party, and we all had a great time.

We had rather palatial living quarters at Hua Hin, furnished compliments of the Agency. The quarters consisted of two large dwellings that were situated right on a prime portion of beach. The property was actually owned by the lord mayor of Bangkok. Our next-door neighbor was the queen's sister.

In spite of wallowing in that high society, our detachment worked long and hard hours at Hua Hin, and spent three-quarters of its time in the field. We adapted our training schedules to reflect the Thai holidays rather than our own, and usually spent days like Christmas and the Fourth of July teaching classes or in the field with the troops. It was very satisfying work, however, and with Harry and Al keeping the sightseers off our backs, we got a lot accomplished.

We conducted several different types of training. We created and taught a senior NCO/junior officer proficiency course, various other refresher courses for the junior NCOs, and special courses—mostly dealing with long-range recon—to members of the PARU.

Hua Hin was the Border Police's main headquarters, and they had many assets that we made good use of. They had their own pilots and aircraft and their own parachute rigger outfit. The Thais parachuted constantly, and our detachment was allowed to jump with them whenever we wished. The Border Police were using American T-10 parachutes with a mild double-L modification, plus toggle lines. The chutes were actually similar to the current MC1-1 parachute. I made more parachute jumps during the two years I was at Hua Hin than I did during all my other time in the Army combined.

I worked through the Christmas of '67 and the American New Year celebration, then got some time off for Tet. Bill Spencer and I went into Bangkok together, and on the morning of the first day in February 1968, we were sitting at a table in the Opera Hotel coffee shop when we read in the *Pacific Stars and Stripes* about the big Communist offensive taking place in Vietnam. There was fighting in all the major cities, and the U.S. Embassy in Saigon had even come under attack.

As usual, I had ambivalent thoughts as I read the early reports of the battle. In one way, I was glad to be sitting at a table in Bangkok, out of danger and uninvolved. I'd been pretty burned-out by the time I'd left Vietnam the last time. In another way, I felt guilty and wished I were back there. I recognized that Tet was one of the major battles of the war, and hated to be missing it.

Once we got into the groove with our training at Hua Hin, time seemed to pass quickly. Every couple of months we got some time off between training cycles and could go into Bangkok if we wanted, but since we were already living in a beach resort anyway, I often just stayed there. And one radio operator had to always remain at camp, to make the daily scheduled contacts.

Although the tours of duty in Thailand were officially "unaccompanied"—meaning the Army wouldn't pay to have the married guys' families brought over—many men brought their wives over at their own expense. Bill Spencer brought his wife, Irene, and infant son over, and they alternated living in Bangkok and in quarters down with us at Hua Hin.

After the first year ended, several of our detachment returned to the U.S. and were replaced with new members. Wally Sargent left, and Master Sergeant Leo Kelland took over as team sergeant. Leo had served time with the old 11th Airborne, and recently fought in Vietnam with Project Delta. Sergeant Charles Thomas took over Bowe's demo slot, and Sergeant First Class Chuck Floyd took over Jamerson's position as senior medic.

Chuck soon brought his fiancée Cathy to join him in Thailand, and they were married in Bangkok—the first of two weddings we celebrated on the team. Willie Chong began dating our civilian secretary, a beautiful young woman named Nagmtaa, shortly after we got to Hua Hin, and before a year had passed they were married in a big, classical, Thai ceremony right there in town.

Duty with the Thai Border Police was relatively safe compared to duty in Vietnam, but there was enough danger from Communist terrorists, some of them North Vietnamese commandos, to keep things interesting. In April of '68 a Border Patrol camp at Ban Haui Khu in northern Thailand was overrun. Only two of the police survived. That summer, Udorn Air Base was attacked by NVA sappers who managed to take out a couple of American C-141 and F-4D aircraft, along with an HU-43.

Our civilian bosses, Munck and Friend, were also in charge of other training taking place up near the Laotian border at Phitsanulok, where most of the exciting stuff took place. Even down in Hua Hin we occasionally had some action, however, as that part of the Thai peninsula is very close to the Burmese border. One evening, just at sundown, one of the Agency operatives was ambushed by a small band of CT on the highway just south of the town. Luckily, he survived unscathed, but the attempt kept us on our toes.

In the meantime, as the war in Vietnam continued at an ever-heightened pace, the antiwar crowd back in the U.S. was becoming louder and more obnoxious all the time. The American news media had transformed the devastating military defeat the Communists suffered during their Tet offensive into a huge, psychological victory for the enemy. Back home, more and more U.S. civilians were thinking the war was a mistake.

To me, it seemed the U.S. media had always been on the side of the enemy. They never appeared to be bothered much by Communist atrocities, which happened often. But when our side occasionally screwed up, our newsmen were always anxious to splash it across the front pages.

All of the antiwar, anti-American, and antimilitary propaganda and sentiment back home was having the effect you would expect on the troops in Vietnam. To those of us in Special Forces, who were more attuned to this new type of politico-psychological-military war, it appeared obvious that the antiwar groups in the U.S. were either (1) dupes of the Communists, or (2) knowledgeable Communist sympathizers.

The North Vietnamese were obviously using the exact same strategy they had used to successfully defeat the French: bleed the larger enemy, and let the pro-Communist supporters in the enemy's own country achieve for them the political victory they knew they could never win on the battlefield. And that strategy was working beautifully.

As I continued to read of one antiwar demonstration after the other, and as each new self-seeking politician and publicity-hungry celebrity joined the peace movement, I became more depressed and alienated from my own country. Many of us in

Special Forces were feeling like a kind of forgotten American Foreign Legion, because we could easily empathize with what that famous French unit had so recently gone through.

Adding to the feeling of alienation in the Special Forces community was the fact that many conventional generals, and other senior officers in our own U.S. Army, hated us. The American army has never much cared for special or "elite" units. There is a huge amount of politics involved in officer promotion, especially when you get to the higher ranks, and when one particular unit starts getting a lot of publicity and attention in the civilian press, then jealousy, hatred, and political back-stabbing are sure to follow.

When Colonel Aaron Banks first developed Special Forces in the fifties, it had been a small, clandestine, low-profile unit. There was no great chance for officer promotion or career advancement in Special Forces then, and officers who chose to serve with the unit did so simply because they liked the work. Then, in the early sixties, things dramatically changed. First came the award of the Green Beret by President Kennedy, then came "The Ballad of the Green Beret." Special Forces suddenly became a celebrity unit.

Special Forces always attracted a different sort of person than the regular units. Since we were "unconventional," we attracted unconventional, freethinking, creative people, some of them pretty wild, outspoken, and—to the conventional Army's way of thinking—undisciplined. But because there happened to be a nice, bloody ground war going on, we were tolerated. Many guys in Special Forces really were war-lovers, just as the antiwar bunch said, and we came in real handy for jobs no other unit could, or would, do. I'm sure that many senior Army officers figured that as soon as the war in Vietnam was over, Special Forces could be done away with just as the Rangers had been after WWII.

As long as General Westmoreland was running things in Vietnam, Special Forces felt as if it had a friend. Although "Westy" had no prior Special Forces training or experience, he was an old paratroop officer, a charter member of the paratroop mafia that had fought the political, budget, and strategy wars following WWII, and he probably understood better than any other conventional officer the nature of the war we were fighting.

Several months after the Communists' abortive Tet offensive, it was announced that Westmoreland was being promoted to Army Chief of Staff and would be leaving Vietnam in a few months. His replacement was to be General Creighton Abrams, a very capable and experienced, but superconventional, officer. He also was known for his dislike of Special Forces.

Special Forces units worldwide watched these developments with mounting premonitions of doom and gloom. President Johnson, bowing to antiwar pressure, offered to begin peace talks with the Communists, and at the end of March said he would not run for reelection. For me, and many others, the handwriting was already appearing on the wall.

Chapter 4

One day in early April 1968, several of us were having lunch at an open-air restaurant in downtown Hua Hin. Parks, Spencer, Leo Kelland, and I were just finishing up and getting ready to go back to work when one of the Agency guys came in with that day's copy of the Bangkok *Post*. "Look at this," he said, handing it to us.

That's how I heard about the assassination of Martin Luther

King, Jr. "This is not good," the Agency guy told us, needlessly. Coming as it did only a few years after the assassination of John Kennedy and the Vietnamese president, Diem, this new political murder back in the U.S. gave everyone a very uneasy feeling.

"Jeez, who's gonna get it next?" someone asked.

Only a couple of months later we found out, when on June fifth the news of Robert Kennedy's assassination reached us. Back at home, things seemed to be going to hell in a hurry.

I tried to ignore all the riots, demonstrations, and killings back at home, and stopped reading the blatant enemy propaganda in the mainstream press; I'd recently discovered *National Review* magazine and ordered an airmail subscription. It was just about the only publication at the time that reflected what I considered to be the reality of the situation in S.E. Asia. Until that time, I had remained basically apolitical—if anything, considering myself to be a liberal Democrat, especially on social issues. Now I changed sides. Bill Buckley is a very persuasive fellow.

In my own little world there at Hua Hin, one course of instruction flowed into another, and time passed swiftly. We had a few more personnel changes on the team, with Mike Rose taking the junior medic slot, Lieutenant Mike Carpenter filling the XO position, and Belcher being replaced in the intel slot by James Stephanski. A few years earlier, Carpenter, then an enlisted man, had earned the Distinguished Service Cross while on an A-detachment in Vietnam. I remembered Stephanski from a couple of years before in Vietnam, when we'd both been with special projects.

Harry Munck's family lived in Bangkok, and he often brought them down to Hua Hin for weekends on the beach. Harry's wife, Jean, was an experienced Special Forces officer's wife, and was used to our carryings-on. Harry and Jean had four teenagers—Vicki, Pam, Cheryl, and Bobby—who also sometimes accompanied them on their visits. Occasionally, especially when our team was on stand-down between training cycles, the visits turned into lavish house parties, rivaling something the late, great Jay Gatsby might have thrown.

Often, special guests blew in from all over S.E. Asia. During one such bash, we entertained a couple of SAS guys from the British Embassy in Bangkok, an Israeli couple who were working with some sort of rural development project, Lieutenant Colonel Millet (famous for his Cavalry moustache, among other things), retired CSM Matteo (who had retired from the Army, but not the war), a couple of Navy SEALs, and the crew of an Air America helicopter who flew in from somewhere and landed in our yard.

We were only a short walk down the beach from the Railroad Hotel, where American and European women tourists could always be found, and we spent a lot of time that weekend giving them joyrides in our detachment's speedboat and in the Air America helicopter.

On the second afternoon of this particular party, I was glancing though a current *Time* magazine that the chopper crew had brought with them, and read aloud one of the articles, which was all about draft dodgers back in the States. Kelland was sitting there with me at a table on our veranda, which overlooked the ocean. Giggling, bikini-clad tourist girls sat on either side of him. "I don't blame 'em for dodging the draft," he said, pouring his beer, "this goddamn war is *hell*!"

All of us watched the presidential race that year with interest and a good deal of trepidation. After Robert Kennedy was killed, old-line liberal Hubert Humphrey pretty much had the Democratic nomination sewed up. He was definitely a "peace" candidate, but for some reason the Marxist-controlled punks and thugs who called themselves yippies staged a riot during the Democratic convention in Chicago. I believe that it was this televised show of disorder that ensured the election of Richard Nixon in November '68.

By then it was pretty obvious to everyone that the U.S. was going to have to get out of the war. The only real question was exactly how we were going to go about it.

Nixon was for a more gradual, fighting withdrawal, allowing us to talk peace with the Communists from a position of power. As Nixon began slowly bringing home "our boys," he actually increased strategic bombing, and Melvin Laird came up with the term "Vietnamization of the war," which soon became Nixon's official doctrine. While slowly pulling out American troops, we would attempt to strengthen the Vietnamese forces so they could continue to fight the war by themselves.

The peace freaks were all for our simply deserting the South Vietnamese as quickly as possible. As I've said, it's my opinion that many of the peace-and-love crowd were actually Communists who were interested in "peace" only if it went along with an immediate, humiliating, American and South Vietnamese defeat.

Naturally, Nixon's plan for a slow withdrawal, and continued fighting, didn't go over at all with the antiwar bunch, and their "peace demonstrations" grew larger, more violent, and eventually openly featured wild-eyed college students waving Viet Cong flags and chanting how "Ho, Ho, Ho Chi Minh, Ho Chi Minh is gonna win!" There were blood drives for the NVA, American flags were routinely burned in the streets, and a movie star went to North Vietnam, swore her undying support for their heroic revolution, and posed for a photo op while sitting at an NVA antiaircraft gun.

My morale was in free fall by that time anyway, but in late summer of that year, a huge scandal involving U.S. Special Forces in Vietnam hit the news. . . .

Earlier that summer, a new commander, Colonel Robert Rheault, had taken over the 5th Special Forces in Vietnam. I'd never personally served under the man, but had heard nothing but good things about him. Rheault had commanded the 1st Group on Okinawa immediately before assuming command of the 5th in Vietnam and served with the 10th Group in Germany before that. He was a rarity for those days, a West Point graduate who also had a sound Special Forces background.

A couple of years before, back in '66, Project Gamma had spun off from C-5. Gamma was an intelligence-gathering unit that targeted NVA/VC base areas in Cambodia. Originally consisting of only a handful of men, by 1968 it fielded nine collection teams, working from A-team camps along the Cambodian border, which were handling almost one hundred agents. Gamma was producing about three-fourths of the intelligence coming out of Cambodia.

About the same time Colonel Rheault was assuming command of the 5th Group, Gamma personnel uncovered a double agent who was doing tremendous damage to the unit. Many agents were being killed, and others simply vanishing. The double agent, Thai Khac Chueyn, was arrested and brought to Gamma headquarters in Nha Trang, where he was interrogated and pronounced guilty. He was eventually shot in the head, placed in a large sack with some chains and tire rims, then dumped into Nha Trang Bay.

This is pretty grim stuff, right out of some damned gangster movie, but you also have to remember that there was a war going on. The "perps" of this execution put out the cover story—which was told to Colonel Rheault—that the agent had been sent on a "one-way mission," but the real story soon came to light.

General Abrams had never liked Special Forces in the first place, and when he found out about this gruesome caper, he was enraged. From one account that I read at the time, Abrams had turned to his staff and said, "Let's clean 'em out!"

Abrams had the intel operatives, plus Colonel Rheault and members of his staff, arrested and charged with murder. Poor

Colonel Rheault had not only been completely uninvolved with the incident, but also was fed the same cover story as everyone else.

Abrams then gave command of the 5th Group to a conventional Army colonel who was not only non–Special Forces qualified, he was not even parachute qualified—in other words, a "leg"!

Eventually all the charges were dropped, because the CIA, "in the interest of national security," refused to allow any of its people to testify. Of course, the damage had already been done. The media had a field day with it all, and Colonel Rheault retired immediately afterward, depriving Special Forces of one of its best officers.

One of the squealers in the case was quoted as saying that the CIA had told him to "terminate the double agent with extreme prejudice," and the term "TWEPing" someone became a popular joke phrase in Special Forces. Here are the lyrics to a little ditty best sung to the tune of "The Ballad of the Green Beret."

> Fighting soldiers from the sky,
> Fearless men who jump and die.
> You'll get to TWEP a spy someday,
> If you work . . . with the CIA!

This scandal affected the morale of Special Forces units worldwide. It had an especially bad impact on me, because I personally knew many of the men who had worked, or were working, with Gamma. Many of them, like Carl Hargus, had been with Gamma off and on since its inception, and it was not an easy job.

My natural cynicism and sarcasm now reached new levels, and my attitude continued to deteriorate. At least once a month I got word that another person I knew had been killed in the war. We were all fighting and dying for a lost cause, it seemed to me, all the while being stabbed in the back not only by traitors back at home, but by enemies in our own Army.

That fall many of us at Hua Hin began getting orders for Vietnam. Spencer, Parks, and I all got our orders at the same time, but we had different report dates. Spencer and Parks were to go over before Christmas, but I was not due to go until after the start of the new year, on the first of February 1969. Spurgeon and Rose also got orders not to go serve their first tours there.

When Parks left, he was replaced in commo by Staff Sergeant Joe Gamez, a guy most of us on the team already knew. Spencer was replaced by SFC "Don" Soriano. Soriano was one of those Hawaiian boys who had learned to soldier the old, hardcore way. He had spent several years on the Army rifle team, was a member of the elite bunch of shooters known as the President's 100, and was probably the best marksman I ever met in the Army.

By that time I had three years in grade as a staff sergeant (E-6), and was eligible for promotion to sergeant first class (E-7), but I was still surprised when I was told to report to the promotion board for an interview. There were only a couple of promotion slots available, and I didn't think I had much of a chance, as it was my first time even to be considered. About ten other men were to go through the interview process, and because we were called in alphabetical order, I was the last one to be called in. The questions seemed pretty easy—just basic military knowledge—and I breezed through them.

A couple of weeks later I found out I'd been promoted to sergeant first class. I was still only twenty-seven years old, and at that time must have been one of the youngest SFCs in the Army. Because of the war in Vietnam, it was pretty easy to move up quickly to the rank of staff sergeant, but sergeant first class was one of the top three enlisted ranks, and it was a lot harder to get.

In November, Thomas and I were split off from the team in

Hua Hin and sent up to Nakhon Phanon, which was on the border. The air base there was home to many of the Air Force's AC-130 gunships, nicknamed "Blackbirds," and also housed a SOG* launch site. Thomas and I, and four others, moved into the local Border Police camp outside of town and began giving classes.

Just after we got there, the air base was hit by a team of North Vietnamese sappers. The way this attack was carried out is illustrative of both the strengths and the weaknesses of the NVA.

The sapper team consisted of twelve men. Very soon after they crossed the border from Cambodia into Thailand, they had been spotted and reported by Thai civilians. The air base went on full alert around noon, and as soon as it got dark, the security force at the base began firing illumination rounds and stepped up patrols around the perimeter.

The NVA sappers must have known they'd been compromised and no longer had the element of surprise, but they continued their mission anyway. Either they were wildly overconfident or, as I believe, were unable to call off their mission once it had started. The sappers were very good, and made it through the perimeter and onto the air base before being discovered. A wild gun battle between the infiltrators and base security forces ensued that lasted for about an hour.

In the end, all the sappers were killed before they could place any of their explosive devices. One of the last killed was apparently trying to get back out through the perimeter wire when he was shot. The rounds either set off the explosives he was carrying or he set them off himself, because he blew up. The biggest part they could find of him was his scalp, which was left hanging on the perimeter barbed wire.

The enemy troops had been very well trained and were the

* An acronym from the cover name Studies and Observation Group (aka Special Operations Group). They specialized in running mixed teams of SF advisers and Montagnards on recon missions into denied areas and "cross border" into North Vietnam, Laos, and Cambodia.

best-equipped NVA sappers I'd ever heard of. They wore black camouflage uniforms with so-called "ninja" face cowls. They carried special wire cutters, clips to hold the perimeter barbed wire back once it was cut, and each of them was armed not with the normal AK-47, but with a Czech Skorpion machine pistol.

The Air Force's security police did a great job of wiping these bad dudes out before they could blow up some AC-130s, and the APs certainly earned my respect for it.

Most of my friends from Hua Hin who had already begun tours in Vietnam had gone to MACV-SOG. With the exception of Parks, who was with SOG Command & Control North, the others had all ended up in Command & Control Central at Kontum. Spencer and Spurgeon got there first and were eventually joined by Rose and Thomas.

That was Bill Spencer's second go-round with special projects. He and I had both had experience with those high-risk operations several years earlier, and we'd often talked about how damned hairy they could get. I thought about Bill often, and hoped he was holding up to the stress.

Although my own Vietnam report date wasn't until February first, I was given the normal thirty-day furlough, plus fifteen days' travel time, to enable me to return to the U.S. So it was around the middle of December that I returned to Lopburi to begin out-processing the 46th Company.

Once I cleared the unit, I took several months' pay, converted it to baht, and headed for Bangkok. The last place in the world I wanted to go was back to the hippie-yippie-infested U.S.A. Instead I moved into a hotel on Petchburi Road and began a very wild, exhausting, forty-five-day furlough in Bangkok.

Chapter 5

What can I say about a forty-five-day binge in Bangkok? For readers who are Vietnam veterans and were lucky enough to spend a five-day R&R in that city, picture that experience times nine! For younger readers, some of whom might have recently had the opportunity to visit Thailand, I need to remind you that things were very cheap there in the sixties. My hotel cost five dollars a day. At the Navy commissary a quart of twenty-five-year-old scotch cost four dollars. A so-called "steam bath" cost about five bucks, and there was no AIDS epidemic.

I reached Bangkok just in time for the start of the Christmas holidays. The Christmas parties blended into the New Year's parties in a disjointed, drunken blur. Then, right after the first of the year, I ran into Willie Chong, who happened to be in town for a couple of days, and he told me something that put a damper on my good times.

"You hear about Bill Spencer?" he asked.

"What did he do, get the Medal of Honor?" I said.

"He's dead," Willie told me. "Got greased right after Christmas. From what I heard, he took a direct hit from a fucking RPG-7."

Somehow that just seemed to be the final straw, and my morale reached rock bottom. The remaining thirty days of my furlough became, basically, a month-long wake for my buddy, Spencer.

From talking to different men who had been with Spencer at

the time, I pieced together what happened. When Spencer first got to the SOG CCC, he'd taken over a recon/commando team and begun running operations across the border into southern Laos. On an operation just before Christmas, his team had gone in for a five-day mission but, due to bad weather, was forced to spend ten days sneaking around in the fog- and mist-shrouded jungle before they could be exfiltrated. They had food and water for only five days, and so spent the second five days in what amounted to escape and evasion mode, eating and drinking whatever they could find.

After they finally got back, Bill began suffering stomach troubles and, as a break, was assigned to the recon platoon of a reaction unit. That unit went on operation right after Christmas. Although you couldn't call the reaction-force operations safe, after running with a six-man recon team, being with a company-size unit probably seemed pretty tame to Bill.

On December 29, Bill's recon platoon was the lead element when they made contact with the enemy. To get a better look at the situation, Bill moved up to the point man, who had been wounded as soon as the shooting started. I think the enemy was hoping that one of the Americans would do this, because an NVA soldier fired an RPG from about twenty-five meters away, and the antitank rocket hit Bill in the chest. He died instantly. Thomas Belcher had recently returned to Vietnam, and he accompanied Bill's body home.

One drunken day followed another as my report date to Vietnam approached. A new western movie, *The Wild Bunch*, was playing at one of the theaters in town, and I probably sat through it twenty times during that furlough. The movie's theme was about the ending of an era, and about men who know they are part of a time that will never be again. That message really hit home because it reminded me of my own situation.

I had a gloomy, fatalistic feeling about my final tour in Nam. There were rumors that the entire 5th Group would be leaving the country in the near future, so even if I didn't get killed, it would be my last trip to Vietnam anyway. "We got to stop living by our guns," William Holden said in the movie, "those days are over." I knew just what he meant.

Fate had one more surprise in store for me before that long furlough was over, however. It was the last thing I ever expected to happen and caught me completely unprepared. What happened was, I fell in love . . . with an *American* woman, for God's sake!

Colonel Munck's oldest daughter, Vicki, had graduated from high school in Bangkok a year or so before, and went to work in the embassy as a secretary. I hadn't paid a lot of attention to her, because to me she was just a kid. Vicki was about nineteen then, and although I was only twenty-seven at the time, there seemed to be a huge age gap between us.

Vicki and Bill Spurgeon had dated a few times, Bill being the youngest guy on the team and closer to her age. It became common knowledge on the team that Vicki had a heavy crush on Bill, and I remember having one of those wise-older-brother type of conversations with Bill in which I advised him to stay clear of silly, American teenage girls.

I was sitting in the coffee shop of the Raja Hotel about five one afternoon, sipping a Singha beer and talking to a taxi driver I knew. The last couple of days had been especially rough, and I was feeling, and probably looking, particularly seedy and disreputable. I happened to look out the window just as Vicki arrived at the hotel in a taxi. She was wearing one of the short skirts that were the style in the sixties, and her wholesome, American good looks and figure made her stand out in the otherwise Thai crowd.

I was interested in why she was at the hotel, and watched her walk to the front desk and ask the clerk something. He pointed over to the coffee shop, and Vicki came in and sat down with me.

"Hey, Vick, what's happening? Who you looking for?" I asked her, trying not to slur my words.

She looked innocently across the table at me. "I'm looking for you," she said.

I should have run like hell, but dealing with women has never been one of my strong points.

The waiter came over, secretly leered at me, and asked Vicki what she wanted. She ordered a beer, just like a big girl, and when it came, we sat making small talk. She told me she'd heard about Spencer getting killed, and we talked about how crummy it was. She asked me if I'd heard anything about Spurgeon, and I told her that he was with SOG at Kontum and doing just fine. She said one of our mutual friends told her I was in Bangkok and had been on a real bender, and she was worried about me. By this time it was getting dark outside.

"It's getting kind of late," I said, hoping she'd get the hint. "Your parents are probably worried about you."

"I have my own apartment now," she said, batting her long eyelashes.

I quit trying to get rid of her. Time passed pleasantly while I was with her, and I have to admit it was fun to have an American girl to talk to for a change. Plus, being seen with a "round-eye" gave me a certain status with the Thais working at the hotel; they had watched me cavorting with an endless string of not-so-nice Thai women for the previous four weeks.

There was a pretty good nightclub attached to the hotel that catered to both Thais and foreign tourists. The place had a small rock-and-roll band, and you could dance. Believing that she would say no, I asked Vicki if she wanted to go over there, and to my surprise, she immediately agreed.

If I'd been in Vietnam, walking along a jungle trail, alarm bells would have been going off in my head. As it was, I continued to stumble along like a lamb to the slaughter.

We stayed at the club until it closed, dancing, drinking, and horsing around. Toward the end of the evening we ended up necking in a dark, secluded corner booth. I felt like a child molester, but I have to admit that Vicki didn't seem too childish right then.

After the place closed, we walked out to the street and I put her in a cab. We made a date for the next night to do it all again. Feeling a little confused, I went to bed alone that night for a change. Things were going on that I didn't really understand.

We started going out almost nightly, and on the morning of the fourth or fifth day of that routine, I woke up to the horrid realization that I was in love with her. Or at least I thought it was love. I'd lived twenty-seven years without ever experiencing the sensation, so I couldn't be sure. In fact, until then I had been convinced that romantic love was all bullshit. I'd thought it was something that giggling young girls talked themselves into believing, not something that could just happen to you—like catching a disease!

Great, just great, I thought as I staggered into the shower. There I was, in love for the first time, and I was getting ready to go back to Vietnam in five days. Maybe, I decided, that was the best thing. I still was not anxious to get involved in a long-term commitment with a woman, love or no love. Besides, I tried to reassure myself, the new development made my coming return to the war more interesting—just like a war novel. But reading fiction is one thing; living the reality is quite another.

The last morning of my forty-five-day bacchanal finally arrived, and as I sat morosely in the coffee shop with my taxi driver buddy, Harry Munck and Vicki stopped in to say goodbye and wish me good luck.

After they'd left, the taxi driver took off one of his Buddha charms and gave it to me. It was a very good charm, he told me, his best one. "You have danger, just hold Buddha in hand, ask for help, then be okay."

I thanked him and attached it to the heavy, five-baht gold chain around my neck; I was already wearing six other Buddhas. I finished my cup of cold coffee and stood up.

"Let's go?" the driver asked.

"Why not?" I said.

Chapter 6

I returned to Vietnam in great style, managing to catch a hop with a general and his staff in his little two-engine plane. It was a short trip, and soon I was looking out the window at the familiar, crater-pocked landscape surrounding Saigon. When we landed, the general was immediately picked up in a waiting staff car and whisked away, and after gathering up my duffel bag, I found a civilian taxi and gave the driver the address of the Special Forces compound downtown.

I'd been gone for two and a half years, and things had greatly changed during my absence. All the changes were for the worse. Saigon appeared to be twice as filthy as before and probably five times as crowded. American troops were everywhere, many of them obviously in the process of packing up to leave. There were sandbagged emplacements in front of practically every building and on most major intersections, but many of them had already been abandoned by the departing Americans and were quickly deteriorating in the harsh tropical weather.

A convoy of departing American troops passed me on their way to Tan Son Nhut, all of them waving and laughing, happy to be going home. Saigon reminded me of a woman who had been raped, then left by her smirking attacker.

The Special Forces compound was a new one to me, built while I'd been away. It was manned by a B-detachment, whose main duties involved logistics and administration. When I went to the orderly room to sign in, it caused a good deal of confusion because I'd arrived back at the war in a very unorthodox manner. New troops weren't supposed to fly in from Thailand, but from Travis. They were supposed to be in big groups, not alone, and they were supposed to land at the replacement center in Cam Ranh, not in Saigon.

I was told I'd be allowed to spend the night there in Saigon, but the next morning someone would take me back to Tan Son Nhut, and I'd have to make my own way up to Nha Trang. I was assigned a bunk in the small transient quarters, and after dropping off my bags, I wandered over to the club to see if I could find anyone I knew. The first old friend I ran into was a man I'd originally met back in 1963 when the 5th Group was still at Fort Bragg.

He told me he was a short-timer and would be leaving in a few weeks. It was his fourth or fifth tour, and he was glad it was over. When I told him I was just starting a new yearlong tour, he laughed and shook his head. "Hey, man, ain't you heard the damned news? The war's over, and we lost!"

When I gave him what must have been a blank stare, he went on to explain it. "Sure, what would you call it? The Americans are all leaving, and the NVA are all staying—it's fucking *fini*, buddy."

That phrase, "The war's over; we lost," pretty much summed up the attitude in the 5th Group during that last year the unit spent in Vietnam. It was not a real happy time.

The old, freewheeling days of Special Forces were just about over too, I discovered. General Abrams was cracking down on Special Forces, I was told, and everyone up the chain of command was running scared because of it. There were lots of new rules that all troops in Saigon had to follow, and that included Special Forces. Evidently there was a huge problem with drugs, especially among the younger troops.

I had never seen any evidence of drug problems in Special Forces units, and tried to make a joke about it, but I was warned not even to mention the word "drug" in a joking manner or I'd get myself in a world of trouble.

I found out that to leave the compound, I had to first request a pass, and if one was granted, it would only be good until dark. There was no place to stay overnight downtown anyway, I was told. I was warned to be back by the stated time or I'd be reported AWOL and receive an Article 15. Christ almighty, I thought, why in the hell did I ever come back here?

I changed into civvies anyway, went through the hassle of getting permission to leave the compound—which included a mandatory briefing on all the sins I should avoid while downtown—signed out and headed for Tu Do Street.

Tu Do hadn't changed a whole lot, but there didn't seem to be as many GIs wandering around as before. Of course, it was just afternoon, and things usually didn't get hopping until later. I wondered at the real motive behind keeping the place off-limits at night to the enlisted swine. Was it really done for the young troops' safety, and to help keep order, or was it done to make the bars on Tu Do quieter and more pleasant for the senior officers, reporters, and visiting big shots?

I went to the Sporting bar first, said hello to the girls I remembered there, and checked out the latest gossip and casualties with a couple of old buddies. After a beer at the other Special Forces hangout, the Morning Star, I decided to try to find a bar girl named Lyn I'd first met seven years before.

Actually, I didn't think I'd have any luck, because I hadn't seen her in several years, and the girls moved around a lot. I went to the bar that she'd been managing the last time I was in town, but she wasn't there. The male bartender pretended not to understand me when I asked about her, but I sat at the practically empty bar and had a beer anyway.

I'd just finished my drink and was getting up to leave when she walked in. She recognized me right away, seemed genuinely glad to see me, and when she saw I had an empty bottle in front of me, she told the bartender to bring me a new one. I told her I'd just started a new tour but that I only had a few hours to spend in town and would be leaving the next morning. She asked me if I'd get to come to Saigon often, but I had to tell her I didn't know.

I inquired about her family, and she told me her brother, an officer in the ARVN, had been badly wounded during Tet, but recovered. One of her sisters was married, and her mother was in good health. The bar business wasn't as good as it once had been, she said, but she was still making out okay. I asked her if she had a boyfriend.

"I always tell you, you my only boyfriend," she said with mock seriousness. "Why you no believe me?"

I bought the next round and we talked some more, but it didn't seem like there was much to say. I asked her if she still had the apartment around the corner, and she said she did, but would probably have to move soon. Evidently her landlord had been offered a huge sum for the place by an American official, and it was an offer he couldn't refuse.

When I looked at my watch, it was already time to be getting back to the compound. "Things are a lot different in Vietnam now than before, aren't they?" I asked her.

"Yes," Lyn said, "and I think pretty soon get worse."

I got to the air base early the next morning and put my name at the bottom of a long standby list for hops to Nha Trang. The waiting area was a big, barnlike room with only a few chairs, all of which were taken. Bored, dejected, and exhausted-looking troops sat and sprawled all over the filthy floor. There was one water fountain and one toilette for everyone. Finally, at 1400 hours that afternoon, my number came up and I got on a C-130 for the ride north.

The Special Forces headquarters hadn't changed much since '67, but it had grown some. It looked more permanent, less like a wartime headquarters and more like something you might find at Fort Bragg. It was too late to do anything that day, I was told by the charge of quarters who signed me in, but the next day I would in-process. He warned me that things had tightened up around Nha Trang too, and that I'd have to have a pass to get out the gate if I planned to go to town. There was a bed check at 2200 hours. It was so crowded downtown that it wasn't worth the effort anyway, the CQ said.

The next day I went through the dreary in-processing procedure. It seemed that there were more levels of bureaucracy than ever, but everyone was pretty efficient. The only hitch came when it was time to get my assignment for the upcoming year.

I'd assumed that I would be assigned to SOG again because I had experience with the operation and because that seemed to be where all the other transferees from Thailand were being sent. I planned to request duty at Kontum with Command & Control Central because of my friends there.

But my radio operator MOS came back to haunt me again. There was a critical shortage of operators, I was told, especially senior radio operators who had A-team experience, and all commo assignments were controlled by the signal officer. When I talked to him, he told me that SOG had all the volunteers it needed. Arguing was futile, he said, and by that time I just didn't give a good shit anyway.

"Okay," I said, "put me wherever you want, but at least make it an A-detachment. I don't get along very well at the B- or C-detachment level."

The signal officer told me that it would take until the next day before they knew where I'd be going, so I spent the rest of the afternoon looking around the headquarters area for people I knew. I went over to Project Gamma's headquarters and bumped into a man I'd known six years earlier back on Okinawa. He told me that I'd just missed Carl Hargus, who had gone home a few weeks before. I asked him about the "TWEPing" debacle, but my friend would tell me little. He said morale in Gamma was shot, and everyone was ready to get the hell out of Vietnam.

I also heard that Bill Martin was at Nha Trang, and found him that evening in the club. He was a short-timer too, and would be leaving in a couple of months. "I was sitting right here at the bar one night, when the goddamn CID and MPs come in and arrested the men sitting on either side of me," he said. "Christ, scared the shit out of me. I couldn't figure out what was going on! Jeez, they drug the goddamn *Group commander* off and threw him in Long Binh jail.

"Things are better now that Colonel Healy took command of the Group and replaced Abrams's hatchet man," Bill continued. "At least Healy's a jumper. I still pity you, having a whole year of this shit to look forward to. Things definitely ain't what they used to be—the goddamn war's over, and we lost."

The next morning I was told that I'd be going to A-242 at Dak Pek, an all-Montagnard camp up in the Central Highlands near the tri-border area. The C-detachment was at Pleiku, and the B-team was at Kontum. Oh well, I thought, at least I'd get to see Spurgeon and some of the other SOG CCC guys on my way through. And after all the tours I'd spent in Nam, I'd finally be getting to work with Yards.

Spurgeon heard I'd been looking for him, and drove over to the Kontum B-team from the SOG compound across town. He was in a good mood, and said that morale in the various SOG units was still pretty high. The men assigned to SOG didn't have to get involved too much with the workings of the rest of the 5th Group, he said, so they were more insulated from the bullshit.

The special projects had grown a lot since my experience with them in the mid-sixties. In late '67, SOG absorbed Sigma and Omega—Delta remained separate—and the unit now was divided into SOG North, Central, and South. SOG units had built on hard-learned experience of those early-day pioneers. From what Spurgeon told me, SOG apparently had its tactics and techniques down pat, and things were running smoothly. It was still extremely dangerous work, however, and all the SOG units, from recon/commando teams to the larger, Hatchet forces, continued to take heavy casualties.

Bill had a bunch of new war stories to tell me. He'd just been given command of his own team, RT-Texas. On one infiltration, he said, his team and another had been assigned the mission of pulling off a prisoner snatch. The two teams were infiltrated simultaneously, but at different LZs. The idea was for both teams to sneak over to the Ho Chi Minh trail and set up ambushes about five kilometers apart. Bill's team would initiate its ambush first, causing a diversion, and shortly afterward the other team would try to snatch the prisoner.

"Both teams got in okay, and my bunch made it to the trail and got into position by the second night without being seen," Bill said. "The other team got compromised before they got there, though, and had to be exfiltrated. Since we were already set up, I decided to go ahead and knock off a truck. We had an AC-130 Blackbird overhead for backup, so I wasn't too worried.

"We were lying on a little high ground right by the trail, and I'd set up two claymores at what I figured was the height of a truck cab. On that operation I was carrying an M-79 grenade launcher loaded with grapeshot. There was lots of traffic on the trail that night and we didn't have to wait too long.

"Pretty soon we hear this truck chugging along toward us. The bastards drive without lights, so they have to go slow. We were right on top of a hill, and the truck driver had it in low gear, really winding it up. He gets to the top of the hill, and just as he threw that baby into second gear, I set off the claymores.

"All the guys opened up on full auto, and I put two of those grapeshot rounds through the front windshield. The team covered me, and I ran down to look at the damage and see what was under the canvas in the back. I jumped up on the running board and checked out the cab first. The driver and his assistant looked like two piles of raw hamburger. I ran around to the back and looked in, hoping to see something interesting like secret weapons or something. The whole fucking truck was full of rice.

"About this time, two other trucks come roaring up and stop a hundred meters away at the bottom of the hill. It's their damned reaction force. They're yelling and screaming orders, and when they all get on the ground, it looks like there's at least a platoon. I watched 'em get in a skirmish line and start up the hill, then we took off running like hell.

"I still wasn't very worried, because I figured the gunship would cut the bastards to pieces while we made our getaway. I'd just made a commo check with the aircraft an hour before the ambush, and he'd come in loud and clear."

"Let me guess what happens next," I said. "You try to call the aircraft and suddenly there's no answer."

"Yeah," Bill said, "how did you know?"

"Because that's Murphy's Law of Combat Communications," I told him. "In combat, commo is always great until you really need it."

Bill and his team had managed to evade the enemy in the dark jungle without aid of the gunship, and were successfully exfiltrated the next morning with no casualties.

Spurgeon could tell I was in a sour mood, and to help cheer me up, he took me on a little tour of some of the local joints in Kontum. Most of the bars were crowded, and the girls working in them were ugly, appeared dirty, and were obviously very overused. In years past, those sorts of places had seemed exciting, fun, and interesting, but by that stage in the game, all they did was depress me more.

I was anxious to get out to my new A-team and go back to work.

Chapter 7

Helicopters flew from Kontum up to Dak Pek quite often, and after a day at the B-team, I threw my stuff in one and headed to my new home. By the time I arrived at camp that March of 1970, it had been in operation since 1962. Dak Pek was one of the first A-team camps built by Special Forces at the very beginning of our involvement in Vietnam, and it had a colorful history. The camp was in the beautiful Dak Poko Valley, next to a river and near an abandoned road the French had been working on when they left.

My HU-1B pilot flew up the valley between towering mountains. We orbited the camp once and I took the opportunity to check out the terrain below. The valley floor consisted of rolling hills that had been stripped practically bare for farming and, I presumed, to afford better fields of fire. Camp Dak Pek was built on seven hills. To me, the camp was eerily reminiscent of Dien Bien Phu, although unlike the position of the French, the fortified hills of Dak Pek were much closer together and could offer mutual fire support in case of an attack.

Over the years, Camp Dak Pek had been steadily improved and more heavily fortified, and by the time I got there, it was one of Special Forces' showplaces. It was one of the few camps in-country with its own paved runway. It could take planes up to the size of a C-123.

I got off the chopper and asked the young American NCO who had come down to meet the aircraft where the rest of the team was. He pointed to the nearest hill, the lowest of the seven, and said I'd find everyone there. I lugged my bags and equipment up the hill to a square, rock building that was the only surface structure. It was, I discovered, the team mess hall and club. A lieutenant was sitting at one of the tables writing something, and a couple of NCOs I didn't know were playing darts. I introduced myself to the lieutenant and said I was the new commo supervisor.

"I'm Lieutenant Alexander, the CA/Psy Ops officer," he said, looking up. "Didn't even know you were coming. Captain Walther is the CO, but I don't know where he's at right now. Sergeant First Class Weeks just took over as team sergeant, and I think you'll find him down in the TOC. You can just dump your bags and stuff in the corner until we figure out where to put you." Alexander showed me how to find the entrance to the TOC, which was right out the back door.

I walked down a flight of concrete steps to get to the underground operations center. It was nice and cool down there and still smelled like freshly poured cement. I found the team sergeant talking to another lieutenant named Andrews, the detachment executive officer. They both said they hadn't been expecting me either.

"The way things have been going lately with replacements, we didn't think we'd get another radio supervisor for a long time—if ever," Weeks said. "I was the senior weapons man, but now I'm the team sergeant. We don't even have an intel sergeant. You and I are the ranking NCOs on the team. Come on, let me show you around and introduce you to the rest of the guys.

"This is the American hill," Weeks said as we climbed back up the TOC steps. "We have a handpicked platoon of security with us and they're good, loyal troops. The LLDB [ARVN Special Forces] team lives over there on that other hill . . . seems to work out pretty well that way."

As we began our tour of the camp, Tom Weeks and I filled

each other in on our backgrounds. Although I'd never met Tom before, we knew many people in common, and I was glad to find out that he had a lot of previous combat experience in Vietnam. I liked him immediately.

One of the very first people we ran into on our tour was a Vietnamese civilian named Minh, whom I already knew. Minh, the camp electrician and generator operator, had worked for me at camp Vinh Thanh five years before. I found out that he had recently been married and was living in a bunker near the generators with his pretty, young wife and new baby.

As we walked, Weeks told me a little of the recent past history around Dak Pek. "Well, as you know, the camp has been here since 'sixty-two," he began. "Up until the big American troop buildup, it was a pretty hairy place, as you can probably imagine. The 4th Infantry moved into the area a few years ago and things quieted down a lot."

Tom pointed to a large, prominent mountain several kilometers south of camp. "They used to have an artillery unit dug in on top of that mountain, and they could cover the whole damned valley. Their infantry used to run a lot of sweeps and operations in the mountains, and that took the pressure off us so we could put most of our efforts into working with the Yards. We really went heavy on the civic affairs bullshit."

I told him I'd met Alexander. "Yeah," Tom said, "a lot of the A-camps have a permanently assigned CA/Psy Ops officer now." Tom showed me a new cement-block building with a tin roof that sat at the bottom of the American hill near the airstrip. "That's Alexander's pet project," Tom continued, "the new school. The Yard kids come from all over the valley to attend. None of them have ever been able to go to one before."

We ducked into a large bunker built into the side of the American hill—the camp hospital and dispensary. I met Sergeant First Class Wolf, the senior medic, and his assistant, Spec Four Erickson. Along with a couple of Montagnard female nurses, they were both busy with the daily sick call. Tom told me that the entire medical crew had been up most of the night helping one of the Striker's wives with a complicated birth. Mother and child were both doing well, Weeks said.

"The 4th Infantry was pulled out of the valley about six months ago as part of the American reduction of force," Weeks continued as we left the medical bunker and continued the tour. "Of course, as soon as they left, the NVA came pouring back into the AO, and things are getting hairy again. We've got a company from the Pleiku Mike Force in camp right now, and they've been running operations for about a month. They'll be pulling out in a few days, though, and we'll be fully on our own again."

I asked Tom how good our CIDG troops were.

"Well," he said, "they're Yards, so they're pretty dependable. Most of them are part of the Jai tribe, who never had as warlike a history as, say, the Jarai. The Jai were mostly artisans, sort of like the American Navajo, I guess you'd say. American Special Forces has been here training them since 'sixty-two, so we don't have to do a lot of that anymore. Camp strength stays at right around 450 men. I guess the main problem is that while the big American infantry units were working here in the valley, our troops didn't see much combat action and they got a little lax and a little soft."

"So, you have no intel sergeant at all?" I asked, changing the subject.

"We have no senior intel NCO," Weeks said. "We still have an assistant intel man, a spec five, and he's pretty sharp. Guy by the name of Frier—used to be a West Point cadet, but something went wrong and he joined the Army as an enlisted man.

"Besides the Mike Force, we also have a semipermanent SOG launch site here," Weeks told me. "They have their own people for security, and they're set up down there on the edge of the runway," he said, pointing.

Weeks introduced me to the two weapons men, Staff Sergeant Fry and Sergeant Charlie Young. "They're young," Weeks said, "but they know their shit. I still help out with the mortars now and then too."

I told him the last A-camp I'd been at back in '65 had a 4.2-inch mortar, and asked what the biggest thing around Dak Pek was. "We got that 4.2 beat," he said. "Look over there on that saddle between the two biggest hills."

"Christ," I said when I saw what he was pointing at, "looks like a couple of 105 pack howitzers."

"That's exactly what they are," Weeks said with a smile. "We got a 106 recoilless rifle too. See it up there on top of that tallest hill?"

I told him I was impressed.

"It's all stuff that's been scrounged over the years," he said. "None of it came through official channels. We got a couple of rocket pods off a helicopter too," he said. "They're set up to fire electrically. Use 'em for indirect fire."

I remembered a similar experiment we'd conducted with 3.5-inch antitank rockets at camp Tan Phu way back in '63. That one hadn't turned out so hot, but I didn't say anything.

"This camp and its CIDG have been selected for conversion to a regular ARVN unit," Weeks said. "It's the so-called Vietnamization program, and it's what you'll be doing for the rest of your time here. All the Yards have finally been reequipped with M-16s, M-79 grenade launchers, and M-60 machine guns. If things keep going smoothly, the ARVN will take over the camp in a few months, and you'll go back to Nha Trang and spend the rest of your tour sitting in the NCO club!"

Weeks himself was a short-timer and would be going home in about a month.

The last man Weeks introduced me to was a young guy named Hull, who was my junior radio operator. He was surprised, but happy, to find out he'd have help with the radio duties again. Hull was busy working on one of the antennas, and I said I'd get back with him later to help with the nightly situation report.

"I guess this will be your new home," Weeks said, showing

me a large bunker on the edge of the inner perimeter. "It's an important position. Besides being the alternate commo bunker, it's got a .50 cal that covers this draw here." We went down four or five concrete steps and I looked things over.

The bunker had a cement floor, concrete-block walls, and heavy beams in the ceiling. It was fairly spacious, and had been divided into two sections by a cement-block wall. Against that wall was a folding canvas cot. In one corner there was a field table that held an ANGRC-74 radio and a PRC-25. Antenna leads ran down from the ceiling and were attached to the radios. I ducked my head and went into the other part of the bunker, which held the .50 caliber Browning. There was plenty of ammo stored there, and in one corner I spotted an M-14 rifle. It had one of the odd, experimental, straight-line stocks with a pistol grip, and was fitted not only with a bipod but with a Starlight scope.

The .50 pointed out of a firing aperture about the size of a bay window, and I immediately envisioned an RPG-7 rocket flying in through it.

"Yeah," Weeks said when I asked him about it. "It really isn't finished yet, but you can work on it while you're here." He went on to tell me that the executive officer from the Vietnamese Special Forces team, who lived on our hill as sort of a liaison officer, occupied the bunker next to mine. Weeks pointed out an electrical firing device with leads that disappeared out the left side of the firing aperture.

He laughed. "That goes to another one of our secret weapons. We got ten CS tear-gas grenades set up on a little improvised launcher. That firing device blows a small explosive charge, and if it works right, the grenades will be lobbed down the hill and go off at the bottom.

"You're kind of hung out here on your own," Weeks continued. "The only American sleeping areas that aren't connected together by tunnels are this one and the medical bunker over on the other side of the hill. Erickson sleeps over there. Come on, let me show you."

The tunnel system started at the TOC, wound back through several underground sleeping rooms, and came out at the other end in the American team's 81mm mortar pit. I told Weeks it was very impressive and said it looked like everyone could sleep soundly without worrying about incoming mortar rounds or rockets.

"The combat engineers say we got enough overhead cover to protect against anything up to about the size of a 155 round," Weeks told me. "That is," he added, "unless they start using some sort of delay fuse, in which case we'll be fucked!"

I asked him what kind of indirect fire weapons the NVA had been using lately, and Weeks said that besides 82mm mortars and an occasional 120, the enemy mostly fired 122 rockets. "They've been using more and more 140s too," he said. "I'll tell you the scariest damned thing we heard lately," he added, stepping closer and lowering his voice. "I guess you noticed the protective mask hanging in your bunker?"

I told him I had, and assumed it was because of the improvised CS gas dispenser nearby.

"It's more than that," Weeks said. "Not too long ago we got an intel report that one of the SOG teams had found a cache of 140 rockets over in Laos that turned out to be filled with fucking nerve gas!"

We walked down the American hill and through the gate in the perimeter wire. A large sheet-metal structure that resembled a pole barn sat on some flat ground there, and Weeks told me it was the supply building. It was conveniently near the helipad, and a dirt road ran from it directly to the airstrip. The supply building was full to the brim with tiger-stripe camouflage uniforms, indigenous rations, mosquito nets, and so on.

"The supply problems we used to have in the early days no longer exist," Weeks said. "Especially since this Vietnamization program started, the crap has really been rolling in. The arms room is up on the American hill inside the perimeter. Ammo is pretty much spread out among the different hills."

"This is the first A-camp I've been at that has its own run-way," I told him. "Makes it a lot easier than having to deal with parachute resupply or helicopters for everything."

We walked through another, larger gate, which was the main one to the camp, and continued on past a large bunker complex, which turned out to be the Vietnamese Special Forces living area. Weeks said they had a pretty good bunch of LLDB. "There's a different sort of atmosphere now that this Vietnamization crap started," Weeks told me. "When the Americans leave, they all stay and get to assume complete command. We're slowly turn-ing everything over to them, and I think they're finally figuring out how much of a load the Americans have been pulling all these years. I actually think they'll be sad to see us go."

We followed a trail past the LLDB area and up the saddle to the pack-howitzer emplacement. The little guns were surrounded by a low wall of sandbags. Weeks said that over the years, the Americans had trained a Yard artillery crew, and that they did pretty well. Just past the two guns, we passed through another gate and more defensive wire, and trudged up the steep side of a tall, cone-shaped hill.

"One full company occupies this hill," Weeks said. "They're one of our best units, and because this is the highest hill in camp, it's one of the most important." We walked up to the very peak where the 106 recoilless rifle stood on a tripod mount, surrounded by a sandbag wall. There was a small ammo-storage area built into the side of the emplacement, and I asked Weeks what they had for rounds. "We got everything," he said, "beehive, HEAT, WP, the works."

There was a great view of the valley from the top of the hill, and also a commanding view of the entire camp. I could look di-rectly down into the American mortar pit on the other, lower hill.

"If the bastards ever take this hill and this 106, we're going to be in a world of hurt," I said.

"Well," Weeks replied, "they never have yet. They'll have to get across about a kilometer of bare ground, then attack practically straight uphill through five rows of defensive wire which is full of trip flares, while all our guys are in fortified positions shooting the hell out of them and lobbing grenades."

I admitted it was a great defensive position.

" 'Course, just in case they *do* manage to get through, the recoilless rifle crew knows they're to disable the gun." Weeks pointed to a couple of thermite grenades at the base of the bipod. "They'll stick one of those in the breach."

I didn't say anything more, but I'm a born pessimist. Besides, I'd grown up listening to my father tell stories about Hawaii before the war. He said that in the year preceding the Pearl Harbor disaster, he'd sat in monthly briefings listening to people say why Hawaii was invulnerable to surprise attack.

Weeks and I walked around the trench that circled the hill. The ground was very hard on the hill, making the trench and the fighting positions dug into the front edge of it that much more sound. The troops had been continuously improving the defenses for eight years, and had done a very good job of it. I mentioned to Weeks what good work they'd done.

"Yeah," he laughed, "these Jai might not be the most aggressive Montagnard tribe, but they're the best at building fortifications."

Weeks took me back down to the TOC and, with the aid of the map, gave me a quick rundown on the enemy situation. "As you can see, we are only a couple of klicks away from the Laotian border. The northern border of Cambodia is right down here, close to camp Dak Seang, which is more or less our sister camp."

Weeks traced a line with his finger across the border, sweeping down the valley toward Kontum. "We're sitting right in the middle of a primary infiltration route from the Ho Chi Minh trail, and interdicting enemy movement across the border has always been one of Dak Pek's main objectives." Weeks indicated a myriad of red—enemy—unit indicators surrounding Dak Pek, with the biggest concentrations just across the border. "As you can see, there is no lack of targets to shoot at in this AO," he said with a laugh.

"These little blue, platoon symbols in the valley are those fortified villages I showed you when we were on the other hill. Back in the early days, when we were pushing the strategic hamlet concept, our predecessors had very good luck rounding up the friendly Yards and moving them to these villages. Each village has its own, militia-type unit to guard it, and the villages are surrounded by earth walls, punji stakes, and stuff like that. They're all under command of District."

I asked Weeks if they'd been reequipped with new weapons like our Strike Force, and he said they hadn't. "Those RF/PF [Regional Forces/Popular Forces, pronounced ruff-puff] units are still low man on the totem pole as far as support goes," Weeks said. "They still only have carbines and rifles, but they don't do any offensive patrolling, only local security. They're a good source of intel information," he added as an afterthought, "and we run med patrols around to them a couple of times a month."

"So does this mean that any Yards we run into who are still up in the mountains are Viet Cong?" I asked.

"Probably, but not necessarily," Weeks said. "Some of 'em still live up there and try to stay neutral. About the only way to tell whose side they're on is if they start shooting at you."

That part of the war hasn't changed, I thought.

Weeks turned me over to Sergeant Hull after that so I could learn the current commo situation. It sounded pretty reassuring.

The main commo room was built into one corner of the underground TOC. We had one of the Collins single sideband radios for primary and an ANGRC-74 for the alternate. The alternate commo bunker, where I would be living, also had a 74 and a PRC-25. All important traffic was still sent via Morse code and encrypted on one-time pads. The Collins also had a voice mode, but was used only for administrative messages and in case of emergency.

"We don't have any problem talking to anyone," Hull assured me. "We get Kontum and Pleiku on voice with no sweat, even at night, and usually have no problem talking directly to the SFOB in Nha Trang." He took me upstairs to the top of the bunker and showed me the antenna setup.

We had a couple of doublet antennas that could be used with either the Collins or the 74, and three 292 ground-plane antennas for the PRC-25s. Hull told me that most of the time we could talk to Camp Dak Seang on the PRC-25s, and that both camps could always monitor each other on the FM radios (the PRC-25s) even when our transmission signals wouldn't get through. Hull told me that, in case the main, aboveground doublets got shot or blown down, they even had an underground antenna that worked pretty well.

As far as commo went, I thought, things had certainly improved since the bad-old early days. I remembered how much trouble we'd had back at Tan Phu in '63 trying to communicate on an ANGRC-109. Back then, we couldn't even get standard 292 antennas for our almost worthless PRC-10s, but had to make do with improvised "field expedient" versions.

"Do you have any problems making commo with your combat operations?" I asked him.

Hull seemed surprised I'd even ask. "No, no problems at all. Each operation carries two or three PRC-25s, and even when they're way back in the mountains we always get through."

My mood was actually starting to brighten up. It looked like this tour would be a damned cakewalk. All we had to do was keep the NVA off our backs long enough to turn everything over to the Viets, then spend the last few weeks or months back at the SFOB getting ready to leave. Hell, like everyone said, this friggin' war was over, we'd lost, and it was time to start getting used to the idea!

Chapter 8

A few days after I arrived at camp, the Mike Force unit terminated its operations in our AO and pulled back into our perimeter. Other than a few minor enemy contacts, they hadn't seen any NVA. The Mike Force told us their gut feeling was that there were plenty of bad guys out there, but that they were avoiding contact.

The standard operating procedure at Dak Pek was to keep one or two combat operations in the field at all times, one of them accompanied by Americans. Since I was the new guy on the team, I was at the top of the list to go next, and was told to be ready to move out a day or two after the Mike Force departed.

The CAR-15 was still a fairly new weapon in those days. Also known as "the bank opener special," it was a short-barreled M-16 with a telescoping stock that made it even shorter and handier. The CAR-15s were standard issue to the SOG teams by 1970, but not general issue down at A-team level. The American team at Dak Pek had managed to scrounge two of the little weapons, however, and they were what we usually carried when out on operations.

"They got a hellacious muzzle blast, and they ain't real accurate," Weeks told me, "but they sure are handy and easy to carry. The AO you'll be working in is thick jungle and straight up and down mountains. You can't see any farther than about twenty-five meters anyway, and the CAR is good at that range."

Well, I thought, this is another improvement over the old folding stock, M-2 carbines (capable of automatic fire) and 9mm submachine guns we used to carry. Also for the first time, the Americans and Strikers were all armed with the same 5.56mm (.223 caliber) weapons, so there was no longer a need to carry huge amounts of ammo.

"We also managed to scrounge a few of those new thirty-round magazines," Weeks said.

I picked up one of the CAR-15s, along with magazines from the armory. Down at the supply building I drew a set of standard web gear, canteens, compass, indigenous ruck, two sets of tiger-stripe uniforms, insect repellent, and several indigenous rations. I'd brought my own knife with me from Thailand—an M-3 trench knife that I'd been carrying for a number of years.

I had a few other odds and ends that I'd kept from my days with special projects, such as my signal mirror, air-to-ground panel, pen-flare gun, and miniature flashlight. I packed them all away in the pockets of the small ruck, then started thinking about the usual problem of how to carry the hand grenades.

I was carrying two smoke and two frag, and after some consideration, I decided to pack the two smoke grenades in the ruck, on top of the poncho and rations, where I could still get to them in a hurry. I attached the frag grenades to my web gear behind the magazine pouches.

I always had the fear that when moving through real thick jungle, one of the grenades' pull rings would get caught on something and accidentally arm the damned thing, so I'd gotten in the habit of putting green tape around the pins and another piece of it around the safety lever. That would slow me down getting one ready to throw, but in my experience, shucking a 'nade was not something you needed to do with blinding speed anyway.

When I'd been in Kontum talking with Spurgeon, he showed me the new, experimental minigrenades SOG had recently been issued. They were about the size of a golf ball and could be thrown a long way. They used the same explosive charge that was in the 40mm, M-79 round.

Special projects always got all the neat, new stuff first, and as I packed up to go on my first Vietnam operation in almost three years, a mild wave of jealousy swept over me. Oh well, I'd been there and done that already. Besides, the war was over, and it seemed fitting to spend my last tour where I'd started fighting the damned thing in '63—back on an A-team with the CIDG.

We were running operations of seven days' duration at Dak Pek. There was plenty of water in the area, and the dehydrated indigenous rations we carried didn't weigh much. The terrain was very rugged, though. Seven days of continuous movement through it was exhausting, and we started incurring noncombat casualties such as heat prostration, twisted ankles, diarrhea, and so forth, if we stayed out much longer.

Weapons, ammunition, water, and a little food were about the only things we carried. The new lightweight nylon ponchos were being issued by that time, and most of the men carried one, but not to stay dry—which was an impossibility. The ponchos were used to make emergency litters, to wrap up in at night to keep from getting chilled, for use as a ground cloth, and to use as shrouds for friendly KIA.

We didn't carry any extra clothing, but some of us got in the habit of taking along a few safety pins to hold together ripped and torn uniforms. Early on in the conflict, Special Forces discovered that underwear and socks caused more trouble than they were worth, and simply stopped wearing them at all. It was impossible not to get your feet wet, and they stayed healthier, and dried faster, if they weren't covered by a soggy, wet sock. We had originally picked up this trick from the British SAS in Malaya, but it was something all our Vietnamese and indigenous troops already knew.

Toward the end of March 1970 the Mike Force company was airlifted out of Dak Pek and returned to what they expected to be a week or two of rest and relaxation in Pleiku. They had been deployed on almost constant operations for the past several months and were worn-out.

The day after they left, I was told to report to the TOC for my operations briefing. When I walked in, our detachment CO, Captain Walther, Sergeant Weeks, and Erickson, the junior medic, were already huddled around the situation map.

Although the lowest-ranking man on A-242, Specialist Fourth Class James Erickson had more firsthand combat experience in the Dak Pek AO than just about anyone else on the team. Medics are always thought of, at least by the civilian world, as being noncombatants. It's ironic that on Special Forces A-detachments in Vietnam, the medics went on more combat operations than anyone, because when Americans accompanied an operation, we usually sent one of the American medics. The duty of going out on operation rotated, but since there were only two medics assigned to an A-detachment, they went out on every other one. And Erickson had been at Dak Pek a long time.

Weeks handled the briefing, with Captain Walther adding occasional comments. It was to be a company-size patrol, standard seven days' duration, and we'd be working the area to the west of camp.

"You'll pull out of camp at first light tomorrow morning," Weeks said. "We're sending 101 Company, which is one of our better units, and they'll be ready to go and waiting for you down by the front gate.

"This is the first big operation we've run in some time, but there shouldn't be any problems. The LLDB weapons man is going along, and you'll have one of the interpreters." Weeks used a pencil for a pointer and showed me the general route of march we should take. "You'll move up this valley, along the sides of the mountains. There's lots of old trails up there. Basically, your mission is to check the trail networks, interdict movement on them, and try to find out if the bastards are starting to form up en masse."

The area he was pointing to on the map was right on the Laotian border. "How much latitude do we have as far as crossing the border goes?" I asked. Special Forces had never paid a lot of attention to trying to stay precisely inside Vietnam before, but what with General Abrams in command, and all the new rules and regulations, I didn't want to start a shit storm of trouble. After all, we weren't a SOG unit.

"Don't be too concerned about it," Captain Walther said. "Try to stay in bounds the best you can. There isn't a fence with signs or a chalk line in the jungle," he added with a laugh.

"I know you've got a lot of time in-country, Sergeant Wade," the captain said, "so you know that the LLDB and the Yards will want to let you run things. Part of this Vietnamization bullshit is to make them start doing it themselves, so try to bring them into the process as much as possible."

The captain must have seen the looks on Erickson's and my face, so he added a qualification. "If they're screwing up and you think they're about to get everyone killed, then of course you do what you think is necessary. You will still handle the American radio and control any American fire support from camp or American Tac-air, medevacs, and all of that."

That evening, Erickson and I walked over to the 101 Company's hill and talked with the Yard company commander and a couple of the platoon leaders. They assured us that they had everything under control and were prepared to move out. Erickson and I checked a couple of the weapons, basically just out of habit, and they were all clean and well cared for.

I got a good night's sleep, unconcerned about having to dodge incoming mortar rounds, and at oh-dark-thirty the American pulling guard duty woke me up. As was my habit since Tan Phu, I slept in full tiger-stripe uniform, complete with boots, so all I had to do was roll out of bed, put on my web gear, and pick up my ruck and CAR-15.

Erickson was already in the mess hall talking with our cook,

Ute, who had gotten up early with us to make sure we didn't leave on an empty stomach. Ute was a Yard, but after working for the Americans at Dak Pek for many years, he'd become a pretty good cook. I wasn't very hungry, and only had some coffee and a biscuit left over from the previous night's supper. As we drank coffee and ate, we could hear the troops from 101 Company forming up down by the gate.

Still wiping sleep out of his eyes, Sergeant Weeks came in to join us. We double-checked the radio frequencies, call signs, and the transposition codes we'd be using. There was a separate air-ground frequency in case we needed a medevac or air strike.

"We'll be tracking you with the mortar and the 105 howitzers," Weeks reminded us. "Every time you stop for any length of time, let us know your coordinates, and the coordinates of danger areas where you might need some indirect fire."

"What's the situation on getting air support and medevacs these days?" I asked.

"No problem," Weeks said, "not like it used to be. We can usually even get a dust-off for wounded Yards. Depending on what's going on, you can call for armed choppers or Air Force Tac-air. The SOG unit down in Kontum has their own armed choppers, and if they don't happen to be using them for one of their own shows, they're good about coming up to help the A-teams. 'Course, we got their launch site here, so that gives them another reason to give us a hand."

"What about at night?"

"Unless it's a wounded American and unless it's a real matter of life and death, don't try to get a medevac out in the AO at night. They'll come into camp at night, but trying to fly into a clearing up in those damned mountains is just too tricky. As far as air support at night, if you get in a real bind, we can probably get you a flare ship and maybe even an AC-130—they fly out of Thailand," Weeks added.

"They use the call signs Specter and Blind Bat?" I asked.

"Yeah, you worked with them before?"

I told Weeks I'd recently been stationed at Nakhon Phanon and had met some of the air crews socially.

It was time to leave, and Erickson and I saddled up and went down the hill to join the waiting company. We positioned ourselves with the command group, which was about a third of the way back in the column. The Yard commander had a quick conference with the LLDB weapons man, then we moved out the gate.

As I mentioned earlier, Camp Dak Pek was situated in the center of a valley floor that was almost entirely free of cover or concealment. This made it difficult for enemy units to sneak up on the camp, but also made it difficult for us to sneak up on them. We knew that our unit's movement out of camp was not going unnoticed by the enemy observers in the surrounding mountains.

The sun was already coming up over the eastern edge of the mountains, and it quickly burned off the few lingering wisps of ground fog. At first it felt good on my back, but very soon it was hot and my camouflage uniform was sweated through. As we slowly trudged along toward the western mountain range, I felt all the old survival instincts flood back. My sight and hearing seemed to improve along with my sense of smell. The trickle of adrenaline also perked up my reflexes, and I knew that at the sound of the first shot or explosion I'd be moving for cover before I was consciously aware of it.

We had a forty-five minute march across open ground before we'd get to the edge of the jungle-covered mountain, and I felt very vulnerable. I turned around to Erickson and mentioned that I hoped the commies hadn't learned to shoot any better than they had before.

Erickson said that in general they hadn't, but then went on to relate in a low voice a sniping incident that had occurred a year or so previously. An operation had been moving out of camp, heading to the west, just as we were, when one shot rang out. It center-punched the American officer accompanying the unit.

He died instantly. The shot had come from quite a distance away, something like two or three hundred meters, and the conclusion was that it had been a specialist, maybe a Russian, using a scope-sighted rifle.

"Yeah," I said, agreeing with the medic, "doesn't sound like any eighteen-year-old Viet Cong with a beat-up, Chicom AK-47." We continued to march, and I hoped like hell that the shooter had moved out of our AO. Until we got into the trees of the foothills, I envisioned some son of a bitch looking at me through a scope with the crosshairs centered on my chest.

When we got into the shade of the trees, we took a short break. I was glad, frankly, because my forty-five-day party in Bangkok hadn't done a lot for my physical conditioning. I was feeling tired and weak, and we hadn't even gotten to the hard part yet.

The company had stopped on top of a small hill that was already surrounded by old fighting positions. Some unit, probably the American 4th Infantry, had dug in and then abandoned the holes. The Yards efficiently moved into a defensive position, utilizing the handy foxholes without much direction from their leaders. The Yard carrying our PRC-25 had automatically joined the command group in the center of the perimeter, and I called in our location to camp. Sergeant Hull answered immediately, and commo was loud and clear.

After catching my breath and washing down a salt tablet with a swig of warm, iodine-laced water from my canteen, I inspected the perimeter. I was favorably impressed. The machine guns were where I'd have put them, and the guys carrying the M-79 grenade launchers were equally spread out.

It took me only a few minutes to decide that they were the best CIDG troops I'd worked with so far in Vietnam. This shouldn't have been any surprise, I suppose, because most of the troops at Dak Pek had been in training and in steady combat since 1962.

I rejoined the command group as they were talking and looking at the map. The Yards, of course, knew the area perfectly, having been born and raised there. The Yard company commander was showing the LLDB sergeant on the map where a good trail ran. The trail was not indicated on the map, but if the Yard said it was there, then it surely was.

It was very dangerous to move along the trails, of course, but that was just about the only choice either we or the enemy had. A small unit such as a recon team could slowly move crosscountry through the thick jungle, but to make any time, you just about had to use the trails and hope for the best. There were many trails to choose from, and with a little luck we could pick one that wasn't watched or guarded by the NVA.

Our break lasted only about ten minutes—just long enough to adjust equipment, get a drink, and catch our breath. Even so, by the time we started moving, I was already feeling a lot better. The recuperative abilities of youth are amazing, although at that time I was an old man, pushing twenty-eight years of age, and didn't snap back as quickly as I once had.

The next leg of our march led us practically straight up a prominent hill that stood on the edge of the mountain range. This hill had a commanding view of the valley and of the camp, and had played a role in many a battle around Dak Pek. As we finally reached the military crest, we found old bunkers and fighting positions and saw numerous craters from artillery and bombs. I was very glad the positions were vacant, and wondered what it would be like to try an assault on the hill, which was very difficult to climb even without being shot at.

The climb hadn't physically affected the Yards in any obvious way, and I was embarrassed at my own gasping and panting. One of our M-60 machine gunners, who weighed maybe 120 pounds, was right in front of me, and I'd watched him effortlessly make the climb with the gun carried muzzle forward, across one shoulder. Besides the gun, he was draped with ammo belts and grenades, and his rucksack was stuffed with what appeared to be all his worldly possessions. Several times during the ascent, he'd heard me panting and cursing, and turned around to grin, give me the thumbs-up sign, and assure me that this was definitely all "number-hucking-one!" For the millionth time I promised myself to quit smoking and boozing and to go on a health kick.

We didn't stop at the top of the hill, but continued on down the other side to a short saddle, across it, and then started up into the mountain range proper. By that point we were out of direct sight of the valley and the camp, and the danger of enemy contact became even greater. About then I somehow got my second wind, and was able to concentrate on the tactical situation and to forget about my personal physical difficulties.

I'd attached an M-1 carbine sling to the little CAR-15, with the front of the sling threaded through the front sight pedestal. The carbine sling had a snap connector on that end, which could act as a quick release. I carried the CAR slung across my body, with the sling let out to full length, and during most of the hard climbing I'd pushed it around to hang at my back so I could use both hands. As the trail leveled out and we began following it along the side of the mountain, I brought the weapon back around and let the weight rest on the right, front magazine pouch while still keeping my right hand on the pistol grip and my thumb on the safety.

Most infantry grunts in Vietnam used variations of this method to carry their M-16s. Of course, when performing small unit reconnaissance, ranger/commando type raids, and so forth, the book says to remove the sling completely. This is not only to reduce noise and the likelihood of getting it caught on stuff, but also to make sure the soldier is carrying it in his hands at the ready position instead of at sling arms.

We slowed down as we progressed deeper into bad-guy territory, and stopped often to scout out suspected danger areas. We'd gained altitude, so it was cooler, and not much sun made it through the double and triple canopy. Now when we stopped moving, the sweat-soaked uniforms became cold and clammy, causing everyone to shiver. The trail we were on was not large and appeared not to have been used recently. Still, with the steep mountainside rearing on the right flank and the sharp drop-off to the left, it was ambush city and pretty damned spooky.

All joking and grab-ass had long since stopped, and any talking was done in low voices or whispers. Even though our tribe of Jai Montagnards had no great history as warriors, they still carried the genes of many past generations who had fought and survived in that terrain and appeared to react automatically to the situation.

We took our time, moving cautiously toward the border several kilometers away. A little after noon we formed a defensive perimeter on top of a small hill, ate lunch, and sent out a few local reconnaissance patrols. One of the patrols reported finding fresh footprints on a trail to our north. The tracks appeared to have been left by a squad of NVA and led back toward camp.

At 1500 hours we pulled out of the temporary patrol base and continued moving to the west, on the same trail, for another two hours. Then we climbed up the mountain to another hilltop overlooking the trail and established our night bivouac.

Erickson and I decided on a couple of good concentrations for the indirect fire weapons back at camp. We were just about at the maximum range of our 81 mortar, but the little 105 howitzers would still reach us reliably. I radioed the coordinates back to camp, along with our remain overnight (RON) coordinates, then Erickson and I took the interpreter and wandered over to listen to what the Vietnamese Special Forces weapons man and the Yard commander were planning for the night's defenses.

"We send one ambush go here, cover back trail," the LLDB sergeant told me. "Maybe VC follow our tracks."

"How many men are you sending?" I asked.

The LLDB sergeant and the Yard commander had a short discussion. "We send eight men. Set two claymore mine."

If I'd been on that ambush, I'd have wanted some sort of light machine gun with us. Because Dak Pek had by then rearmed with the American TO&E of M-16s and M-60 MGs, we no longer had a squad automatic weapon, such as the BAR (.30-cal. Browning Automatic Rifle), which would have been the gun of choice. Our CIDG company was equipped with only three M-60s, and we needed them for perimeter defense, so the ambush would have to make do with M-16s.

After a little more discussion, we decided to send another group of four men to establish a listening post on a lower adjacent hill that covered a likely avenue of approach from the northwest. They were also close enough to the trail to detect any enemy movement in our direction from the border.

The southern edge of the company's defensive position was close enough to the trail to function as a large ambush, should the enemy attempt to come at us from Laos. Erickson and I watched the Yards placing the claymores and trip flares, and double-checked where they'd put the machine guns. We could find nothing wrong with their tactics. I was starting to feel more like a training cadre than a combatant.

It got dark quickly as the sun set behind the mountain range to our west, and it started getting downright chilly. Soon fog and mist began to form, making it seem even colder than it was. We had no entrenching tools so were not dug in, and, though we spent a quiet first night with no enemy activity, I didn't get a hell of a lot of sleep.

Chapter 9

The next morning we continued our march to the west, and that afternoon we made our first enemy contact. We had once again stopped and established a patrol base. I'd just finished eating, and was trying to decide if I should risk taking off my boots to doctor several new blisters. Suddenly, about half a kilometer to the southwest, we heard a single shot from an AK-47. There was a short pause, then several short bursts of M-16 fire. Fearing an attack, everyone dropped what they were doing and found better cover, but there was no more firing.

The LLDB sergeant was jabbering on the HT-1 squad radio, and the interpreter told me that one of our patrols had killed a trail watcher.

It was a common tactic of the VC and NVA to post trail watchers along obvious routes of march and, occasionally, on possible helicopter landing zones. The trail watcher's job was simply to stay alert and give the signal of approaching enemy by firing a couple of shots. These shots usually never hit anyone—may not even have been aimed—but had the desired effect of causing a short delay while the unit fired on dove for cover, giving the trail watcher a chance to run like hell.

In this case, we had lucked out, the enemy soldier apparently having dozed off or something. He allowed our guys to get too close to his position before firing his warning shots, and the Yard patrol was able to run him down and kill him before he could make good his escape.

Actually, that sort of thing was not uncommon. The NVA and VC were good troops, but often they became overconfident. After days of watching a trail and never seeing any enemy, they sometimes became lax. There was one popular war story making the rounds of Special Forces camps about a small patrol that had snuck up on an unsuspecting VC in a hammock. The young soldier was so unsuspecting, in fact, that he was lying there, contentedly flogging his dong. One of the Americans on the patrol supposedly lobbed an M-79 round at the masturbating VC just as he reached the short strokes. The round was a direct hit. We all laughed about the poor VC reaching what must have seemed the ultimate climax!

Our patrol came back in carrying the dead trail watcher's AK-47. The enemy soldier's only other equipment was a plastic canteen. The patrol leader reported that although the dead enemy was dressed as a VC, with no discernible uniform or insignia, he was Vietnamese. Since there were no Vietnamese living in those mountains, only Yards, that meant he was an NVA regular.

So now we were in that position I always dreaded. The shooting had undoubtedly warned the enemy of our presence in the area. We didn't know how many of them there were, or their exact location, but knew they must be within hearing distance of a rifle shot. Of course, they didn't know exactly how big a unit we had or our position either, but we were far from our base of support and close to theirs.

Erickson and I had a short conference with the LLDB and the Yard commander and decided to do something the enemy might not expect. We were right on the Laotian border. The enemy would probably think that we'd either stay where we were or pull back east toward the camp. We decided to do the opposite, and moved instead to the top of a large hill farther to our west. That put us about a kilometer and a half inside Laos.

We were, of course, in a very precarious position, and spent extra care in preparing our nightly defense. We had moved out of Dak Pek's artillery fan, so would only be able to depend on our organic weapons in case of an attack. I wasn't counting too much on the possibility of getting a gunship overhead.

Before it became fully dark, we once again had a discussion with the command group, and made a tentative plan for the rest of the operation. We decided to move southeast, which would put us on the other side of another large mountain. We would begin working our way generally back toward camp, following the contour of the land, and eventually reenter the Dak Pek valley at a point several kilometers south of camp. By coming from the direction of Laos, we hoped to confuse any enemy we made contact with into thinking we were on their side. That would give us a slight edge at the very beginning of the ensuing firefight.

As things turned out, all our plans were for nothing. That night, I was lying with the handset of the PRC-25 radio next to my ear. We'd put up the long antenna to give us some more range, and I started picking up bits and pieces of radio transmissions from aircraft, our camp, and occasionally from Americans whose voices and call signs I didn't recognize.

It sounded like there was a hell of a battle going on someplace, and before long we heard rumbles of large ordnance going off to our south. Before the night was over, we'd determined that our sister camp, Dak Seang, was under attack.

The next morning I got a short message from Sergeant Hull that confirmed our conclusion. He couldn't send many details, but we gathered that the attack at Dak Seang had been no mere probe, but a major attack, and it was still in progress. We advised camp that we were continuing our mission, and began to make our way very cautiously on our planned route of march.

By about 1400 hours we were back across the border in Vietnam and, finding a particularly good defensive position on yet another hilltop, decided to make it our RON position. Once again we sent out a few small patrols, and after checking the perimeter defenses, Erickson and I had nothing really to do. We kicked back, using our rucks for pillows, and as we monitored the PRC-25, listening to scattered transmissions from the continuing battle to our south, we watched the clouds float by overhead.

"Jeez, look at that," Erickson said, pulling me out of a light doze.

I opened my eyes in time to see, far overhead, three B-52 bombers fly in trail toward Dak Seang. "That must be a real shit storm going on down there for them to get fucking B-52s," I said. Less than a minute later we heard the rumble of the Arc Light strike going in, and even from that distance we felt the earth tremble beneath us.

By then I was less concerned with our own situation. I figured that if a big battle was going on down at Dak Seang, just about all the NVA in the area had to be involved in it in one way or the other. That meant that the only units still in our AO would probably not be very large, stray VC guerrillas or an occasional NVA recon element.

An hour or two later one of our patrols made contact with just such a unit. The patrol was lying in an ambush position next to a large well-used trail that ran west to east farther down the mountain from the smaller trail we'd been using. A group of four NVA in khaki uniforms came walking along from the direction of Laos, and our guys fired them up, managing to kill one of them. The rest of the enemy broke contact and got away in the jungle.

I always had cynical doubts about afteraction reports from our troops. If our patrol had really been in a good ambush position, and alert, they should have killed all four of the enemy. What I suspected was that they were lying off the trail, taking a break, all but one or two asleep, when the enemy came in sight. They'd probably just lucked out in zapping the one unfortunate NVA.

We spent another uneventful but tense night. The next morning we received a message from camp ordering us to immediately terminate operations in that AO and pull back closer to camp. We marched all day with only short breaks. By that evening we emerged from the mountains and were once again in the foothills within sight of camp. Our troops all knew about the big battle going on to our south, and I could tell they were relieved that we'd pulled in closer to home.

We spent the remainder of that operation working the foot-hills along the western edge of the valley floor. Over the course of the last eight years of fighting, just about every good defensive position in the area had been occupied by troops at one time or another. Most of the hilltops already had foxholes and other fighting positions, which we gratefully occupied at night. We saw no more sign of any enemy in our area, which didn't surprise me because the battle still raged twenty kilometers away at Dak Seang.

The sixth night of the operation, we RONed on a hill only a kilometer from camp. We moved out early the next morning and were marching through the front gate in time for breakfast. Erickson and I were starved, and old Ute's cooking never tasted so good.

"They're fighting at least a regiment down there," Weeks told us, "probably the NVA 28th Infantry, augmented by artillery."

I told Weeks we'd been hearing parts of the battle on the radio and asked him when the fighting had started.

"The thing kicked off at first light on April first—fucking April Fool's Day," Weeks said.

"They must have really had their shit together to start the attack during daylight," I said. "Before, these things always began about midnight so they could use the darkness and not have to worry so much about our Tac-air."

"You're right," Weeks said. "The bastards seem real confident, and are being aggressive as hell. The initial bombardment was with mortars *and* recoilless rifles. Blew the shit out of several buildings and knocked out part of the camp's commo. The

NVA tried their first assault right after that, but were beaten back when they got to the wire.

"Luckily, not all the commo was down, and the camp managed to alert higher of the situation. The C-detachment sent in some reinforcements right away. They airlifted in a company from Plateau Gi right outside the wire, but they got surrounded before they could move into camp—spent the whole night pinned down, and almost got overrun themselves."

"That first night is when Erickson and I started monitoring the battle," I said.

"The reinforcements finally got into camp the next morning, after the Air Force naped the shit out of the area," Weeks continued. "The damned NVA didn't seem to mind and made two more daylight assaults that same day. There's about a hundred bodies hanging in their wire down there, and the NVA are still trying to take the camp. The reports are that the damned bastards are dug in about thirty meters from the perimeter wire."

"That's the same tactics they used to take Dien Bien Phu," I said.

"Yeah," Weeks said, "why fix it if it ain't broke? Anyway, the Mike Force was inserted by chopper yesterday. They're a couple of klicks from camp and moving in behind the enemy. The camp is still under constant bombardment from rockets, mortars, and those damned recoilless rifles. You know that big fucking mountain right outside camp?"

Erickson and I nodded, completely enthralled with the details of this major fight.

"Well," Weeks went on, "the American 4th Infantry had that baby secured when they were still here. There was a battery of 155 artillery dug in right on the top of the thing. So now the peak is cleared and there's room to land one or two choppers at a time."

I said I'd noticed it from the air when I'd flown over it on my way into Dak Pek a couple of weeks earlier.

"Well, the NVA moved right in behind the 4th when they

pulled out of this AO, and now occupy that mountain. You can see directly down into Dak Seang from up there, so they know everything that's going on in the camp. They're directing the artillery from up there too.

"Yesterday our guys tried to get tricky and attempted a vertical envelopment. The plan was to insert one of SOG's 'hatchet force' platoons on the peak. They were going to secure the LZ so a company of Mike Force could be put in.

"Before the attempted insertion, the Air Force blew the holy-living-shit out of the area around the summit," Weeks said. "We were listening to it on the radio, and they must have put in five sorties of nothing but fucking napalm. The hatchet force was being airlifted by a Jolly Green Giant, and the chopper followed right in behind the last napalm run.

"It was still no good," Weeks told us. "Just as the bird flared out to land, one fucking NVA, who was somehow still alive, took out the chopper with an RPG-7 rocket. It blew up and burned. Killed them all."

After I cleaned up and changed clothes, I joined several other team members in the TOC to listen to the battle on the radio. We had a speaker hooked up to the base FM radio, and with the tall 292 antenna, we were able to hear both the soldiers on the ground and the aircraft supporting the battle.

The Mike Force element, which we could identify by its call sign, China Boy, made heavy contact with the enemy before they were able to relieve the besieged camp.

Rather than get flanked, and deciding not to run, part of the large NVA unit wheeled around to engage the new threat. The Mike Force was soon surrounded themselves and fighting for their lives. They were taking many casualties, and we listened as one by one the American leaders of the unit reported getting wounded.

In the meantime, the camp was still fighting off direct ground assaults by infantry and sappers, which came not only during darkness, but right in the middle of the day. The enemy was showing that he was not intimidated by our air support.

It was obvious to me that this was indeed an extremely large and dangerous enemy force—and the twenty kilometers that separated our two camps no longer seemed like that great a distance. The rest of the American team, and the LLDB too, were feeling the same way, and despite the fact that we had seen no signs of a major enemy presence in our AO, Camp Dak Pek went on heightened alert. We were not expecting a major assault; we thought the NVA might hit us with a probe to take some of the pressure off their unit at Dak Seang.

Another day or two passed, and pressure on Camp Dak Seang lessened slightly. The enemy apparently had decided to turn his full attention on the pinned-down Mike Force. All the American team members at Dak Seang had wounds of varying severity, and with the slackening of incoming rounds, the more seriously wounded were medevacked. Several American volunteers from other A-detachments were airlifted into the besieged camp, one of them being our team commander at Dak Pek, Captain Walther. We also loaned Dak Seang about half a company from our Strike Force to beef up its depleted unit.

Chapter 10

The day of April 11 passed uneventfully at Dak Pek, and that evening, after supper and showers, some of us gathered to sit outside in the cool twilight. A couple of the guys from the SOG launch site down by the runway wandered up the hill to join the bullshit session. One of them showed us the gun he'd recently bought off a guy who was on the way home, a modified Model 97 riot gun. Someone had cut the stock off, leaving just the pistol grip, and then sawed off the barrel so it was even with the end of the slide handle. As a final touch, the weapon had been chrome plated.

The gun was quite a novelty, and the owner fired it for us one-handed a couple of times, just to demonstrate that he could do it—no one else was particularly interested in trying it out.

Curfew in the valley was at sundown, and the locals knew that after sundown they were supposed to be inside their forti-fied villages. Anyone moving around the area after dark was considered fair game. On that particular evening, as we were all outside, someone spotted a man in civilian clothes walking along-side the river that flowed just below the camp.

It was only a few minutes after the start of curfew, and none of us was concerned, so we yelled at him to get going and fired a few shots in his direction to help make the point, and the man disappeared from our view.

Since Erickson and I had returned with 101 Company, we'd sent no more large operations out of camp because we were waiting to see how things transpired down at Dak Seang. We had taken a little heat from higher for this, as the SOP was that we should have an American-accompanied operation in the field at all times. As a compromise, we decided to start sending an American or two out with the nightly ambush patrols. On the night of April 11 it was the senior medic's turn, Staff Sergeant Wolf. Just before it became fully dark, we watched his small pa-trol depart camp and head for a position about a kilometer away.

That evening, I prepared for bed as I always did, by remov-ing only my camouflage shirt, leaving on my boots and trou-sers. It was more out of habit than anything else, because ever since I'd been at Dak Pek, I'd actually felt pretty secure at night. My bunker was very sound and well built. It had a cement floor and walls, which were dug completely into the side of the hill. I had a good five feet of overhead cover with large, sturdy beams holding it all up. I was not particularly worried about the enemy's indirect fire weapons.

By that late stage in the war, all the A-camps were constructed with an outer and an inner perimeter. My bunker was part of the inner perimeter, and to get to me, the enemy would first have to infiltrate through four rows of wire that were saturated with trip flares; through the outer perimeter trench line and bunker system, which was manned by our handpicked security platoon; then finally through another row or two of wire. That assault would have to be made uphill, over bare ground, while being raked by machine gun and M-16 fire and blasted by claymore mines and hand grenades, which were easy to lob downhill.

My only concern was with the large, window-size firing aperture for the .50 caliber machine gun, which I still had not gotten around to fixing. The aperture would make a good target for any sort of direct-fire weapon, including a recoilless rifle—many of which were being used at Dak Seang—or one of the very effective RPG-7s the enemy carried in increasingly greater numbers.

I slept in the inner portion of the bunker, though, and had a cement-block wall between me and the large, inviting target the opening made. My folding cot was against this wall, and the backup radios for the camp were in the far corner. As I prepared to sack out that night, I placed my M-16 and web gear in the corner nearest my cot, where they would be handy.

Since 1965, when the Special Forces A-teams in Vietnam had been equipped with the Collins SSB radios, the camps had maintained a round-the-clock radio monitor. This was possible because the Collins had a voice mode, and knowledge of Morse code was no longer a prerequisite just to send and receive routine traffic.

Messages of tactical importance were still encrypted and sent as code, however. At Dak Pek, one man pulled a whole night of guard duty, and was then given as much time off as possible the

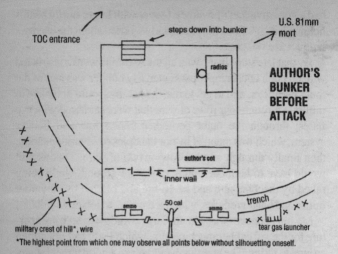

TOC entrance

steps down into bunker

U.S. 81mm mort

radios

AUTHOR'S BUNKER BEFORE ATTACK

author's cot

inner wall

trench

ammo   .50 cal   ammo

tear gas launcher

military crest of hill*, wire

*The highest point from which one may observe all points below without silhouetting oneself.

next day to get some sleep. His main duty was to monitor the radio and to wake up one of the team radio operators if higher headquarters came up on voice to say they had some encoded traffic to pass.

As I recall, the man on guard that night was our XO, Lieutenant Andrews. "Wake up, Sergeant Wade," he said, shining his flashlight on me. "The B-team has an ops-immediate message for us."

An "operational immediate" message was the second-highest priority, and I wasted no time getting over to the TOC where the main commo was set up.

The message was short and only took a couple of minutes to receive and decode: Electronic surveillance in your AO indicates heightened enemy activity. Be prepared for possible attack.

The message didn't seem all that fucking important to me, and I was pissed off that I'd had my sleep interrupted for it. Hell, in a goddamned A-camp, we were *always* ready for a possible attack.

The lieutenant agreed with me. For the past couple of nights we'd been on a fifty percent stand-to at night, and we both decided that would be good enough.

I walked back up the steps of the brightly lighted TOC and stood a moment or two in the dark to get my night vision back. I decided to smoke a cigarette before returning to bed, and sat down on the top of my bunker, looking out over the peaceful valley. It was a very dark night, and I couldn't see much.

I detected nothing wrong. But as I sat there awhile longer, alone in the dark, I began to get a strange feeling of danger—something quite different from just the usual cautious alertness. When moving around inside the inner perimeter at night, I always carried some sort of weapon, usually just my .45 pistol stuck behind my belt. Unconsciously I pulled the weapon out and sat with it in my lap as I finished off the smoke. A shiver ran up my spine, and I hastily made my way down the steps to the protection of my bunker.

I found the Starlight-scoped M-14 rifle in the corner, next to the .50 cal, turned on the power, then slowly used the scope to sweep the outer perimeter wire. The night-vision scope turned everything a weird green, but it was as easy to see objects through it as if it were day. I saw nothing out of the ordinary, and going back through the small doorway to the main part of the bunker, I lay down on my cot and immediately went to sleep.

It wasn't a very deep sleep, and at the first sounds of the incoming artillery, I jerked awake and rolled off the cot to the hard, cement floor. I was crawling over toward my rifle and web gear, which sat only a few feet away, when my bunker blew up.

I was knocked unconscious for a few moments, and when I came to, I thought I was in hell. I was still lying there on the floor, but my bunker was destroyed. The cement-block wall that separated the .50 cal from the rest of the bunker was gone. Where the big Browning had once stood there was nothing but a gaping hole. And a fierce fire was burning there, the remaining ammo

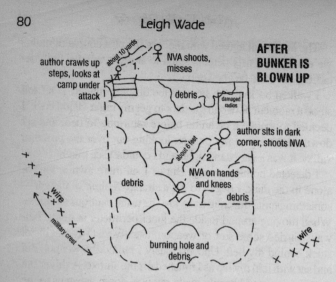

AFTER BUNKER IS BLOWN UP

author crawls up steps, looks at camp under attack

about 10 yards

1. NVA shoots, misses

debris

damaged radios

about 6 feet

author sits in dark corner, shoots NVA

2.

NVA on hands and knees

debris

debris

wire

military crest

wire

burning hole and debris

cooking off and detonating. The air was filled with dust and oily black smoke.

I realized I'd been hit in several places but I couldn't tell how badly off I was. At that moment, it didn't seem to matter, because I found I could still move all my body parts and wasn't really in much pain. I crawled over to where I'd last seen my rifle and web gear, but it was gone—buried under part of the collapsed wall.

I had no idea exactly how my bunker had been destroyed, but thought the enemy must have put some sort of large rocket through that damned firing aperture. The exploding .50 cal rounds were throwing slugs and the brass casings all around, and I crawled through the rubble as far away from that end of the bunker as I could.

I was hearing many other explosions and small-arms fire outside, and knew I needed to get the hell out of where I was. Then, to help me decide to evacuate, my demolished bunker began to fill up with tear gas that choked and blinded me.

Still on all fours, I went up the bunker steps and stuck my

head out to look around. I'll never forget my first impression of what had previously been one of the showplace camps in Vietnam. The entire American hill appeared to be engulfed in flame. The rock building that had been our mess hall and club was completely destroyed, and a fire raged in the ruins. Mortar rounds and grenades were exploding all over the hill, and tracers laced through the air.

I saw a crouched figure moving through the smoke toward the entrance to the TOC. I thought it was one of our troops from the security platoon and yelled at him to get under cover before he got himself killed. "Hey! Over here!"

The still-crouching figure heard me and made an odd sort of grunt, which sounded rather like a startled pig. As he turned to face me, I saw the unmistakable outline of an AK-47 silhouetted for just an instant against the fiery background.

Everything seemed to go into slow motion then. The enemy soldier appeared to casually bring the AK into a firing position and aim it in the direction from which he'd heard the American voice. In the meantime, I had already whirled and was flying through the air, diving headfirst back down the bunker steps. I heard the burst of AK-47 fire ripping the air where my head had just been.

I landed very hard, and once again briefly lost consciousness. Survival instincts brought me immediately back, however, and I scrambled as far away from the steps as I could get. I was sure the NVA sapper would toss in a hand grenade—just as I would have. I had no place to hide and could only get a few feet away from the gaping, bunker entrance.

My luck held, and no grenade came bouncing down the steps. Maybe he thought he'd killed me with his burst of fire, or maybe he was just preoccupied with the probable mission of knocking out the TOC.

I was beginning to suffocate from the thick smoke and tear gas, and suddenly I remembered the protective mask that had once hung in the corner, next to the radios. I was in luck again, because that was the only corner of the bunker still standing, and after a brief, blind search through the rubble, my fingers closed on its familiar shape. I put the gas mask on, cleared it as I'd drilled so often, then hungrily sucked in the filtered air.

I was still unarmed and had to find my weapon, even though that meant crawling over where the fire raged and ammo continued to cook off. I could see a little better with the protective mask on and was able to recover my M-16, which held one twenty-round magazine. Unfortunately, I could not find my web gear, which contained the rest of my ammo and my canteens.

There was still a huge volume of automatic-weapons fire outside, and it crossed my mind that I could very well be the only American left alive. I made my way back to the corner where the radios still sat on their table, partially covered with debris. I found the PRC-25 and the short whip antenna and, holding my breath, flipped it on.

It still worked, and I immediately heard an American voice on the handset! It was our detachment XO, busy talking to an incoming gunship. I was relieved to know that I wasn't the only one still alive and functioning.

I called on the radio to report that I was still alive. Sergeant Hull answered and told me they'd thought I was dead. Most of the other team members, with the exception of Wolf, who was out with the ambush patrol, and Erickson, who was either still holding on in the med bunker or dead, had gathered together in the American 81 mortar pit and were in a fight for their lives.

I said I needed to try to join up with them, as my bunker was still exploding and burning and I had only twenty rounds for my rifle. After a short pause, Weeks came on the radio and said I'd be better off where I was. "There's NVA everywhere, and we're shooting every fucker we see. You got a good thirty meters of bare ground to cross to get to us here. If the Cong don't kill you, we probably will. Try to hold out until it gets light!"

I sat cross-legged on the floor with my back to the only remaining corner in the bunker, put the M-16 across my lap to cover the exit, and dragged the PRC-25 over next to me on my right. I left the radio on and continued to monitor the situation up top. The thought that things couldn't get much worse than this had just flitted through my terror-filled mind . . . when they did.

Whoomb! KERWHAM! Two deafening explosions went off over where the .50 used to be. Crap flew everywhere, but somehow managed to miss me. For a second I couldn't figure out what was happening, but then I remembered that besides the many rounds of .50 cal ammo, there had also been about half a case of grenades sitting next to the gun.

WHAM! Another one went off, then another. A piece of frag hit me in the leg, near my knee, but in my excited state, I felt no immediate pain.

Before Erickson and I had gone on our operation a week earlier, I'd attached the Buddha charm that the Thai taxi driver had given me to my dog-tag chain. It was still there, and remembering it, I reached up and held it in my hand. If I ever needed any outside help to survive a situation, that was the time, and I muttered the only true prayer I ever attempted in combat. I promised to do anything for my survival—boy, did I grovel!

When I got done, I noticed that the explosion of the last grenade had somehow blown out the fire in that end of the bunker and the munitions had suddenly ceased cooking off. But I didn't have much time to marvel over the power of prayer, because there was a sudden commotion on the radio.

"This is Lima Sierra, they're in the open, coming across the runway!" one of the guys from the SOG unit was yelling through the handset.

"Stinger, do you copy Lima Sierra? Enemy on the runway!" the XO said, talking to the gunship.

"Roger, Camp. Understand confirmed enemy troops in open on runway—coming in hot."

A Stinger gunship was one of the old C-119 cargo planes that had been converted for ground support. The C-119 resembled a

bumblebee anyway, and with the newly added Bofors 40mm
cannon sticking out the tailgate, the illusion was complete. This
particular gunship had been on-station over Dak Seang when our
battle began, and immediately diverted and flew up the valley
to aid us. The Stinger arrived only minutes after the shooting
started, and had a tremendous, beneficial impact on the outcome
of the battle.

From my bunker, I heard the repeated impacts of Stinger's
cannon as the gunship flew over the long axis of the runway,
cutting the enemy's assault to pieces.

There were wild cheers and congratulations on the radio as
the SOG position called in the results. "You creamed the fuckers good! They've pulled back to the eastern edge of the runway,
make your next pass just off the asphalt!"

As the battle went on unabated aboveground, I suddenly realized that I had a new problem to contend with. Now that the
fire was out, there were two openings for the enemy to attack
me from. I could look right out the hole where the .50 had been,
and began to see occasional, dark forms moving back and forth
just outside. That area of ground was the military crest of the hill,
and could not be covered by the direct fire of the other guys in
the mortar pit—so naturally, that's the place the enemy gravitated.

I huddled quietly in my dark corner, hoping they would think
they'd already killed me, and tried to watch both bunker openings at the same time.

"They're in the fucking supply building!" someone yelled
on the radio. I hurriedly turned down the volume for fear the
enemy just outside would hear it. "Tom, there's about twenty of
'em down at supply," the voice on the radio said again, talking
to our team sergeant. "You won't believe this, but they got a
human chain going, taking stuff out . . . can you bring in the 81
that close?"

Weeks told me later that he'd had to stand the 81 mortar practically straight up and down, and was firing zero charge, but had

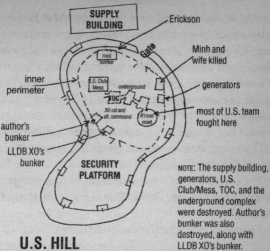

U.S. HILL

NOTE: The supply building, generators, U.S. Club/Mess, TOC, and the underground complex were destroyed. Author's bunker was also destroyed, along with LLDB XO's bunker.

managed to put seven HE rounds with delay fuses right through the tin roof. The rounds exploded inside with excellent effect.

"Yeowww!" the voice on the radio howled gleefully. "Arms, legs, and fucking indigenous rations went flying everywhere!" What little remained of the supply building after our mortar attack then caught on fire and burned to the ground, incinerating all the luckless NVA who had attempted to take cover inside.

During a short lull in the radio chatter, a whispering American voice suddenly came on the air. "Camp, this is Ambush, over."

Hell, it was poor Sergeant Wolf out there on ambush with only ten Yards for company. In the confusion, everyone had forgotten about him. He reported that there were approximately fifty million NVA wandering all around his position, but so far they didn't know he was there. He asked what he should do.

"Just lay low until it gets light," he was advised. "If we don't all get wiped out, try to come back in after sunup. If you stop hearing American voices from camp on the radio, contact the aircraft and ask for a chopper exfiltration."

Now that I was forced to remain immobile down in my own hidey-hole, I took some time to check my wounds to see how badly I was injured. The powdered CS tear gas had gotten in the wounds and was causing them to burn like hell. There was a lot of blood in my hair, but it seemed to be mostly dried. There was a piece of cement still sticking out of a hole near my elbow, and I pulled it out with my fingers, which caused it to start bleeding worse. I had nothing to use as a bandage, so just said to hell with it. There were some more small pieces of frag embedded in various other parts of me, but as far as I could tell, I was in amazingly good condition. "You were right," I said, whispering my thanks to the Thai taxi driver, "that is one good, lucky, fucking Buddha!"

The enemy attack had begun at 0200 hours. By now it was almost 0400, and although the shooting continued at what seemed an undiminished pace, I could tell we were winning. There were fewer and fewer radio reports of large enemy concentrations, and the consensus was that at least some of the enemy unit was attempting to withdraw. This withdrawal of the sapper unit might only have been the prelude to a large-scale attack by their regular infantry, however. Meanwhile, the ammo supply was getting critically low.

I was sitting there in the dark thinking about all of this when a dark, crouched shape suddenly appeared at the opening of my bunker. It was an NVA. He seemed disoriented and was looking for cover.

He was only three or four yards away, but didn't see me sitting there in the dark corner. He got on all fours and started to crawl in toward me. My M-16 was in my lap with the muzzle already pointed right at him, and I didn't even have to move the weapon. I fired once, and the bullet drilled him right through the top of his head.

A wild wave of exultation swept over me and I got a little giddy. The thought of my bullet entering his head, going through his body, then shooting out his asshole, seemed very amusing. I started to giggle.

"Sorry, dickhead, no room left. This spot's already taken," I whispered to myself, and giggled some more at my great humor.

The shooting outside had died down to only occasional bursts and single shots. I began to be able to see better, and realized it must be getting light. I didn't know if that was good or bad. Down at Dak Seang, the main enemy assault had come at dawn.

I cautiously crawled over the scorched, blackened rubble to the hole in the front of the bunker. I could see a few dead NVA lying around but no live ones. I dragged the one I'd shot to the edge of the opening and dumped his body over the side to join the rest.

Now that I could see, I was able to find my web gear and dug it out from a pile of broken cement. I also spotted my camouflage shirt lying in the mess and put it on. The feel of the cloth over my bare skin gave me an odd sense of security—fighting a war half naked ain't the way to go.

I suddenly realized I was thirsty as hell, but discovered that both my canteens were empty. I went back to where the .50 had once been and piled up a few of the bigger chunks of broken cement in an attempt to build some sort of berm to shoot over. I pulled the gas mask away from my sweaty face and cautiously tested the air. Although there was still a heavy smell of CS, the air was breathable, and I gratefully peeled off the mask and hung it on my web belt. Then I sat back down, suddenly exhausted, and waited for the enemy's main assault.

I was feeling a little light-headed and groggy, but the sound of stealthily approaching footsteps coming around the corner of my position snapped me back to alertness. I swung my rifle just as Sergeant Trin, the commander of our security platoon, stepped around the corner holding an M-60 machine gun. We came within a hair of blasting each other.

"Ahh, Trung-si Wade, you still alive!" Trin said, breaking into a smile. Trin was closely followed by his personal flunky and bat-boy, who carried a can of machine gun ammo in each hand. They came over and sat down next to me, and Trin shared some of his dwindling supply of water with me.

"Last night kill beaucoup VC," Trin told me with a pleased smile. Later, Sergeant Weeks told me that Trin had spent the entire night running around in the open, firing the M-60 "John Wayne style," and had indeed personally killed many enemy. Trin was awarded the American Silver Star for his valor that night.

Trin and his ammo bearer left after a few minutes, but a short time later I heard an American voice calling down the bunker steps. "Sergeant Wade? You still alive?"

"Just barely," I answered, crawling back through the litter to the entrance. It was Erickson, the medic. I went up the steps to meet him and we crouched behind cover, talking, looking around at the devastated camp. Occasional bursts of AK fire were being directed our way, and at first we couldn't figure out where they were coming from.

Erickson had spent the entire night in the med bunker, where he'd been sleeping when the attack started. The bunker's firing port covered the area around the front gate and the supply room, where there had been so much enemy activity.

"The sons of bitches were everywhere," Erickson said. "The clickers for the claymores covering that side of the hill are in the med bunker, you know, and I blew them first. There was a big mob of the bastards standing right in front of the mines, and I'm sure I must've killed ten or fifteen of the suckers right then.

"In the first ten or fifteen minutes, I fired up almost all my M-16 ammo. I'd just loaded my last magazine when the bunker door slams open. I whirled around and it's my goddamned Yard nurse. Came within an inch of shooting her."

Erickson had to pause a moment, as we both ducked another burst of fire that came very close to our heads, then he went on with the story.

"Christ, she looked like some sort of wild, Amazon woman

out of one of those fantasy novels. She's got this scary look in her eyes. Her long, black hair is flying every which way, and she's carrying a smoking M-16. Except for her web gear, she's bare from the waist up.

"She'd been in her hootch with her mother and father clear over on the other side of the hill when the shooting started, but knew she was supposed to come to the med bunker in case of an attack. She grabbed her shit and fought her way over all that damned open ground. Crap was blowing up, slugs were shooting past her, and NVA sappers were running every fucking where! She said she knows she killed at least one of them."

"Jeez," I said, "that's what you call dedication to duty."

"Well," Erickson told me with a smile, "you know she has this sort of crush on me . . ."

Suddenly we heard the sound of incoming choppers, and looking south down the valley, we saw them coming in: Cobra gunships were in the lead and on both flanks, with slicks in the center of the formation. It was quite a sight.

"Those have to be from SOG," I said. "No one else could get here that damned fast."

"Helicopters come take us away?" a Vietnamese voice asked.

Erickson and I turned to look behind us, and there stood the cook, Ute, carrying an M-16 and wearing his harness with a full basic load. We didn't have any noncombatants at Dak Pek.

I'd just told Ute that we didn't know exactly what was going on, and warned him to keep under cover, when there was another burst of AK fire which again just missed my head.

"That shit's coming from 203 hill!" Erickson said in disbelief. The 203 Company hill was the large one that dominated the entire camp. I immediately remembered the 106 recoilless rifle over there, and was relieved to see that it still stood, unattended, with its muzzle pointed safely in another direction.

"Did the shithead CIDG up there turn against us?" I said disgustedly.

We heard a moan, and looking over at Ute's position, saw for the first time that the Yard had been wounded by the last burst of fire. He sat dumbly holding his upper thigh, trying to stop the bleeding.

"Jesus Christ, Ute," Erickson said, moving over to see how badly the cook was hit, "we told you to stay the fuck down!"

While the Cobras buzzed around the camp's perimeter, the slicks landed on the runway and the SOG unit began evacuating. The Cobras were finding plenty of targets, and had immediately come under heavy ground fire themselves.

Erickson finished putting a battle dressing on Ute, stuck him with some morphine, then rejoined me. The top of the American hill was oddly quiet all of a sudden, and as Erickson and I looked around, we could see no other team members. We looked down at the runway where troops were madly boarding the choppers, then looked back at each other. We both got the same idea at once.

"All the Americans are being pulled out . . . they're leaving our asses here!" Erickson said.

Luckily, some team members in the 81 mortar pit began shoot-

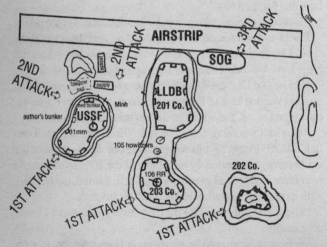

Attacks on the night of April 12, 1970, at Dak Pek

ing back up at 203 hill at just about this time, and we figured out that only the SOG launch site was being extracted. I carried the PRC-25 up to the top of the bunker steps so Erickson and I could listen to what was going on.

"There's a whole shitload of 'em in the school," Weeks told the Cobra pilots.

"Understand we have enemy in the school," the Cobra flight leader answered. "Is that the building just off the chopper pad?"

"Hey, don't blow up my school building!" Lieutenant Alexander, the CA/Psy Ops officer suddenly said, breaking into the radio transmission.

"Fucking school's closed for the summer, Lieutenant," someone told him, voice dripping with sarcasm. "Blast 'em outta there, Cobra!"

"Commencing rocket run from south to north," the pilot said.

After the salvo of rockets from the Cobra, there wasn't much left of the new school, and before the dust settled, two more of the armed choppers made strafing passes with 7.62mm machine guns and the nose-mounted 40mm cannons. Weeks dropped a few rounds of 81 HE in on the mess just as a grand finale.

"We built the goddamned thing, so I guess we should be able to destroy it if we want to," I heard Erickson mutter under his breath.

Chapter 11

Down on the runway the SOG extraction was going swiftly and smoothly, but mortar rounds had begun bursting on the tarmac. The rounds were hitting some distance from the choppers, but the NVA gunners began walking them in closer, trying to get the range. Just after the last slick rose in the air with its load of troops, several rounds landed exactly where the bird had been sitting.

Several months later, when I next talked to Bill Spurgeon, he told me he was greatly ashamed that the SOG leadership decided to pull the men out.

I told him that their extraction hadn't bothered me or anyone else on the A-team: "Hell, Bill, we knew that those were all highly trained troops and that SOG has a special mission. No need to risk getting them all wiped out by using them as grunt infantry. Those guys on the launch site took the brunt of several mass attacks that night, and probably saved us from losing the rest of the camp.

"Besides," I added, "we were so glad to see those Cobras that morning, it was worth trading the air support for a few ground troops."

The unarmed SOG HU-1Bs circled up to altitude, then headed off back to Kontum. The Cobras stayed to help us until the first flights of Air Force Sky Raiders and jet fighter-bombers got there. Sergeant Wolf, still outside the camp with his ambush patrol, was able to mark his position by means of a signal mirror, and the choppers gave him air cover while his small patrol successfully made it back into camp.

The mysterious voice that had told Alexander "school was out for the summer" once again came on the air, and I realized it was Major Ramos from the B-team. He was orbiting in a HU-1B, and acting as both an air/ground radio relay and as a forward command and control. He asked us if we were able to reestablish direct radio contact with Kontum. "Stand by, C and C, I'll check out the situation," I told him on the PRC-25.

The TOC and the radios down there were wiped out. Thick black smoke still poured up out of the entrance. I ducked back down into my bunker to check on the status of the alternate radio, an ANGRC-74, and discovered that a large piece of ceiling beam had landed on it, smashing it flat. The damned fire had started burning again.

Back up on top, I looked over to where the main generator bunker had once stood. It was demolished and still smoking. The alternate generators were next to the entrance to the TOC, and I went over to check them out.

Pow-pop-bang! Shit, I'd forgotten about the enemy on 203 hill. I ducked behind the generators for cover, and while I was there, looked them over. They were both shot full of holes and out of commission. I went back to my bunker entrance, this time at a crouching run, and reported the commo situation to the C&C chopper.

When I got done with my message, Sergeant Hull radioed in our first afteraction report and indicated we were very low on all sorts of ammo. He reported we had no Americans killed so far, but many wounded, and that there were many other friendly and enemy KIA and WIA, the exact number unknown.

Just about this time, a couple members of the Vietnamese Special Forces team, accompanied by several Yards, made their way through the incoming mortar rounds from their position in the center of camp over to the American hill. For the first time, we found out exactly how things stood. The situation was not good.

Half the camp was in enemy hands. The enemy held 203 hill and two lower supporting hills. Apparently, the sappers had been able to get through the defenses undetected and had killed many of the Yards before they could even react. A rout had ensued and our troops fled off the hill, across the saddle to the center of camp.

Several of our troops, along with their families, had been captured, brutalized, then executed. One young girl, the twelve-year-old daughter of the 203 Company commander, had managed to escape in the confusion of battle. She told of being gang-raped, then of having one eye gouged out by an NVA bayonet. Her father, she said, had been decapitated.

Apparently, the enemy unit that had been successful in over-running and holding part of our camp thought they'd won the battle at the time they performed these atrocities. I got grim satisfaction thinking about their consternation that morning after the sun came up, when they discovered they were stuck there, cut off from the rest of their people.

Paybacks are a bitch.

However, our camp seemed to be the only part of the valley still in friendly hands. While we'd been under attack, most of the fortified hamlets in the valley—thirteen in all—were overrun. A look through binoculars verified that all the villages we could see had VC flags defiantly flying from their flagpoles. There was a *shitload* of NVA out there!

As the LLDB continued talking, I watched a six-man unit run from cover on the LLDB hill, dash across the open ground of the saddle, and make it to our 105 howitzer position. "We tell crew turn guns, shoot at 203 hill," the Vietnamese Special Forces weapons man told us.

The gun crew was successful in getting one of the little howitzers turned and pointed up the hill at the nearest trench line, which was less than fifty meters away. They touched off a round that effectively tore into one of the enemy-held bunkers, but were answered immediately by a RPG-7 rocket. The enemy rocket landed among our men, successfully knocking out the howitzer and wounding or killing most of our gunners.

"Humm, is number ten," the LLDB grunted as surviving gun crew members retreated back down the saddle, dragging their dead and wounded.

Erickson had gone down to check on Minh, our generator operator. He too had been forgotten in the confusion. A few minutes later Erickson came back up to the 81 pit carrying Minh's crying, infant son.

"Minh and his wife are both dead," he told us disgustedly. Erickson said that it looked like a sapper had jumped into the bunker where Minh lived with his family and riddled them with his AK. Erickson found the crying baby underneath the dead mother, who, in the last seconds of her life, turned and shielded her baby with her body, taking the burst of AK fire in her back.

We began talking about the night's action, trying to sort out exactly what the hell had happened.

"When the shooting started," Sergeant Weeks said, "I grabbed my stuff and headed through the tunnel to the 81 mortar. Young was right behind me. I'd just stepped out into the open when I looked over toward Wade's bunker and it was already blown up, two NVA were standing on top of what remained of the roof, and they were stringing up a goddamned VC flag on one of the antenna poles! I killed them both with one burst."

As soon as the battle began, Hull and the lieutenant had gone immediately to their positions in the TOC. "There were big explosions going off aboveground," the lieutenant said, "and I thought we were under rocket attack. At first the generators were still running and the lights were on. I was standing there right in front of the bunker steps, when I look up and see this fucking sapper come walking down them."

The lieutenant shook his head in wonderment, then went on. "He saw me standing there about ten feet away with my M-16 pointed at him and he hesitated. I'll never forget the look on his face just before I blasted him—emptied most of the magazine in his chest. Just after that, the lights went out and one of the fuckers tossed a grenade or something down the steps. Hull and I took some frag, and the bunker started burning. We decided to beat-feet, and ran like hell through the dark tunnel to the other exit and came out into the 81 pit with Weeks and Young."

After hearing those stories, and others, I finally figured out that my bunker hadn't been destroyed by artillery after all, but by hand-delivered satchel charges. As we talked it over that morning in the mortar pit, we reconstructed the early-morning attack.

There had been a short mortar barrage as a diversion, just to make everyone duck for cover, and at the same time the large sapper unit assaulted through the wire. Apparently, they had infiltrated right up to the edge of it before the NVA mortars started firing.

The enemy sappers were very, very good. Their objectives were the American hill, 203 Company hill, and the two supporting hills. The sappers made it through the perimeters of all objectives before we defenders realized they were there. We later determined that some of our men on the outer perimeter defense line that night had been enemy sympathizers or traitors and had let many of the sappers in. We found a few other Yards down on the outer perimeter still in their hammocks, throats cut—killed as they slept on guard duty.

The sappers had made their first attack from the west, and shortly afterward there were more attacks from the east. We never discovered if the later attacks were also attempted by the sappers or by regular NVA infantry. Down on the airstrip, the enemy had the misfortune of running into the SOG unit that, unlike our own troops on 203 hill, refused to retreat. The hapless attackers had also gotten a taste of Stinger.

It seems that when the sappers blew my bunker, our improvised CS launcher had gone off too. Although the gas had almost done me in, the consensus was that it hurt the enemy more than us.

Also, many weeks later, we received an intelligence report stating that on the night of the attack two of the enemy units had run into each other in the dark, which had touched off a lethal firefight among themselves. That particularly tickled me, because I'd imagined that only our friendly forces and us ever screwed up like that.

A few determined defenders can withstand a much larger attacking force, as the American team had demonstrated by holding our hill against overwhelming odds—even after first getting overrun!

* * *

That morning of April 12, we were still expecting another large-scale assault by NVA infantry and I returned to my position at the demolished bunker. After turning Minh's orphaned baby over to his nurse, Erickson rejoined me. To pass the time, we began singing current Beatles songs, changing the words to make them more relevant and interesting.

The stupid, vulgar lyrics we ad-libbed helped relieve the built-up tension, and soon we were howling with laughter.

"*Incoming rockets!*" one of the guys at the 81 pit yelled.

The 122 and 140mm rockets the enemy used made a lot of smoke when they launched, so if you were lucky enough to see them taking off, you had some time to duck for cover. Erickson and I spotted several clouds of white smoke rising from the mountainside where we'd only recently been with our combat operation.

Swoosh! The goddamned things went over our heads, missing by what couldn't have been more than six feet, and impacted in the center of camp.

WHAM-BAMB-BOOM! "Those got to be 140s," I told Erickson.

The intel man, Frier, had been making his way over to our position from the 81 pit, and was standing out in the open when the big rockets sailed directly over his head. Now he stood erect, shook his fist, and screamed to the enemy in the surrounding mountains. "Ha-ha, you missed me, you stupid fuckers!"

Shortly after that, Erickson and I heard muffled cries for help. At first we couldn't figure out where they were coming from, but soon discovered they originated in the pile of rubble that had once been the bunker next to mine—the one occupied by the Vietnamese team's executive officer. Since his bunker was completely collapsed, everyone had assumed the man was dead, but somehow he had survived. With the help of a few others, we dug the poor bastard out.

The officer had spent the entire night buried alive, and hadn't been sure if the enemy had successfully taken the camp or not.

It wasn't until he heard Sergeant Frier yelling in English that he dared to cry for help. The LLDB lieutenant was badly shaken by the experience and always acted a little weird afterward.

Several Sky Raider aircraft suddenly appeared at the mouth of the valley, flying low, between the mountains. They were closely followed by a C-123.

"Dak Pek, this is Alpha Delta Three," the pilot of the cargo plane said on the radio. "We have some stuff you asked for, where do you want us to drop it? Over?"

Weeks tossed out a yellow smoke grenade that started burning several feet from the mortar pit. "We've tossed smoke," Hull said on the radio, "Identify color. Over."

After the pilot identified our smoke correctly, Hull told him to drop the resupply directly on it. The C-123 began making very low passes, and the brightly colored cargo chutes came floating down on top of us. Several men ran out and began breaking out the ammunition and carrying it to fighting positions. All the bundles landed inside our perimeter wire and none was lost to the enemy.

The C-123 was taking heavy ground fire, and the Sky Raiders, using our directions, began hitting some of the many enemy concentrations. A lot of the fire was coming from the enemy-held 203 hill, and we called in the first of what were to be many, many air strikes against that position.

An Air Force forward air controller also arrived on the scene about then. The FAC pilot had just swooped down and marked 203 hill with a smoke rocket when Weeks came on the radio. "Bird Dog, can you see the 106 recoilless rifle on the very top of that hill you just marked?" Apparently I wasn't the only one worried about that damned 106.

The FAC answered that he could see it, and Weeks told him to have one of the Sky Raiders try to take the weapon out. That would be the first of many such attempts to destroy the thing during the battle, all of which proved futile. It was very hard to hit the peak of the hill directly, and although there were many near misses, in the end the gun still stood there, defiantly silhouetted against the sky.

Besides ammunition, that first parachute resupply also contained a pallet of water cans. With the much-needed ammo and water distributed, and Tac-air on the scene, I was no longer concerned about being overrun again. If the enemy had failed to take us at night, with everything in his favor, he surely wouldn't be able to do it during the day.

Our many dead and wounded troops were being carried to the med bunker, and Erickson said he'd better leave me and go help Sergeant Wolf. The sun was higher and it was getting hot. As I sat in my position, awaiting developments, I again heard Major Ramos on the radio, calling from the returning HU-1B. He said the bird was coming in to land and drop him off, and he wanted to know if the main LZ was secure.

By that time in the war, we knew the enemy monitored our voice radio transmissions. Although the SOG units had begun using newly issued online encryption devices, no other field units had them yet. During a battle, we just did the best we could, using brevity codes and simple transposition when possible, but sending a lot of stuff in the clear and hoping the enemy couldn't react fast enough for it to do them any good.

We'd been taking mortar rounds all over the camp since the battle began early that morning. The large enemy rockets continued to sail in frequently also. We knew the enemy had the runway zeroed in and probably marked for future reference, but we didn't know if he had registered the small helipad that stood just outside the gate.

We told Ramos we didn't want to throw any smoke that might indicate to the enemy where the intended LZ was, and he said the pilot had flown into camp many times in the past and would come in without it. The chopper dropped in on the main helipad, doing a touch-and-go, and Major Ramos, wearing helmet and flak vest, hopped out lugging what looked like a ton of equipment. Another American, whom I didn't recognize at first, jumped out with him.

The chopper had just gotten out of the area when the first enemy mortar rounds hit near the LZ, and the two Americans made a mad dash for the bunkers by the front gate. They somehow got to cover unscathed. A couple of our guys went down to help them lug the equipment—a new ANGRC-74, antennas, and fresh batteries for the PRC-25s—up the hill to our position.

When they got closer, I saw that the other American was our team leader, Captain Walther, who had been down at Dak Seang helping them. We were all glad to see him come back.

"Christ," the team leader said, still panting from the run up the hill, "I spend almost a whole year here and nothing happens. Then, as soon as I go down to get some action at Dak Seang, all hell breaks loose back here!"

I returned to the 81 pit, and we had a short conference about the commo situation. Although the main generators that supplied power to the camp had been destroyed, the LLDB sergeant told us that they still had their small 1.5 KW in operation. That was big enough to supply power for a few lights and to run both their commo and ours. We decided to reestablish the communications center over in the center of camp.

The LLDB said they had room in their main bunker complex on the other hill, where I could set up the new ANGRC-74. The remainder of our team would stay and defend our old positions for the time being. So, with the aid of the LLDB and several Strikers, we made the rather scary and exhausting move.

We waited for what seemed to be a lull in the enemy's mortar fire. "Okay, let's go!" I yelled, and we took off like broken-field runners in a bowl game.

Down the hill we went . . . watch out for the mangled bodies . . . ugh, what happened to *that* one . . . past Minh and his wife, side by side, wrapped in ponchos . . . *blammo*—oh fuck, the mortars are starting again . . . through the other gate . . . look at those sumbitches hanging in the wire . . . up the other hill . . . just a little bit farther . . . *blammo-blammo-blammo* . . . good try, assholes, but you missed me again! We jumped into the safety of the trench.

My new temporary home was adequate. It had good overhead cover and there was even a cement floor. The bunker was built directly off the inner perimeter trench that surrounded the LLDB position. The only downside was that the new position was only about fifty meters from the enemy-held trenches of 203 hill. The Vietnamese Special Forces radio operator ran in a power line for me and loaned me a folding field table and a chair. I hooked everything up, turned on the power, and was in business. Except for one small item.

I still had to go out and try to string a doublet antenna, and the area where I had to hang it was the one where most of the goddamned rockets were hitting.

I waited for another lull in the bombardment, then cautiously moved out into the trench and peaked over the rim, checking the surrounding mountains. No telltale white smoke clouds. Although many of the LLDB's antenna poles had been knocked down by then, a couple of them were still standing.

I took a deep breath, then climbed up on the bare, exposed ground above the bunker. Feeling vulnerable as hell, I ran over to the first pole. Reaching up as high as possible, I tied the insulated end of the doublet to the pole. With frequent nervous glances over my shoulder at the mountains, I ran over to the other pole. Hurriedly pulling the antenna wire tight, which caused it to rise about eight feet off the ground, I tied off that end. Then, feeding out the center co-ax cable behind me, I jumped down in the trench and back into the safety of the bunker.

I'd just hooked the antenna to the radio when there was a deafening blast from the ground above. Dust floated through the door of the bunker. The severed end of the antenna lead-in told me my work had been in vain. Now I'd have to do it all over again. I envisioned the NVA rocketeers up in the mountains snickering and laughing.

Chapter 12

By 1000 hours that morning of April 12, here's how things stood: the enemy held half of our camp, plus all the surrounding valley and mountains; there was still a huge concentration of NVA twenty kilometers to our south at Dak Seang; and the enemy's main base of resupply lay only five or six kilometers to the west, over the border in Laos.

As the famous "Mad Dog" Shriver might have said, "Now we had the bastards just where we wanted them!"

This is actually not as absurd a statement as it sounds, for although things didn't look all that great there on the ground at Dak Pek, as far as the generals, and particularly our Air Force, were concerned, it was a perfect setup. Throughout the entire course of the war, one of our main strategies was to use our ground forces, particularly Special Forces A-camps, for bait, causing the enemy to concentrate his forces so we could hit him with overwhelming firepower.

By late morning we had more air support overhead than we could direct at one time. The flights of jet fighter-bombers and prop-driven Sky Raiders were stacked up three and four levels high, waiting to come in and deliver ordnance. In the mountains to the west we heard the rumblings of the first B-52 strikes going on.

who I'd figured were surely dead from the air strikes, mysteriously came back to life and began shooting us to shreds.

The forward edge of that first attack made it about halfway across the saddle before the Yards broke and ran back to safety.

I decided this wasn't going to be as easy as I'd thought.

As the sun inched lower and lower behind the mountains to the west, a lot of my self-confidence evaporated. One by one the sorties of Tac-air dropped their loads and flew back to their bases for the night, until the sky above us was once again clear of aircraft. As the shadows grew longer and darkness approached, the full extent of our situation again came crashing home.

Because the enemy still held the largest hill in camp, a good portion of our perimeter was not under our control. That amounted to having a large, unsecured back door. During the daylight hours, with all the Tac-air overhead, the door was closed. At night, with only a gunship overhead, it was going to be much harder to [...] that break in our perimeter.

[...]he enemy had two options. He could use the darkness to [...]ate his men from positions inside our perimeter, or he [...]nfiltrate more reinforcements and make another attempt [...]the rest of the camp. So far the enemy had shown no [...]acking away from the attack, and we knew the battle [...]where near to being over with yet.

[...]sk, Stinger arrived over the camp. I recognized the [...]radio as the same one from the night before. We ad[...]the situation, and he assured us he would keep a [...]the portion of the perimeter that we could not [...]round. As soon as it got fully dark, the attacks [...]gain.

[...]rted from the east, down by the runway. The [...]rse, that the SOG unit had been pulled out, [...] that area was undefended. Because the [...]perimeter had shrunk, however, we'd had [...]at danger area with troops. The runway

At that stage in the war, the most common fighter-bombers used were the F-4 Phantoms. They were great planes and were very versatile. They worked well in a Tac-air mode because they could carry such a varied load of ordnance. And, from what I understand, they did pretty well against enemy fighter planes too.

The pilots who supported us at Dak Pek did a marvelous job. During the first few days of the battle, we had enemy positions not only just outside our perimeter wire, but still *in* our perimeter. The jets arrived carrying varied loads, and would call to tell us what they had. Some came with bombs only—500 and 750 pounders. Some carried bombs and napalm, and some carried all napalm. Most of them had a 20mm Vulcan for strafing. The pilots delivered all of this lethal stuff with pinpoint accuracy and killed many enemy soldiers.

Sergeant Hull was still over at the other hill, and was handling most of the air-ground commo on one of the PRC-25s. With so many aircraft in the area, this was a tricky job, and my young assistant radio operator was doing a great job. Just before noon, we started bringing in medevac choppers, and things got even more complicated.

The medevacs were very dangerous for all concerned. We could only use the main helipad because it was closest to the medical bunker. But the enemy had the helipad zeroed in with mortars and was close enough to place it under fire with small arms and machine guns. The dust-offs took ground fire coming in, while on the ground, and while taking off. The evacuations were extremely dangerous for our medics too, because they accompanied each litter party to the chopper.

Erickson was in charge of the evacuations, while Wolf worked on the steady flow of wounded. James Erickson, at that time a lowly specialist four—that is, not even a true NCO—eventually handled twenty-seven evacuations under fire. It wouldn't have been so many, but on the very first medevac that Sergeant Wolf performed, he was badly wounded himself. I recently talked to Erickson about the fighting that day, and he told me how it had gone.

"Each trip down to that goddamned LZ got worse than the one before. We tried all sorts of shit to trick the NVA but nothing did much good."

I told him I remembered that one time he'd had Sergeant Young go down to the airstrip and throw smoke there. When the next evac chopper landed at the usual place, the enemy gunners bombarded the smoke on the airstrip instead.

"Yeah," Erickson said, "that worked pretty good—but only one time."

Erickson said he'd just pulled off three real fast evacs in a row, and that he'd been exhausted when the next dust-off radioed in to tell them to get ready. "Sergeant Wolf took that bunch down," he told me. "It was his very first time, and he took a goddamned AK-47 round through the arm. Almost blew it off. So, of course, that required *another* trip down to the LZ to evac Wolf. And after that, I was the only American medic in camp."

Sergeant Wolf was the first American team member to require evacuation due to the seriousness of his wound. Though by that time in the battle just about everyone on the team had been hit, all had elected to stay and fight. That wasn't as much due to gung-ho bravery as it was to good sense—it was too damned dangerous to try to get out from that LZ!

At about 1300 hours we made the first of several attempts to retake 203 hill. The Air Force had pounded the hill with two air strikes by then, the first sortie dropping bombs, the second one coming in with napalm followed by strafing, and we didn't think there could possibly be much resistance after that.

We were quite wrong.

The LLDB team leader was adamant in insisting that the defeated members of 203 Company be the ones to retake the position. The Vietnamese team leader was angry that the defenders had broken and run, and at the time, I thought he was simply

being mean and vindictive in insisting that the defeated men lead the charge up the hill. On later consideration I realized he was right. The members of 203 Company needed to be given the chance to regain their self-respect, otherwise they would have remained a demoralized and worthless unit.

All of our assaults on the hill followed the same general routine. First, we rounded up all the American and LLDB team members who weren't busy doing something else, and put them on the front rank. Next, 203 Company, augmented by whatever Yards from the other companies we could spare, formed up in a mob, and the group moved to the saddle between the LLDB hill and the enemy-held hill.

Our men had to charge across the open saddle, which was only about twenty-five meters wide, then through a ten-me wide break in the wire surrounding 203 hill, then uphill o other thirty meters of open ground to the enemy-hel and bunkers. Of course, all this had to be done enemy fire.

Charging hills and taking trench lines was Montagnard troops had any experience w for. Their forte was jungle warfare, no needed a lot of prodding. I accomp the hill. As I recall, Weeks, An went along. As we huddled un we began trying to encoura

"Are we ready?" the ers, screamed at the fr

"Yes!" the troop like they meant

"Are we r "Yes!" t "Charge!" company cadre i We'd gone only abo

attack was on the opposite side of camp from the enemy-held 203 hill, and we assumed it was a feint to take our attention away from the "open back door" of our perimeter.

We resisted the impulse to have Stinger attack the threat on the runway, and instead told him to continue watching the western side of 203 hill. That turned out to be the proper response on our part, because Stinger soon reported large movements in that area and opened fire. Our camp mortars took care of blasting the attackers down on the runway, and within an hour or so the shooting died out.

We had won that night's first round.

The evening dragged slowly on toward midnight. Stinger orbited overhead, occasionally dropping flares that lit up the valley floor and gave us a sense of security. Just after 0001 hours, the Stinger pilot radioed that he was out of fuel and would be departing for the night, but told us that a replacement would be on station shortly.

As the sound of Stinger's engines faded away in the distance, I again became very nervous. I made a radio check with Kontum on the ANGRC-74 because, with the aircraft gone, that was once again our only means of communications with the outside world. Kontum came in five-by-five on code, but we could not communicate in voice mode. The B-detachment assured me it was standing by for developments.

Not five minutes after Stinger had flown out of the valley, the NVA attacked again. This time they directed their main attention to the American hill, then followed up with a very aggressive probe by the unit holding 203 hill, which attacked across the saddle and attempted to penetrate the defenses of the LLDB hill.

The probe was beaten back at our wire, but the enemy retreated only as far as the abandoned 105 howitzer position, and held that for the rest of the night. Luckily, the guns were out of commission, or we would have really been in a world of shit.

I was monitoring both the 74 radio and the PRC-25. "Camp

Dak Pek, this is Spectre," the pilot of the approaching AC-130 called in on FM. "I'm due west of your location, ETA about zero-two, over." Sergeant Hull answered him from the other hill and said he couldn't have arrived at a better time. If the NVA had thought Stinger, with its one Bofors cannon, was a bitch, they were about to meet their worst nightmare!

The AC-130s were a fairly new weapon in 1970, and because experimentation was still going on, they were configured in several different ways. Some were armed with just 20mm Vulcans. Others had a combination of Vulcans and 7.62 miniguns, while others, especially those hunting tanks over on the Ho Chi Minh trail, also had a damned 105mm howitzer—an artillery piece!—sticking out the side. The one that showed up in our valley that night had the 20mm/minigun combo. Man oh man, could that baby lay down some lead!

Hull directed the aircraft to the largest enemy concentration, which was only about 150 meters due west of the American hill's wire. When I heard the pilot say he was coming in for a hot run, I hurried outside into the trench to watch the fireworks display. I don't know how many guns the plane had, but the entire side of it appeared to light up as a sheet of red tracers shot out. Seconds later the accompanying roar, which gave the gunships their nickname, Spooky, reached us. It was truly a hideous sound, something a flying dragon on the hunt might make.

As usual when I watched such displays of American firepower, I was overcome by a wave of grim satisfaction that caused me to cheer and laugh out loud.

Reassured once again, I returned to the bunker to sit out the rest of the night.

Chapter 13

We continued to fight off probes the rest of that night, but the awesome firepower of Spectre seemed to have cooled the enemy's ardor somewhat. We did continue to take an almost constant barrage of mortar and rocket rounds, however, and my radio antenna was knocked down again, the third or fourth time.

As the sun came up that morning of April 13, a thin layer of smoke from the flares, rockets, mortars, and small-arms fire still hung in the air. Spectre called and said he'd see us later, and within minutes of his departure, the FAC was again orbiting overhead, telling us to get ready for the first flight of Phantoms.

By that second day of the battle, I was becoming aware of the particularly foul odors in the air around Dak Pek. For one thing, the powdered CS was still detectable, and every time a chopper came in, the rotor downwash blew the stuff back up in the air and recirculated it. Another factor that led to the stench was the smoke I mentioned earlier, which came not only from expended munitions but from the numerous fires that still smoldered at Dak Pek and at many of the strategic hamlets in the valley.

The *worst* smell, however, was coming from the hundreds of quickly decomposing bodies that littered the area. The enemy was usually very good about recovering its dead, but had been unable to get to the ones in the immediate vicinity of our perimeter or the ones hanging in our wire.

The bodies of the enemy we'd killed inside the perimeter had simply been hauled as far off to one side as possible and stacked in piles. We had not been able to do anything about our own dead either, except lay them in rows and cover them the best we could.

Our dead Montagnards would eventually be buried there in the valley, which was their home. Dead Vietnamese, such as Minh and his wife, or Yards not from Dak Pek, had to be flown out for burial elsewhere. Their sad carcasses lay rotting and bloating beneath the tropical sun for many days before things quieted down enough to fly them out.

That second day of the battle, the enemy gunners and rocketeers intensified bombardment of the camp as soon as it got light enough for them to see it. We directed a few air attacks against the telltale clouds of smoke left by the rocket exhausts, but that appeared to have no effect. We decided that the rockets were probably laid-in on our camp in advance, from camouflaged positions, and then set to go off later using a timer. That would give the enemy gunners time to get out of the launch area before we could return fire.

The mortars and recoilless rifles were much harder to detect and were undoubtedly fired from well-dug-in and fortified positions. A lot of the indirect fire came from the surrounding high ground, where the enemy could look directly down into camp—just as they'd done at Dien Bien Phu. The two big differences between our situation and the one the French faced was that the NVA around Dak Pek had no actual heavy artillery pieces—only rockets and mortars. And perhaps more important, at Dak Pek we had overwhelming air support.

Early that morning I received a coded message from the B-team, labeled "For American info only." It said that we would be receiving reinforcements sometime that day, exact ETA to follow later. The "American info only" tag was for security reasons, as higher headquarters, and probably the reinforcing element, feared the information would leak and the NVA would receive prior warning.

The enemy on 203 hill were very inactive that morning, and we suspected they had managed to retreat from the position during the night. We put together another assault force, again using the survivors of 203 Company as the lead element, and launched a second attack. I was busy on the radio and didn't accompany or even watch the assault, but later talked to a couple of guys who went on it.

"We formed up in the trenches right at the base of the saddle, and there wasn't a peep from the enemy positions," my buddy told me. "We were feeling pretty confident that we could simply waltz up there and reoccupy the bunkers. Ha! They let us get just past the howitzer position, then let us have it. Instead of evacuating like we thought, the fuckers had managed to reinforce and resupply. They hit us with some RPG-7s and maybe even a recoilless. The troops broke and ran back to cover, with us Americans right behind them. I don't know how many damned casualties we took. The poor Yards in 203 Company are starting to get that ten-thousand-mile stare. . . ."

After the particularly heavy barrage of incoming rockets and mortar rounds that morning, things quieted down around 1100 hours. A combat patrol of thirty men, led by Lieutenant Andrews, was launched from the American hill to sweep around just outside the perimeter wire. The patrol had two missions: (1) wipe out pockets of enemy still holding on near our wire, and (2) conduct a body count of enemy KIA.

The business of counting and reporting enemy dead bodies had been an American obsession since the early days of the war. In an attempt to establish the reliability of reported data, higher headquarters recognized several different categories of body counts. The most reliable type was "U.S. count, on the ground." There was also "body count from air," and the least reliable, "body count by ARVN." The last was always considered to be grossly exaggerated, and the numbers received from the Vietnamese were usually taken with a grain of salt by U.S. intel analysts.

After the raw figures got to higher headquarters in Saigon, they were plugged into some sort of formula to determine how many enemy were actually killed and wounded in any particular engagement. If, for example, five enemy bodies were found on the battlefield, that would probably mean there were two or three times that number that were not found. Also, if you had X number of dead bodies, it could be assumed there had been Y number of wounded.

The North Vietnamese must have been breeding like rabbits, because according to some mathematical accounts, by 1970 we had already killed every man in the North Vietnamese Army at least twice . . . which goes to show you the difficulty of counting dead bodies.

Picture some eighteen-year-old American draftee wandering through an enemy base camp that has just been blasted by a B-52 strike. The American is an honest kid and wants to do a good job, but how does he count 'em? There's a leg over here, an arm over there, and staring up at him from between his muddy jungle boots, there's half a face. Is it all the same enemy soldier, or two, or three, or what? The usual procedure in these situations was to count each piece as a separate enemy KIA, but of course, there was no way to know for sure.

As the saying goes: Garbage in, garbage out.

Anyway, on that morning of April 13, Lieutenant Andrews and one of the Vietnamese Special Forces team members cautiously led their small patrol out the gate. They poked around in the still-smoldering remains of the supply building first, where they found numerous charred bodies.

Next they proceeded to the school building, most of which was then in ruins, and found many more dead enemy. Each of the mangled decomposing bodies had to be searched, of course, an obviously disagreeable task, but a necessary one if we were to gather intelligence info on the enemy units we were fighting.

Unfortunately, by the time the bodies were searched, the enemy had spotted the patrol and begun to react with mortar and small-arms fire. Our men only managed to make a hurried circuit of the American hill's perimeter, then, because of mounting casualties, called off the venture and returned to camp.

The Vietnamese Special Forces sergeant who had accompanied the patrol later told me that he'd seen "beaucoup dead VC," which was just about as exact as body counts ever really got. After examination of the gore-encrusted items recovered from the NVA dead, however, we were able to piece together the enemy order of battle.

The first, successful attack, which partially overran the camp, had been made by the NVA's K-80 Sapper Battalion. The other, less successful attacks were attempted by members of the NVA 26th Infantry Regiment. Some weeks later we determined that units from the enemy's 66th Regiment had been responsible for overrunning the strategic hamlets in the valley, and discovered that we had the NVA's 40th Rocket Regiment to thank for the rain of 122s and 140s.

Whereas during the first day of the battle our main objective had been to hold the part of camp we still occupied, it was becoming obvious that we needed to take back that damned 203 hill ASAP. The Air Force continued to pound the enemy positions on the hill, but our Yards had done a real good job over the past eight years of building solid bunkers, and only a direct hit with a five-hundred-pound bomb could completely destroy one.

Napalm was more effective for this sort of situation, and we called in a lot of it against the hill. But nape was also less accurate, covered a large area, and was thus much more dangerous to our own troops, some of whom were within fifty meters of the enemy positions.

We had only a five-minute warning that the reinforcements were on the way. They would be making an air assault, but for security, the message did not tell us where the LZ was going to be. I went out into the trench line to watch them come in.

The flight of HU-1Bs was accompanied by gunships and Sky Raiders, and they didn't fool around. The Sky Raiders entered the valley first, flying aggressively low and shooting up targets of opportunity. The slicks came in next, surrounded by the gunships, and without any hesitation the slicks landed all at once in formation on the runway. The choppers were only on the ground for a few seconds, then immediately *di-di*'d as soon as the troops had unloaded. By the time the enemy gunners were able to react, the well-trained Mike Force troops were already moving through our wire and into our trenches. If I recall correctly, the Mike Force suffered just a few minor wounds during the hazardous combat air assault.

It was only after the reinforcements had successfully completed their insertion that we found out who they were: the 1st Mike Force Reconnaissance Company, augmented by members of the Strike Force from Camp Plei Mrong. We directed the troops to positions in the trench line at the end of the saddle leading to 203 hill and called a conference to decide what our next move would be.

We briefed the American Mike Force leaders on the situation, and they agreed that the main priority was to retake the rest of the camp. By that time darkness was only an hour or so away. We decided to schedule the next assault on 203 hill for 1000 hours the next morning, which would give Tac-air time to maul the enemy again just before the ground attack.

Our LLDB commander still thought that the members of 203 Company should lead the charge, but after some discussion we convinced him to let the better-trained and better-rested Mike Force company be in the vanguard.

Darkness fell once again, Spectre arrived overhead, and we got ready for more fun and games. With the reinforcements in camp, and in position between my bunker and the enemy-held hill, I felt better about my chances of living through that third night of the battle than I had during the previous two nights.

Chapter 14

I've always regretted that I didn't accompany that final, successful assault on 203 hill. I was busy receiving a long, coded message from the B-team as our attack was getting ready to kick off, and didn't find out about it until a Vietnamese Special Forces sergeant came into the commo bunker and told me. I grabbed my shit, ran out to the trench, and was just in time to watch over the parapet as it started. This assault turned out to be one of the most glorious feats of American bravery I witnessed during the war.

Although much more aggressive and better disciplined than our own Strikers, the Yards in the Mike Force weren't that excited about trench warfare either. As a result, all the Americans in the Mike Force cadre, along with every American on our team who could be spared, had positioned themselves in the front rank of the assault force. As I recall, the team members who made the final assault were: Young, Frier, Andrews, and Hull. Directly behind the Americans were the Mike Force Montagnards, and bringing up the rear were the exhausted, glassy-eyed survivors of 203 Company.

Again the Americans went through the ritual of trying to psych up the troops.

"Are we ready?"

"YEESSS!"

"Are we afraid of the Cong?"

"NOOOOO!"

About this time, the enemy defending the hill saw that another ground assault was imminent, and began pouring fire down across the open saddle at the attackers, who still huddled under cover at our end.

"Are we ready to fight?"

"YEEESSS!"

"KILL VC!"

"YES, YES!"

Then, from the Americans on the front rank, I heard the spine-tingling order: "FOLLOW US!"

As one man, the Americans, perhaps ten in all, jumped from the safety of the trench and out onto the bullet-swept, open ground. An enemy recoilless round burst, kicking up a geyser of dirt, but the shell fell short. The Americans, moving at what seemed to be a casual walk, made it halfway up the saddle before they looked back and discovered that none of the Yards was following.

From my perch on the edge of the trench I saw my friends hesitate a moment, glance at each other, then make their decision. "C'mon, let's go!" they yelled back at the cowering troops. Then, seeming not to care whether anyone else was coming, they continued the assault alone!

Witnessing that feat of bravery was too much for the terrified Yards. Their shame overcame their fear. Many placed their Buddha charms in their mouths, others crossed themselves, then, with a loud yell, they leaped from cover and ran to catch up with their leaders.

The enemy fire was withering, and bunched up as they had to be in order to traverse the narrow saddle, our side took many casualties. This time, however, the assaulting force made it through the gap in the wire and up the hill to within pistol range of the enemy positions before the Yards paused and took cover.

After a short exchange of hand grenades with the enemy, our assault force overran the bunker and trench immediately to its front. Our men quickly regrouped, then divided into two elements and began advancing around the hill from opposite sides. Following the enemy-held trench line, they cleared one bunker after the other.

I watched them as they slowly fought their way around the hill, out of my sight. No quarter was asked for by the enemy and none was offered. Rooting out an enemy who is fighting to the death is an extremely bloody, dangerous job, and soon a steady stream of friendly wounded was coming back down the hill, heading toward the medical bunker. I was watching for American casualties, and recognized Sergeant Frier as he was carried by on a stretcher, facedown.

After twenty minutes of furious fighting, the sounds of detonating grenades and small-arms fire died down to a few scattered shots. I watched as several of our men cautiously advanced to the summit of the hill where the 106 recoilless rifle emplacement still stood, then saw them wave their hands, indicating that the hill was once again ours.

Later that day, as he sat in the commo bunker with me, reloading his M-16 magazines, Sergeant Young gave me the firsthand account.

"Well, as you probably noticed, the Yards weren't too anxious to follow us up that goddamned hill," he said. "I guess we were sick of messing around by that time, and decided just to push on by ourselves and hope for the best, and luckily the troops finally jumped up and followed us. After we took that first bunker, and first section of trench, the Yards had more confidence and got more aggressive."

Young placed another stripper clip on top of a magazine, shoved in the rounds, then went on with his story. "We formed up into what were basically just two mobs, and started around the hill from opposite directions. I went to the right, and Frier went with the other group, to the left. It was a real son of a bitch. None of those fucking sappers would give up. A few tried to fall back around the hill to the other side, either to regroup or maybe to retreat off the hill, but once the Yards saw them running, the ol' blood lust kicked in."

"Well," I said, "our troops from 203 hill probably remembered all the shit the Cong pulled with their captured wives and kids that first night of the battle . . . a little revenge was in order."

"That's for sure," Young said. "Anyway, as we moved around the hill, the bastards fought harder and harder. I'd just run completely out of M-16 ammo and was down to bumming grenades from the Yards when Frier comes running back around the hill to my side. 'Quick, give me another rifle,' he was yelling. His own had been shot right out of his hands. Since I didn't have any rounds left anyway, I gave him mine, and he ran back over to the other side. I guess it was just after that when he got hit."

I asked Young if he knew how bad off Frier was and how he was doing. Young said he'd talked to Erickson, and found out that Frier had taken an AK round through the pelvis. Erickson had managed to get him on a dust-off chopper about an hour after he'd been wounded, and as far as anyone knew, Frier would survive.

Frier did survive, as a matter of fact, and after spending several months in a hospital in Japan, he requested to return to Vietnam. When he got back in-country, Frier asked to go to MACV SOG, and ended up in CCC, right back in Kontum. Six or seven months after I'd watched him go down the hill on the stretcher, I ran into Frier in the club at the B-team, and he told me all about it.

"It just seemed like the damned Yards wouldn't move fast enough, and I kept getting out in front of them," he said, sipping a beer. "Three assholes jumped out of a bunker and opened up on us, and one of the rounds hit my rifle and knocked it out of my hands. I picked it back up, but it was ruined and wouldn't work. I yelled at the Yards to give me a weapon, but none of them seemed to understand me. I didn't know what the hell to do, so I ran back around the hill looking for another American, and ran into Young.

"Young was out of ammo, but I still had plenty, and he gave me his rifle. I'd just run back around the damned hill and started over toward the next bunker when I caught a movement out of the corner of my eye. It was one of the bastards we missed, and he was only about ten feet away. I'll never forget that feeling," Frier said, finishing off the beer in one gulp.

"I whirled around and tried to get my M-16 lined up on him, but it was like one of those damned dreams where you can only move in slow motion. He was aiming his AK right at me, and I knew he was going to shoot me first—and he did! I felt the hit and knew it was serious. I actually thought he'd probably killed me, but I finally got my own rifle aimed at the asshole and gave him about half a magazine in the face and upper chest. Then I don't remember much of anything until I was down in the med bunker."

Sergeant Young was also wounded in the assault on 203 hill, and both he and Frier received the Silver Star for valor that day.

By noon of April 14 we'd finally recaptured the rest of our camp. There was another lull in the battle as both sides regrouped and prepared for the next round. The enemy indirect fire even slackened as the gunners waited for word on where to direct their rounds.

The Mike Force troops occupied the positions on the side of 203 hill that faced out toward the enemy. Our troops from 203 Company took the safer side of the hill, which faced in toward camp. The victorious troops then spent the rest of the day trying to clean up the mess.

The men on 203 hill were still taking a large amount of fire from enemy soldiers who were dug in on several lower hills located a hundred meters to the west. The NVA had another recoilless rifle position over there, and several machine guns, and although we pounded them with everything from our camp mortars to air strikes, we couldn't seem to knock them out.

As the third night of the battle approached, the enemy fire

dwindled away to practically nothing, and I was pretty sure the fight was over. We had retaken the rest of the camp, and since the surrounding enemy no longer had any of their friends still holding out against us on 203 hill, I couldn't see much reason for them to continue pushing the attack.

Young and Frye and a couple of other Americans had joined me in the commo bunker by then, so I had someone to talk to. Since the battle had begun forty-eight hours before, none of the Americans on the team had gotten any sleep whatsoever. That night of April 14, with the Mike Force holding 203 hill, and the diminished enemy attacks, we finally felt we could try to catch some rest. There in the commo bunker, we established a roster so we would sleep in four-hour shifts.

I was still trying to get caught up on the backlog of radio traffic flowing between us and the B-team, and took the second sleep period, which began at midnight. I lay down on the cement floor and pulled a poncho around me to keep warm. The hard, cold floor was amazingly comfortable, and feeling more secure than I had since the battle began, I immediately zonked out.

Chapter 15

It seemed like I'd just closed my eyes.

BOOOOM! *Bang-pow!* The bunker shook. There were excited cries from outside, and feet went running by in the trench. I groggily opened my eyes, wanting it all to just go away so I could get some damned rest. I was alone in the bunker again, the other Americans having gone somewhere. Screw incoming rockets, I thought, and rolled over to go back to sleep.

Sergeant Young stuck his head in the bunker doorway and yelled at me.

"Get up! It's another big one, and the bastards have broken through again on 203 hill!"

That woke me up in a hurry.

I got back on the radio and warned the B-team that we were under major attack again. Jeez, I thought, don't these shitheads ever know when to quit?

I was frankly amazed at the aggressiveness the enemy was showing. He no longer had the element of surprise on his side. We had Spectre overhead dropping flares and shooting the piss out of them, and the enemy also knew we had recently reinforced. Yet here he came at us again with another major assault—and he'd actually penetrated our defenses for the second time!

This attack was basically a replay of the first attack on the night of the twelfth. The enemy attacked in force at both 203 Company hill and the American hill. Unlike the previous attack, however, they were successful only in breaking through our lines on 203 hill. On the American hill, the beefed-up defense held fast, and the attackers were stopped at the wire.

Actually, only a squad or so of sappers got through up on 203 hill, but it was apparently a suicide attack, and the enemy managed to kill and wound quite a few of the Mike Force defenders before being wiped out.

"I don't know how they did it," one of the Mike Force sergeants told me later. "Our guys were *raining* grenades down that hill. Spectre had just dropped illume and we could see the sonsabitches coming, but some of 'em *still* made it through!"

The only thing I've ever been able to figure out is that the enemy thought our troops would run again if they managed to break through the perimeter. I guess the sappers didn't know they were facing better-disciplined Mike Force troops the second time around.

As the morning of the fourth day of battle dawned, the litter parties began carrying that night's batch of casualties down from 203 hill. The attack was back on at full force, and the enemy barrage continued with renewed intensity. Evidently they'd gotten in a fresh supply of ammo from the Ho Chi Minh trail that night.

The Mike Force men were exhausted by then; during the previous twenty-four hours they'd been shot up badly. Before coming to aid us at Dak Pek, they had been on almost constant operations. We pulled the Mike Force out of the hazardous positions on 203 hill and replaced them with the survivors of 203 Company, augmented with men from our other companies.

The day continued at the same pace, and the constant bombardment began to seem like normal routine. Down at the helipad, Erickson doggedly evacuated one chopper load of wounded after another. The air strikes around camp continued, and now we were able to direct all of them at the enemy positions outside of our perimeter.

Late that morning, over at the American mortar pit, Weeks and the guys spotted a lone NVA dug in on the top of a small hill. He was about two hundred meters away from our position. Every few minutes this asshole would stick his RPD (Soviet-made Degtyarev light machine gun) over the edge of his hole, shoot a ten- or fifteen-round burst at us, then quickly duck back down under cover. The entire camp began shooting back at the idiot, but he turned out to be very hard to kill.

The NVA gunner popped up at unexpected intervals, and by the time we could shoot back at him with our own machine guns and rifles, he always managed to duck back down in his hole. Knocking him out was going to take a direct hit by one of our mortars, and we discovered that hitting a three-foot-diameter hole at that range was extremely difficult.

Finally, we'd had enough of his harassment. Weeks shot a white phosphorous round from our 81 mortar out toward the enemy position, and it landed about thirty meters from it.

"Bird Dog, this is camp," Hull said to the FAC, "do you see that WP round we just fired?"

The FAC said he could see it.

"We want a 750-pound bomb dropped thirty meters south-west of that burst, over."

The FAC said he understood, and contacted one of the or-biting F-4s. The Phantom dropped down from an altitude of four thousand feet like a Stuka dive-bomber, releasing the single bomb as he pulled up. The bomb landed five or six yards away from the enemy gunner's foxhole, but in that case, as when play-ing horseshoes, close counted.

There was wild cheering and laughter from the American hill. Weeks told me later that he'd been watching through bin-oculars and had seen the body of the enemy soldier blown at least one hundred feet in the air.

An hour or so before dark, Young and I received word that we'd be spending that night up on 203 hill with the Yards. Lieu-tenant Andrews briefed us.

"You'll be the only Americans up there tonight. I know it will be pretty hairy, but we feel like the Yards still need some Ameri-cans with them to put a little steel in their spines."

Young and I grunted to let him know we understood.

"Besides that," the lieutenant continued, looking at me, "I want an experienced American up there with a radio so I'll know what the hell is going on."

Sergeant Young and I wearily put on our web gear and picked up our rifles. I grabbed one of the spare PRC-25s and a fresh battery, then we trudged up toward the trench line on 203 hill. Just past the gate in the defensive wire, we passed a pile of enemy corpses, awaiting burial. They were getting pretty ripe.

In fact, the first thing I noticed about 203 hill was its smell, which was at least twice as rank as the rest of the camp. Besides the smell of putrefying bodies, which I was getting used to by that time, there was also the sickening smell of burned flesh. I realized for the first time how effective our napalm strikes had been. There was another new smell up there that I had a hard time identifying at first. I finally recognized it as the smell a human exudes when terrified—the body odor of fear.

The new 203 Company commander met Young and me on the trail and led us around the hill to the side that faced the enemy. The Yards had already cleaned out and repaired a fighting position for us. One collapsed wall had been shored back up, I noticed, and some new sandbags had been added to the parapet. Only later, when we became aware of the odor, did Young and I find out that the cleaning crew had also tossed several dead NVA over the side of the hill directly in front of the position.

"NVA stay there, and there," the Yard commander warned us, pointing to several nearby hills. "I send one squad go retake outpost over there," he continued, pointed to a small finger of land that jutted out about fifty meters from the main body of our hill. I could look down from our position and see the squad of men huddled in the ruins of the unit's old outpost position. They were in a very precarious position, and I was glad I didn't have to spend the night with them down there.

We still had about half an hour of light, and before it got dark, I wanted to go look at the 106 position on top of the hill. Ducking intermittent sniper fire, I made my way up the slope.

The gun had been knocked over at an angle by one of the bomb bursts but had otherwise remained undamaged by all our attempts to destroy it. The breach block was partially open, and looking more closely at the weapon, I finally saw why the enemy had not been able to use it against us.

To load a round into the chamber of a 106, the gunner must make sure that rifling grooves on the projectile line up with the lands in the rifle barrel, but whoever had tried to load the gun had not done that, and instead attempted to force in the round. The result was that the round had jammed in the breach, rendering the weapon inoperable.

We never did decide if one of our own troops had mistakenly

done that in the excitement of the battle, or if one of the NVA sappers, being unfamiliar with the weapon, had done it in an attempt to use it against us. In any case, the mistake had certainly saved us a great deal of grief.

The shadows were getting long when I made my way back down the hill and rejoined Young in the trench. Spectre had arrived overhead, and I flipped on the radio to make a commo check with him and let him know that I would be talking to him from 203 hill.

Young and I were both worn-out, of course, and we decided to stay awake in shifts. While one of us stayed alert in the firing position, the other would sleep in the still-sound bunker built into the side of the hill behind us.

Young took the 2000 hours to midnight shift, and I took the midnight to dawn watch. With Young on guard, I gratefully retired to the bunker. Besides just being tired, I had another reason to be anxious to start my off-duty hours.

The last time I'd been able to take a crap had been four days earlier, on the morning of the twelfth. Now, finding myself with solid overhead cover, and with a bit of privacy, I dropped my camouflage trousers, squatted in a corner of the bunker, and took the biggest and best dump of my life. Being able to take a safe shit is one of a combat infantryman's infrequent pleasures during a long battle.

When I got done, I realized there was no toilet paper, but there next to me in the rubble, I found the charred remains of an NVA's shirt. Tearing off part of the sleeve, I used that. Then I gratefully flopped down in the opposite corner and immediately went out like a light.

Unfortunately, I got only two hours of sleep before the shooting started up in earnest again. The detonations woke me, and Young's excited yells to get my sorry ass out and help him hurried me along.

When I staggered out to join Young in the trench, he had just emptied a magazine down the hill and was reloading. The Yards on either side of us were blazing away with rifles and machine guns, and many others were tossing grenades down the hill. Spectre had three parachute flares floating in the air above camp, and it was bright as day.

"Looks like two groups of 'em," Young yelled at me above the din. "They've overrun the damned outpost already, and another big group is trying to come up just below us there," he said, pointing.

The guys over on the American hill had also spotted the group of attackers, and were pouring fire on them. While Young and I also directed our attention to this threat, a trip flare suddenly lit up in the wire about twenty meters in the opposite direction.

Oh, hell, I thought, trying to stay calm, they're coming from everywhere! I could see dark, indistinct shadows moving in the flickering light of the parachute flares, and put a full, twenty-round magazine down among them. One of the Yards in the trench directly above the advancing enemy threw a grenade, and he was either very accurate or very lucky, because it exploded right in the middle of the ominous shadows, sending them flying.

Hull, or someone, was on the PRC-25, excitedly directing Spectre against a nearby group that was attacking from yet another direction, northwest of the American hill. An NVA armed with a recoilless rifle let one go at us just about then, and he was firing from a position that couldn't have been more than one hundred meters away. When you get shot at by a recoilless, you don't know the round is coming until it goes off, and this one exploded just above our position, showering dirt all around. The suddenness of it scared the dogshit out of me.

By the time Spectre was finished with Hull's fire mission, the recoilless rifleman was probably long gone, but I had the gunship direct a few of its jillion-round-per-second bursts at where I thought the fire had come from . . . just because I could.

This attack lasted about an hour, then dwindled away to the usual scattered shots. By then it was 0100 hours, and time for my turn of guard duty. I told Young to try to get some sleep in the bunker.

"This fucking place stinks!" my buddy yelled out to me as soon as he went in. "Those goddamned Yards have been *shitting* in here!"

"Yeah," I yelled back, "they're a bunch of fucking animals. You'll get used to the smell in a while, though. Go to sleep."

Small probes continued the rest of that night, and at dawn the rockets started again.

Chapter 16

As it turned out, the attack on the night of April 15 was one of the last major ground assaults the enemy made during the battle. The NVA continued hitting us with small harassment probes nightly after that, but pulled most of their large units off the valley floor and contented themselves with shelling the shit out of us from the surrounding mountainsides.

The battle turned into a kind of stalemate. At camp we could run only small, local security patrols in the immediate vicinity of our perimeter. Large-scale operations would have been blasted to pieces by the surrounding enemy artillery before we could ever get to the cover of the foothills. On the other hand, the enemy had taken horrendous casualties from our air strikes while attempting to remain on the open valley floor, so was forced back into the cover and concealment of the surrounding jungle.

Once it became apparent that we had the battle in hand and that the immediate threat of being wiped out had passed, the

Mike Force company was extracted for operations elsewhere. A couple of engineers from the C-detachment were flown in about a week after things had died down, and even though still dodging incoming rockets and mortar rounds, we began rebuilding the camp.

One of those engineers, Sergeant Bodt, was permanently assigned to the team. A replacement medic by the name of Ellis also arrived about then. I got to know both men pretty well during the next nine months, eventually going on several very action-filled operations with them. James Ellis was a young, blond guy from Vero Beach, Florida, who was on his first tour in Vietnam. Sergeant Bodt was an amusing fellow with dark hair who, if I remember correctly, was from some big city in New England.

Captain Walther completed his tour of duty in Vietnam at the end of April and was replaced as team leader by Captain Gordon Strickler.

By the first of May, the heavy enemy ground fire from machine guns and rifles had died down to the point where getting in and out by chopper was not nearly as hazardous as before. The birds flew in over the surrounding, enemy-held mountains at high altitude, staying up there until directly over the camp. Then they spiraled down to land. To take off and depart the valley, one just reversed that procedure.

Due to the continued enemy bombardment, however, fixed-wing aircraft were still unable to land on our runway, and we still received all heavy resupply items, such as ammunition, sandbags, and new defensive barbed wire, by parachute.

Both the B-team and C-team commanders came out to pay us a visit and pat everyone on the back. We appreciated their effort, because although things had quieted down a lot from the way they'd been several weeks earlier, Dak Pek continued to be a very good place to get your ass shot off if you weren't careful.

When I'd first arrived at Dak Pek a month earlier, I'd had two months' back pay in my pocket. Not knowing what else to do with the cash, I'd stored it in the field safe located in the TOC. Several days after we'd been overrun, when the demolished TOC stopped burning, someone had pried open the safe to see if any of the contents had survived. They hadn't.

My two months' pay now consisted of a carbonized brick. Not knowing what else to do with the ashes, I gave them to the B-team commander to take back to headquarters with him after his visit. This turned out to be a wise move on my part, because six months later, when I was going through the red-tape nightmare of trying to file my claim for personal property lost during the battle, the commander was able to vouch for the fact that I had indeed lost the money during the attack, and I was grudgingly reimbursed.

I never was reimbursed for my thousand-dollar, gold neck chain, however, because I'd purchased it while in Thailand, and couldn't produce a receipt for it. The REMFs back in Saigon who determined the validity of these claims obviously didn't believe that a front-line soldier would be stupid enough to be wearing such a chain—or be wealthy enough to have one in the first place. They obviously hadn't been around very many Special Forces troops.

After surveying the destroyed American hill, our attached engineers, along with the leadership of the American and Vietnamese Special Forces teams, decided to abandon it, and rebuild the American TOC and team living quarters in the center of camp, next to the LLDB positions.

Over at the old American position there was still one solid bunker left that could sleep about six men. The rest of the team moved to the LLDB hill with me, and found floor space wherever they could. We continued to hold the lower American hill for the time being, as our very well-constructed 81 mortar pit was located there and we had no other position to move it to.

A gang of Yards began the laborious task of digging the large holes for the new American positions. We salvaged what building materials we could, such as heavy beams, pierced-steel planking, and so forth, from the destroyed buildings. Rebuilding the positions for the American team became the camp priority, but it was hampered by the continued enemy bombardment. Just to make life even more miserable, the rainy season kicked off about then, and we all lived in a sea of mud.

During the first week of May, the B-team sent us a new Collins single sideband radio to replace the one destroyed in the TOC. They also airlifted in a 1.5 KW generator so the American team would not have to rely solely on the one controlled by the Vietnamese team. Except for times when the antenna was being replaced due to enemy rockets, we once again had good, round-the-clock voice commo with all higher headquarters elements.

Although we could still get an air strike on very short notice, we no longer had planes overhead on a continuous basis. When the NVA realized that our air cover was gone, they again became emboldened, digging in several large mortars on hilltop positions right on the edge of the surrounding mountains.

We had their new positions spotted, and returned fire with our own camp mortars, but that had little effect. We also called in several air strikes against those hills during the day, bombing and napalming the positions until nothing could have survived. Apparently the NVA occupied the hills only during hours of darkness, however, because they kept up an intermittent stream of incoming rounds from the positions each night.

I knew how to solve this problem. My plan was to wait until darkness, when our movement could not be observed by the enemy on the surrounding high ground, then depart camp with a platoon-size combat patrol. A unit that small might be able to make its way undetected to a position just below the top of one of the enemy mortar positions. The patrol would then have the option of ambushing the enemy soldiers at dawn, as they left for the day, or assaulting and overrunning the mortar positions.

The problem with such an operation was that once the enemy

was overrun, our own assaulting force would then be trapped on top of the hill right in the middle of fifty million NVA. I figured that if we did some coordination with our air assets, however, the patrol could either shoot its way back to camp or be airlifted off the hilltop the next morning, before the enemy had time to get his shit together.

I kept this plan to myself, however. For one thing, our Strikers at Dak Pek just weren't that good. To pull something like that off, we would have needed indigenous troops of the same quality as those in the SOG units. Also, I knew that if I put that plan forward and it was accepted and put into action, I would undoubtedly be the prime candidate to lead the hazardous patrol! Four or five years earlier in the war, I probably would have welcomed such a mission. In 1970, however, with American involvement in the war nearing its end, I had decided that my main objective was simply to survive my last tour of duty the best way I could.

By the middle of May we had become accustomed to dodging the occasional mortar rounds and rockets. The trick was always to know where the nearest bunker or trench line was, and to spend as little time in the open as possible. The camp had been pretty well cleaned up, all the dead bodies we could find had been buried, and all the seriously wounded flown out.

Since being overrun, we'd been subsisting primarily on the indigenous combat rations that we supplied our troops. Those meals consisted of instant rice with a packet of seasoning thrown in. A few cases of American C-rations had been parachuted in, but C-rats were so greasy and unpalatable that most of us couldn't gag them down. As can be imagined, our living conditions were filthy, and just about everyone on the team was suffering from diarrhea. Because the supply building had been destroyed, we had all been wearing the same uniforms we'd had on since the night of the first attack, four weeks previously.

One day, after a visit by a colonel from higher headquarters, a chopper came in and dropped off a big bundle of new American jungle fatigues. There were assorted sizes, and everyone on the team found at least two pairs that fit. Wow! It was suddenly just like Christmas around Dak Pek.

Now that we had fresh uniforms, our team medics—sounding a little like stern parents—proclaimed it was also time that we all washed our sorry, filthy, stinking asses. That, however, was easier said than done.

The small amount of water on hand in camp was strictly for drinking. Bathing would require going down to the river, which flowed about one hundred meters outside the perimeter. Our Yard troops were as anxious to clean up as we were, so we instituted a series of "combat bathing patrols," each consisting of two Americans and a platoon of Yards. We ran only one each day, at random times, and each patrol went to a different bathing point at the river's edge. My day to go finally rolled around, and if I remember correctly, Erickson was the other American with me.

Anxiously watching the surrounding mountains for signs of enemy incoming, our little group formed up down by the gate. We made an absurd-looking bunch, armed to the teeth and wearing full combat gear, but each of us carrying a towel, shaving kit, shower shoes, and bundles of clean clothing. We left the protection of camp, walked along the edge of the runway, then down a small embankment toward the clear, inviting river.

Then the fun part started. One American, accompanied by half the patrol, stripped naked and daintily waded out into the cold water. The other half took up defensive positions along the bank. I was in the second group to bathe, which meant that the enemy had more time to spot our little group and react before I exposed myself. When my time came to take off my clothes and walk out into that damned water, I was one nervous dude, believe me.

The water was shallow—only knee deep—but was flowing at a good clip. The bottom was covered with slick rocks too, and it was hard to keep my footing. Splashing and laughing, several of the Yards fell down. We didn't waste any time playing, how-ever, but quickly cleaned up the best we could. I had just fin-ished, and was carefully wading toward my towel onshore, when the first mortar round went off about twenty-five meters away.

With terror-filled eyes, our happy band of buck-naked bath-ers splashed toward the relative safety of the bank. Near the edge, I slipped on the rocks, went down on hands and knees, and had to crawl out of the water in that position. Two more enemy rounds exploded behind us as the gunners tried to get the range. I grabbed my web gear and rifle as I ran past my bundle of new clothing and towel, and flopped down on the dirt bank next to Erickson. A few more mortar rounds went off, and we hugged the ground.

The camp mortars began returning the enemy fire, and the in-coming rounds stopped. I looked down at my naked, muddy body. None of us in that second shift of bathers was anxious to go back out in the water again, and we quickly put on our uni-forms over the dirt. Once back in the safety of the commo bunker, I had to strip down again and brush off the caked mud . . . but at least I didn't stink as much as before.

One day not long after the new uniforms arrived, we also re-ceived a large sack of mail. I never got much mail from the States anymore, but that time there were several letters from Vicki, who was still over in Thailand. With all the recent excite-ment of the battle, I'd forgotten all about being lovesick, mis-erable, and all of that. Now, of course, I remembered.

To her credit, Vicki didn't write love letters at all, but simply chatty, newsy little missives with gossip about people we both knew. She said she'd heard about the fighting in the Central Highlands, and hoped that Bill Spurgeon and I were both un-harmed. Actually, because Vicki worked "upstairs"—code word for the intelligence section—in the embassy in Bangkok, I knew she was privy to the classified battle reports from Vietnam, and figured she probably had most of the details of what had recently been going on.

I wrote her back and said things had been pretty hectic lately, but that Spurgeon and I were still all right. I told her that I would be getting a five-day R&R in about two more months, and that I planned to spend it in Bangkok. Since her letters had contained no lovey-dovey sentiments, I didn't put any in mine either.

Someone back at the B-team had also been nice enough to include a few current issues of *Time* and *Newsweek* with the mail, and I got caught up on all the current events.

For the first time, I found out about the large American and ARVN combat operation to our south that had recently pushed into Cambodia. All right! We were finally moving in on their sanctuaries and wiping the bastards out, something we should have done years earlier.

The start of this major push into Cambodia had occurred during the last week of April, and coincided with the lessening of pressure around the Dak Seang/Dak Pek areas of operation. I assumed the large NVA units surrounding Dak Pek had been fearful of getting flanked and had pulled back farther into Cambodia and Laos. Or maybe they'd been sent south to aid units defending sanctuaries there. Whatever the reason, the Cambodia operation had certainly made things a little less deadly around camp, and we were all thankful for it.

Meanwhile, back at the home front . . .

The college students, led by hardcore Communist agitators, hadn't liked the U.S. excursion into Cambodia at all. Nothing new, of course, because the comm-symps back home never liked anything the U.S. military did that might help us win. The big news story during those first weeks of May was about Kent State University.

During one of the "peace and love" demonstrations protesting the bombing in Cambodia, the flower children had gotten a little out of hand and had burned down the Kent State ROTC building. That was obviously just a case of innocent, youthful overexuberance, the news media reported. Unfortunately, the mean Ohio governor had overreacted by sending in the National Guard (fascist pigs!) to subdue the children.

Trouble was, when this screaming, hate-filled mob of several thousand students surrounded a small group of armed Guardsmen, the undisciplined troops, fearing for their lives, panicked and used their rifles. When the gun smoke cleared, there were four dead and eleven wounded rioters (oops, I mean "innocent, student peace demonstrators").

There was going to be an investigation, the news reports said ominously. The Guardsmen had fired "hundreds" of rounds of ammunition during the confrontation.

"There ought to be a goddamned investigation, all right," I said to some of the team members who had ducked into the commo bunker to avoid a spate of incoming mortar rounds. They were all sitting around on the floor listening to me read the news article out loud. "Apparently these Ohio State National Guardsmen fired up their entire, basic load of ammo. They were shooting at point-blank range. Their targets were untrained, unprepared students . . . and the idiots still only managed to kill four and wound eleven. What they need to investigate is why the National Guard isn't being trained to shoot better!"

We all got a big laugh out of that.

By the end of May the number of incoming mortar rounds and rockets had slacked off to only one or two a week, and we declared the siege over. We began taking cargo planes on our runway again without incident, and our first large offensive operation since the one in early April was launched.

The operation was of company size and was accompanied by Sergeant Young and Specialist Erickson. Although the operation was sent into the area east of camp, which was away from the hotter, border region, the situation was such that leaving the camp perimeter at all was still a pretty hairy undertaking.

As it turned out, the patrol got out of the open valley and into the mountains without taking any mortar rounds. They made only light enemy contact during the seven days they were out, which tended to confirm our suspicions that the large enemy units had left the AO, for the time being at least.

Erickson's diarrhea on that operation was so bad that he was forced to cut a hole in the seat of his camouflage trousers, a trick that had also worked for Merrill's Marauders in Burma during WWII.

Although Dak Pek was once one of Special Forces' showplace camps in Vietnam, after the battle of April 12, we no longer got a lot of visitors. That was actually okay with me, because I'd long before gotten tired of conducting dog-and-pony shows for touring dignitaries. Some of the guys on the team still spoke a little wistfully about the good old days before the battle, however, when the big shots used to drop in to be impressed by the new Montagnard school, the team club room—its wall adorned with captured flags and weapons—the "impregnable" American TOC, and all of that.

Around the first of June, however, I received a message that we would be getting a couple of visitors of a different type. Two Air Force F-4 pilots who had flown air strikes for us during the battle had decided to spend their one week of R&R out at our camp. They just wanted to see what the area looked like from the ground, they'd told our higher, and wanted to get a better idea of what damage their bombing and strafing had done.

Hell, I decided, they were our kind of guys! Anyone can go on R&R to some sissy place like Australia or Bangkok; it took a couple of real nutcases to want to spend their limited rest and relaxation time in a place like Dak Pek.

They arrived one morning via helicopter, and jumped out carrying parachute kit bags full of whiskey, cigarettes, and skin magazines—the bare necessities for a week at a Special Forces A-team camp—somebody had briefed them well. They had flown numerous strikes against the 203 Company hill, and wanted to go up there first. From the air, they told us, the target had looked small, the friendly forces very close. From ground level it seemed worse. "Good thing we didn't fuck up," one of them said.

That evening, with Hull manning the radios, I grabbed a bottle of scotch that one of the pilots offered and retired to our newly reconstructed mess hall to see how much of the bottle I could drink in one sitting. Getting drunk while at an A-camp in Vietnam was a very dangerous and stupid thing to do, but by that stage in the war my morale was such that I just didn't give a good shit anymore. Besides, it was the first alcohol we'd had in camp since being overrun.

About halfway through the bottle, I collected all the knives in the kitchen and began amusing myself by throwing them into the wall. The new medic, Ellis, joined me for a few drinks about that time, and after an impromptu knife-throwing lesson, he also joined me in the fun.

Then Sergeant Young and Erickson showed up to grab a bite to eat, and decided to have a few predinner cocktails themselves. Before long I had about half the team with me, all of us drunk, singing, and having a grand time of it.

Young had just received a Dear John letter from his girlfriend back in Wisconsin, and we made up a poem about her, which we recited over and over again.

Unfortunately, our party was interrupted by an enemy probe that sent our group of merry revelers staggering off toward the alert positions. Luckily, it wasn't anything big, or things might have turned really ugly. The next day, however, we did hear from Captain Strickler about it. He let us know he hadn't been too happy with our performance. Since I'd been not only the ranking man at the party, but also the instigator, I took the brunt of the blame.

Chapter 17

"You and Sergeant Ellis will be taking out the next operation," the captain told me several days later. I presumed this was part of our punishment for the party, but maybe it was actually just our turn to go. On A-teams we tried to always send an experienced man along with a less experienced, and it would be Sergeant Ellis's first combat operation outside the wire at Dak Pek.

We were standing in front of the situation map in the LLDB operations center. Strickler pointed to the area south of us, which included the tall commanding mountain several kilometers away. "You can work out your own route of march and operation plan," the captain continued, "but I want you to go up to the top of that damned mountain. The LLDB suspect that there are some NVA still up there acting as observers."

"How long has it been since Dak Pek Strikers have been up there, Tom?" I said, turning to Sergeant Weeks.

"Been quite a while, actually," the team sergeant told us. "Not since before the 4th Infantry moved into the AO back in 'sixty-seven. We were planning to check it out after they left, but then we had the big battle and all of that . . ." He let his voice trail off.

"We have many men know trails up mountain," the LLDB team leader reassured us. "Before 4th Infantry come, our CIDG go top of mountain many times."

Accompanied by two of the LLDB, Ellis and I would be going with a company and a half of the Strike Force, and would depart camp the next morning at first light. The patrol was scheduled for the usual seven days. After the briefing, I went back to the mess hall and got a cup of coffee from Ute, who had recently returned from the hospital in Pleiku. Sergeant Ellis came in to join me, and I spread out my map on the table.

"I think what we'll do is head out of camp and move to the southeast. That way, maybe the Cong will think we're going to the same area Erickson and Young just worked. We'll have to cross this big stream here," I said, showing Ellis on the map, "then when we're under cover in the foothills, we'll drop straight south. Our first RON coordinates will be here, on this small hill next to the river. Next morning, we'll cross back over the river, go directly to this big fucking mountain the captain wants checked out, and climb it while we're still fresh.

"We'll go up the north side," I continued, "the side that faces the camp. That way, if we run into some shit, it will be easier to get fire support from camp. Also, we'll be in line of sight, and the commo with camp should be no problem on the short whip antennas."

"Think we'll run into anything up there?" Ellis asked.

"No one has any fucking idea," I said. "If we do, I doubt it will be anything big. 'Course, if they're dug in real good on the side of that mountain, it wouldn't be hard for them to defend. If there's a lot of the bastards, we'll just pull back and call in the Air Force," I added. "I'm not interested in re-creating Hamburger Hill.

"Anyway," I went on, "if we're able to make it up there with no problems, we'll spend the second night on the top of that sucker, so you might want to bring a sweater or something, because it will probably be chilly up there."

I paused while I took a sip of Ute's thick, burned coffee. "We'll go back down the next day, and spend the rest of the operation just playing it by ear, working these hills around the base of the mountain."

Ellis said he'd go pack his aid bag and meet me later that

afternoon so we could inspect the troops' equipment and go over our plan with the LLDB and the Yard commander. After he'd gone, I continued studying the map, trying to memorize the terrain features. It was a habit I'd gotten into several years before, when I'd been with special projects.

There was a lot of ground fog the next morning as we left camp, and that helped hide our movement from watching enemy. By the time the fog had burned off, we were entering the edge of the jungle-covered foothills. The point man in the lead squad picked up a trail, and we followed it to the river crossing.

The crossing was a Montagnard-style suspension bridge of ropes and vines. It hung in the air at least thirty-five feet above a rocky riverbed and swayed ominously back and forth in the slight breeze. We had to cross in single file, daring only to put four or five men on the bridge at one time. Even though half the patrol was already across by the time Ellis's turn and mine came, it was still spooky out there in the middle of the bridge, thinking about what an enemy machine gun or even a single sniper could do.

Once we all got to the other side, we formed a perimeter and took our first break. The two LLDB sergeants came over with the Yard company commander, and after a short discussion, we decided to go south at the next trail junction, which was only a kilometer away. The Yard commander pointed out a small hill several klicks down the trail and suggested it would be a good place to stop for the noon meal. All of that agreed on, we once again moved out.

An hour later, as we slowly worked our way along the trail, with flankers out on either side, we ran across the first enemy sign. The column came to a sudden halt and everyone faded off into the vegetation on each side of the trail, taking up defensive positions. A few minutes later the platoon leader from the point element came back to the center of the column where Ellis and I crouched with the command group, and he quickly briefed the Yard commander and the LLDB sergeants in Vietnamese.

"They find many NVA footprints cross trail," the LLDB sergeant translated. "Look like one platoon, maybe more."

I asked him how fresh the tracks were and if they could tell which direction the enemy troops had been moving in.

"Foot prints very new," the Vietnamese sergeant relayed to me after asking the Yard platoon leader. "Think cross last night. Move east."

If we continued our movement due south, it didn't sound like we would be running into that group, but when we resumed our march, we were much more alert. It appeared that the bad guys hadn't all left after all.

It was nearly 1300 hours before we reached our predetermined stopping point for lunch. The rice-burning Montagnards couldn't go too long at any one time without stopping to eat, as their bodies quickly metabolized their mainly carbohydrate diet. Ellis and I were eating pretty much the same things as the troops, so by the time we stopped, we were hungry too.

With half the troops on perimeter duty, the others divided into little groups and started preparing their meals. Several of the men fanned out into the surrounding jungle in search of food items to add to the boring reconstituted rice. The food foragers returned in minutes carrying odds and ends of fruit, leaves, and fresh bamboo shoots.

Each group of men began building its own, small cooking fire, and I wandered over to the nearest bunch to watch. I'd been hearing about the amazing woodsmanship of these hill tribesmen for years, and was anxious to see them in action. What ancient, Stone Age techniques would they use to get the still-damp twigs and wood burning? Would they start the fires by rubbing sticks together or, perhaps, strike sparks from pieces of flint?

The group I watched quickly assembled fire-starting materials, which consisted of: two plastic bags, several pieces of cardboard from an ammo box, and a big hunk of C-4 explosive.

The wet wood was ceremoniously tossed on this pile of com-bustibles, and one of the crafty, native hill tribesmen started it all burning with a flick of his Zippo!

Margaret Mead would have pulled out her hair.

As they squatted around the fire, one of the grinning Yards showed me a delicious delicacy he'd just discovered in the jungle, a big mess of white, sluggishly moving grubs of some kind. "Is number one chop-chop," the man said. "You eat too."

One of the other troops produced a piece of aluminum foil and laid it over hot coals. The other man dumped his grubs on the improvised griddle, and we watched the white larvae squirm just a bit before they began to sizzle and pop. When the grubs were a nice, golden brown, we commenced to eat. I was pretty hungry, and the sautéed critters weren't bad, actually, crisp on the outside, but soft and creamy in the middle.

This time, Ms. Mead would have smiled.

After the meal, I took a quick tour around the perimeter. Every-thing looked pretty good, all the danger points were well covered, and the troops were manning their weapons alertly. I went back to where I'd dropped my indigenous ruck in the center of the perimeter and flopped down on the ground with my back rest-ing against it. I was just thinking what good troops the Dak Pek Montagnards were and how much they'd learned over the past eight years about modern warfare when the silence was suddenly shattered by two explosions.

Grenades!

The detonations came from the bottom of the hill, someplace near the river. We'd sent a squad down there to act as an early warning post, and they must have made contact. All around me the troops ducked for cover, readying their weapons and getting prepared for whatever might come next.

Something wasn't right, though. The unexpected explosions were not followed by the usual bursts of small-arms fire. Down at the river, I heard excited yelling in Vietnamese, then a shouted answer, followed by giggling from some of the nearby troops.

The Yards around me relaxed and went back to what they'd been doing.

One of the LLDB sergeants came over to where Ellis and I were still trying to figure out what the hell was going on. He squatted next to us. "Montagnard troops use grenades kill fish," he said with a disgusted shake of the head. "All Montagnard think about is eat—number-hucking-wenty!"

He was right, of course. Now every goddamned NVA within ten miles knew our location. "Come on," I told the Vietnamese sergeant, getting to my feet. "Let's get the hell out of here before the sonsabitches have time to set up some ambushes for us."

We continued our march to the south, pushing it a little to get some distance between us and where we'd eaten lunch. At 1800 hours we stopped for the day and established our night perimeter. As usual, the hill we'd chosen to defend had been previously used by one side or the other, and had the usual "predug" fighting positions. I radioed our RON coordinates to camp and advised them of two concentrations for the camp mortars.

We were still near the river, which flowed past us at the bottom of our hilltop position. "Tell that Yard company commander that he can send a few water parties down to the river," I said to the LLDB sergeant, "but no more fishing with grenades!"

Chapter 18

A light rain had begun falling before Ellis and I had our poncho hootch strung up. Using one poncho for a roof and the other for the floor, we built the shelter close to the ground, directly behind one of the fighting positions. With our rucksacks up at one end for pillows, we were soon snug and dry.

To keep from getting chilled, we took off our wet camouflage shirts and put on jungle sweaters. We kept our weapons and web gear next to us, and I took the PRC-25 from the Montagnard radio bearer and put it behind my rucksack, with the handset next to my ear. The droning, rushing noise of the side tone, broken by occasional, routine transmissions between the units down at camp, was reassuring.

One of the Yard commander's personal flunkies had an entrenching tool, and made the rounds of the command group's holes, cleaning and slightly deepening each. While on operations around Dak Pek, only one man from each squad carried a shovel, and that seemed to work out okay.

As I lay there under the poncho, watching the rain fall, I remembered back to 1965, when I'd spent a few months attached to the 173rd Airborne. When on operations with that regular infantry unit, I'd had to carry my own shovel and even wore a goddamned steel pot. Of course, while with the American unit, I hadn't had to worry about the troops running away and leaving me, and I'd had no command responsibility either. Also, the 173rd didn't use grenades for fishing—at least, not while on operations.

Sergeant Ellis and I divided the guard duty in the usual manner, with each of us staying awake half the night. I had the second shift, which I always preferred because I enjoyed watching the sun come up. Because of the rain and gathering fog, it got dark early, and I had no problem falling asleep. When Ellis woke me for my shift, just after midnight, I felt oddly refreshed.

Guard duty while with one of these operations didn't amount to much more than staying awake and alert so you could wake up the other American if some shit broke loose. The Americans were always with the command element, which bivouacked in the center of the perimeter, and so didn't have to worry too much about spotting approaching enemy. Even at a Monta-gnard camp like Dak Pek, however, there were always a few Viet Cong sympathizers or agents in the Strike Force, so we stayed on the lookout for possible assassins.

On earlier tours in Vietnam, I'd learned that trying to move around inside the perimeter at night to check on the trigger-happy troops was too damned dangerous. Besides the possi-bility of getting accidentally shot, it would give one of those VC agents I just mentioned a good excuse to kill you and get away with it.

I made the hourly commo check with camp, and the Ameri-can on guard duty there promptly answered, telling me that the commo was still "five-by-five." About 0200 hours there was a little excitement when one of our listening posts thought they heard some enemy movement. I had to wake up Ellis, and we jumped into the foxhole. I decided against calling camp for some 81mm illumination, fearing that it would only give away our position, and I didn't want to call in any HE until some shooting started. After about an hour, nothing else had hap-pened, so Ellis and I crawled back under the cover of the poncho shelter.

Because it had been raining while we'd huddled in the un-covered fighting position, we were wet again, and muddy, but the wool jungle sweaters still kept us warm.

"Awww, it's a great day to be a rompin'-stompin' Special Forces paratrooper!" I said loudly from where I stood, stretch-ing my stiff muscles in the clear, dawn light. The rain had stopped and the air smelled fresh and wonderful. The sun would not come over the mountains for several hours yet, so it was still cool.

Ellis crawled groggily out from beneath the poncho. "Ser-geant Wade," he said, running a hand through his blond hair, "sometimes you're a weird bastard, you know it?"

"What do you mean, Ellis?" I said, flopping down on the

ground and taking a bite of an Army-issue chocolate bar. "This is the goddamned life!"

The funny thing is, I really meant it. From our vantage point on the hill, we had a view of the entire valley. It was a beautiful sight, laid out there before us. Several of the strategic hamlets had been reoccupied, and smoke from morning cooking fires drifted up. Everything was green, and lush, and the morning sunrise turned the rising patches of ground fog a strange, pinkish color.

"If it wasn't for the war, this would be a great place to live," I said. "I'd like to come back here, build me a little thatch hut up on stilts, get me a Yard wife, and just kick back for the rest of my life."

"I think I'll stick with eastern Florida," Ellis said. "It would be nice and peaceful here, all right, but a diet of bamboo shoots, rice, and grub worms would probably get a little old after a while."

"You just ain't got no feel for the exotic, Ellis," I told him with a laugh.

We broke camp and got back on the march before 0600 hours. The Montagnard commander told us there was a good fording place not far from us, where we could get back across the river without getting too wet. We sent a squad of Strikers up ahead to check it out for ambushes and to secure it for the main body.

There was no bridge that time, just some large rocks and a couple of logs to walk on, and because of the recent rain, the river was running higher than normal. By the time we got across, I was wet to my knees. Damned wet feet again, I thought. Always being wet was just one of the many curses an infantryman had to endure. I hoped I wouldn't get any blisters.

As soon as the sun came up over the edge of the mountains, it started getting hot again. By 0800 that morning we had arrived at the base of the mountain, and took a short break to adjust equipment and take a drink of water.

The top of the mountain was still hidden by the low-lying clouds. "Thanks for bringing me on this operation with you, Sergeant Wade," Ellis said. "I always did want to climb fucking Mount Everest."

"I hope it isn't snowing up there," I said. "I forgot my damned ice ax."

We had a short huddle with the rest of the command group to decide what route to take.

"Company commander want take trail," the LLDB sergeant told Ellis and me, tracing it for us on the map. "He say he know way, and not too hard."

This was always a difficult decision to make. Using the obvious trails and routes of march was a good way to get your ass ambushed. On the other hand, moving through thick jungle by breaking bush was a very slow, difficult, and exhausting way to travel. Trying to break bush and climb a slick, steep mountainside at the same time was just about an impossibility, and it would take us several days to get up the side of the damned mountain instead of one.

We finally agreed on using the trail. With the lead squad farther out in front than usual, and the rest of us well spread out, we started the climb.

At first it wasn't so bad because the trail followed the easiest route, and for a while we were on the gradual slope of a finger. We gained a little altitude, then hit the mountain proper. Since we were under the double and triple canopy of the rain forest, we were at least in the shade.

I'd lost about twenty pounds of body weight since my first operation at Dak Pek back in April, and had gotten back into pretty good physical condition just from hiking around the hills of the camp. Still, it was tough going, and even the tough, stringy Yards, who had been climbing the mountains since birth, were having a rough time of it. There was nothing in my indigenous ruck but a poncho, sweater, and a few packs of dried rice, but besides two canteens of water, I was carrying a full load of ammo, plus two frag and two smoke grenades, and all of that stuff was heavy.

I was very thankful to be armed with the light, handy CAR-15 rather than something like the old Garand. Ahead of us I could see the poor bastard with the M-60. He was carrying it in the usual fashion, with the weapon balanced across his right shoulder, muzzle forward, right hand on the flash suppressor. That was not the tactically sound way to carry the gun, but I wasn't stupid enough to volunteer a demonstration of the proper method!

Our straggling column came to one of those unexpected, sudden halts, and I collapsed in the bushes off the side of the trail. There had been no shooting, and nothing exploded, so I took the opportunity to reach around and drag out one of my canteens. It was already half empty, and I knew I would have to be careful as there would be no more water until the next day, when we were down off the mountain again.

The Yard commander was talking in a low voice on his HT-1 radio, and one of the LLDB sergeants translated that the point element was checking out some old fighting positions along the trail ahead.

In a few minutes we resumed the march, and soon came to the old positions ourselves. We needed a break, and that was about as good a place as we were likely to find, so using the previously dug holes, we formed a temporary perimeter. I dropped the ruck off my sweat-soaked back and wiped my face with the large OD bandanna I'd bummed from the medics.

Those bandannas were actually supposed to be used as slings for injured arms, but they came in so handy for various things in the field that most of us on A-teams and in special projects had begun wearing one around our necks on a permanent basis. That, of course, was just one of many uniform violations that never failed to infuriate the rear-area big shots when they made their inspections.

"How's your water holding out?" I asked Ellis as he took a sparing swig.

"This canteen's about empty," he said, "but the other one is full, and I've got one of those two-quart bladders in my ruck."

"Good," I told him. "I'll probably want to take a bath tonight after we get to the top of this fucker."

He flipped me the bird.

It was nearly 1100 hours by the time we began moving again. After another meeting with the company commander, we'd decided to skip the lunch break and push on to the summit. If things went well, we would be there by 1500 hours and could stop for the day.

Of course, things didn't go well.

Something exploded at the front of the column, and we all dove for cover at the side of the trail. At first there was no firing, and I suspected that the point man had simply tripped a booby trap of some sort. Then a short burst of automatic-weapons fire cracked through the limbs overhead and was immediately answered by the point element.

I glanced over at Ellis, and he was all right. The Yard commander was giving orders to one of his lieutenants, who quickly moved off in a crouch up the hill toward the shooting. An M-79 round went off, followed by more firing, all of it outgoing.

Although this didn't seem to be much of an attack, it was just the sort of situation I'd been dreading. There we were, three-quarters of the way up the side of the fucking mountain, strung out for over a hundred meters—and the enemy had the high ground! The two LLDB sergeants had crawled over to the company commander, and one of them was talking excitedly on the HT-1. The Yard carrying my PRC-25 was up there also, and I made the short dash up to join them without drawing any fire.

The radio bearer already had the handset out, and he gave it to me when I dropped down next to him.

"Alpha One, this is Alpha Two," I said into the handset, using the call signs we'd decided upon. Hull answered immediately.

"This is Alpha Two, we've made enemy contact. Over." I was trying to keep my voice calm.

"Roger. Over" was the reply.

I pulled my map out of the leg pocket of the camouflage trousers, quickly checked our location, and radioed the coordinates of our position back to camp. I didn't take the time to encrypt the information, because the enemy already knew where we were.

"Roger, Alpha Two," Hull answered, "I read back your coordinates for possible correction. Four-five-nine-seven-two-two, over."

"That's an affirm. Stand by. Out." If it turned out that we needed to call in fire support, I damn sure wanted the camp to know where *not* to shoot!

The Montagnard lieutenant who had been sent forward came running back down the hill then and reported to the commander. "He say maybe five NVA," the LLDB sergeant translated for me. "Throw one grenade, shoot AK-47."

"Any friendly wounded?" I asked.

The LLDB relayed the question to the Yard lieutenant in Vietnamese, and the lieutenant answered me directly in halting English. "No WIA, Trung-si. No KIA."

So we had five enemy soldiers holding up 150. To punctuate the situation, there was another short burst of incoming AK fire, and we all instinctively ducked. I drew a crude picture of our situation in the dirt with a twig.

"Our point squad here," I said, making a hole in the earth. "NVA here," I continued, jabbing the ground again. "Can we flank the bastards?" I drew a line from our point squad up around in an arc to one side of the enemy position.

"Okay, we try," the Yard company commander said. After a short discussion between the commander, his lieutenant, and the LLDB sergeant in rapid Vietnamese, the lieutenant ran back up the hill toward the point element.

"You call camp, shoot mortar?" the LLDB asked me.

"Yes," I told him, and took the handset from the radio bearer again. I was a little leery of trying to call in the mortars too damned close, because we were at the weapon's max range, and the gunners would be shooting toward the side of the mountain. On the other hand, I knew that a few friendly mortar rounds going off would be a morale boost to our troops and maybe have the opposite effect on the enemy. So, adding a big fudge factor, I radioed the fire mission to camp. I asked for an initial round of HE rather than white phosphorus, because I'd have to adjust the fire by sound.

The first round was on the way in only a few minutes, and it sounded like it landed about where I'd hoped it would. I called in an adjustment of "drop twenty-five, left twenty-five," and told Weeks and the boys to go ahead and give us three rounds for effect.

The rounds also impacted well away, not only from us but the enemy too. The friendly incoming was reassuring, though, and immediately after they went off, our point element began shooting as they started their flanking movement.

Five minutes later the lieutenant came back down the hill and reported that the enemy had retreated. There were no casualties on either side, so after radioing the report back to camp, we continued our march up the mountain. Although it had been a very typical engagement, to me those little firefights never got to be merely "routine." I was constantly aware of the fact that my friend Bill Spencer had been killed in a very similar situation.

Due to the delay, it was almost 1630 hours before we reached the summit. Thankfully, it was unoccupied by enemy, and we merely walked in and took over the old 4th Infantry emplacements.

There was something eerie about returning to the old firebase. It was like walking into a ghost town. The fighting positions, only recently so well maintained, stood empty, the sandbags already beginning to rot.

Only six months before, this mountaintop had swarmed with activity. Choppers had flown in daily, bringing food, water, ammo, mail, and replacements. Sweating men, stripped to the waist, had busily worked on the fortifications and cleaned the 155 howitzers. The top of the commo bunker, now partially caved in, had once bristled with 292 antenna poles, and a constant stream of communications had flowed between the mountaintop and other bases in the area.

All gone. The men who had once manned the hilltop were probably already back in the United States, telling war stories about their "horrible time in the Nam." Those of us down at Camp Dak Pek would be gone shortly too, after Special Forces' almost ten years of occupying this valley. Would the little Montagnards be able to hold it against the regiments of NVA? None of us really believed they could.

I sat on the edge of an old foxhole, my feet and legs dangling down inside. At the bottom of the hole, partially covered with dirt and leaves, was a rusted C-ration can. I picked the relic up, looked at it, then tossed it off the side of the mountain. The can, which was labeled "Ham and Lima Beans," had never been opened.

We spent an uneventful night there in the old firebase. With 150 men occupying the fortified summit, I really hadn't expected to be attacked. Even with our jungle sweaters, though, it got cold up there, and I was glad the next morning when we broke camp and started back down.

Chapter 19

The month of June ended with things about the same. The intensity of enemy activity stayed at a mild simmer, with just enough pressure to let us know that the NVA hadn't forgotten about us. Down at Dak Seang things had finally quieted down too, and they were also working on repairing damage done to their camp during the long siege.

Reconstruction at Dak Pek was already about half finished by the start of July 1970. Following what was by then common practice, the entire American TOC, sleeping, and dining facilities were being built underground with enough overhead cover to withstand a 140mm rocket. The new complex was built in the shape of a U. The new mess hall was at one side, sleeping rooms were on the other, and in between were the TOC and commo bunkers. The new American 81mm mortar pit was constructed right out the door of the TOC, and was reached by a short trench.

Although not as fancy as the old complex on the other hill, it was just as strong. What the new facility always lacked was the feeling of hominess that the other place had. All of us on the team knew that we'd be leaving, turning everything over to the Viets, within months, so we didn't make a lot of effort to decorate.

In fact, you could say that the morale on the team was downright sour. The unofficial team motto was "Tell someone who gives a shit," and one of the guys had scrawled that on a board and nailed it to the wall of the mess hall. The war was over, and we'd lost. The NVA were staying and we were leaving—it was just that fucking simple.

Sergeant Weeks reached the end of his final extension in Vietnam about then and went back to the States. Everyone was sorry to see the experienced man go. The B-team sent in a temporary replacement for him, Master Sergeant John Smith, but due to the draw-down in force, we were told we might not get another permanent team sergeant.

Captain Strickler also rotated out about then, and was replaced by Captain Frederick Britton. Lieutenant Andrews left and was replaced in the XO slot by Lieutenant Terry Scott. Those officers would be with the team until we turned Dak Pek over to the ARVN.

We began sending one or two men back to Kontum and Pleiku for a few days at a time. Several of the guys who were long overdue for their seven-day out-of-country R&R got to go, returning to regale us with tales of wanton debauchery.

One day an officer from higher headquarters flew in and we held a hurried team formation while he pinned an assortment of medals on everyone's dirty, ragged fatigues. I found out later that some of the highest decorations given out during the fighting around Dak Seang and Dak Pek went to REMF officers who had "earned" the medals by observing the battle while flying above it at an altitude of about forty thousand feet.

"Hey, what the hell?" I said to a couple of the team members who were particularly disgruntled after hearing about that. "Someday those bastards will be generals and have their pictures in the newspapers and on TV. Whoever heard of a general without a bunch of medals?"

"Yeah," Erickson chimed in, "tell someone who gives a shit."

"That's the spirit!" I said.

Toward the end of that month we received a report from higher that caused a flurry of excitement. An aerial reconnaissance mission over our valley, which had utilized some new, super-classified, high-tech device, had detected what were believed to be armored vehicles. The unidentified vehicles were parked along the old, abandoned road about six kilometers northwest of camp.

The report was taken quite seriously by all of us, as the threat of enemy armor in that area was a reality. Two years earlier, Special Forces Team A-101 at Camp Lang Vei, up on the Laotian border, had been overrun by an NVA assault spearheaded by PT-76 amphibian tanks.*

Like Dak Pek, the defenders at Lang Vei had a 106 recoilless rifle. Unfortunately, because they hadn't really feared an armor attack, there were only a few antitank (HEAT—high-explosive

* For a survivor's firsthand account, see CSM Bill Craig's *Team Sergeant* (Ivy Books, 1998)

antitank) rounds on hand for the weapon. Besides this 106, the Lang Vei defenders had also recently received a supply of the one-shot, M-72 light antitank weapons (LAWs).

When the attack kicked off right after midnight, the defending A-team used the few 106 HEAT rounds to good effect, immediately knocking out the first three lead vehicles. But the 106 was destroyed by enemy return fire right after that, and the team members discovered that their newly supplied LAWs were practically useless, either malfunctioning or bouncing off the tank hulls without exploding.

"This will be the first air assault ever conducted by the troops at Dak Pek," Captain Britton said to no one in particular.

We were huddled around the maps in the TOC, having a conference with the intelligence (S-2) and operations (S-3) officers from the B-team. "There's got to be a first time for everything," the B-team S-3 said. "In a few months these Yards will be part of the regular ARVN, so they might as well get used to it."

"We've got enough chopper support to put in two platoons," the S-2 told us, "but they'll have to go in on two separate lifts. The LLDB have volunteered to send in two of their men. Which two Americans do you want to accompany the mission, Captain?" the S-3 said, turning to Britton.

Britton paused for a moment as he thought it over.

I was probably the only American team member who had prior experience performing these airmobile operations, and started to say so, but just then Britton said, "I guess it will be Young and Ellis—maybe Frye."

Once again I remained silent, not volunteering. The war was over, and I'd had enough of that shit anyway, I decided. Still, I felt guilty.

The plan was to hit the suspected enemy tanks, which were parked under the cover of some trees, with an air strike, then immediately follow up with the ground assault. The ground assault was going to be mainly a hit-and-run attack, its primary mission being bomb damage assessment (BDA).

"Right after the Sky Raiders make their runs, you'll be airlifted in at this little clearing here," Britton said as he briefed Young later. "You and one of the LLDB will go in with the first lift to secure the LZ. The second lift will come in about ten minutes behind you. This LZ is only two hundred meters away from the tanks, and you should be fresh when you hit 'em. The mission is to make sure the tanks have been destroyed, and to kill or capture any survivors."

"Is that all?" Young asked.

"That's it," the captain continued, either not noticing or deciding to ignore the sarcasm. "Don't stick around the area. Send us an immediate afteraction report on the PRC-25, then head straight back to camp. Come right down the road. The Sky Raiders will still be overhead for air cover, and you'll be able to get an immediate dust-off for wounded. If you manage to take any prisoners, the S-2 will be standing by with a chopper for pickup."

The operation was scheduled for that afternoon. For the plan to work, it would have to be a surprise, and to maintain security, we waited till the last minute before briefing the troops. About 1300 hours the two platoons of Strikers were gathered together and told the news.

"The Yards are scared shitless," Young told me later as we went over the radio frequencies and call signs. "First we put 'em through trench warfare, now we've turned 'em into an air assault unit!"

"Well," I told him, "after the conversion in a few months, they'll be called a Border Ranger unit. Time they started doing some ranger-type shit."

The Americans and the LLDB on the operation were each carrying one of the LAWs. I told Young about what I'd heard of the LAWs' less than stellar performance during the Lang Vei battle, and warned him to call the Air Force back in if the armor wasn't knocked out on the first strike.

The five HU-1D slicks flew in from Kontum and landed on our runway, and our guys did a "hot load," meaning the choppers didn't shut down the engines. The Sky Raiders appeared right on time and made their bomb, rocket, and napalm runs. The first lift of choppers took off, and within minutes reached the LZ, which turned out to be clear of enemy. The second lift went in right behind the first, and they all moved out in the direction of their objective.

Back at camp, the rest of us hovered around the radio, waiting for the first report from the battle area.

"Delta Papa, this is Charlie One," Young reported over the PRC-25. "We have reached the objective. BDA follows . . ."

In the commo bunker, we waited breathlessly for the gory details.

". . . One abandoned French road grader destroyed, one steam roller damaged. Negative enemy contact. Returning to camp, out."

Back in the commo bunker, we all looked at each other with stupid expressions.

As it turned out, this operation wasn't a complete dud, however, because on the way home the two platoons spotted a VC trail watcher and managed to wound him, then run him to ground. The tough old VC was making a last stand in a shallow gully when one of our Yards jumped around the side of the hill and blasted him. Our Yard was carrying a M-79 grenade launcher loaded with canister, and he shot the VC from a distance of about fifteen feet.

"That dickhead was nothing but bloody holes" is how Young later described the condition of the VC's body.

A few months after the "tank-killer attack," I was talking to a man who had been at Dak Pek eight years before, when the camp had first been established. He said they'd known about the abandoned road-building equipment way back then. "If I remember right," he told me, *"National Geographic* magazine even had pictures of that stuff in the article they did on the camp."

As the old Army saying goes: There's always ten percent who don't get the word.

After five months of celibacy, I thought the local Montagnard women, many of whom still went around bare-breasted, were looking better and better. The Yards were a handsome bunch anyway, reminding me a little of the Thais. Back in the earlier days of the war, a few American Special Forces men had gone through the Yard marriage ceremony, and set up housekeeping with some of the young ladies. Fortunately, or unfortunately—depending on how you look at it—the Army didn't recognize the Montagnard ceremonies as legal.

By 1970, with General Abrams in command and everyone back at the Special Forces' rear area running scared, such fun-and-games were strictly forbidden. No more sitting around the rice wine pot with the village elders, drinking potent home brew through a straw. No more trading your .45 for a handmade Yard crossbow. No more fun of any kind allowed, period. Trying to make the war fun was no longer considered "professional."

"You ever hear of this guy Spock?" I asked, reading through one of the weeks-old newsmagazines we'd gotten with the mail drop. Several of us were sitting in the mess hall, harassing the cook, Ute, and talking mainly about pussy.

"You mean Dr. Spock, the guy who wrote the book on baby care?" Ellis or someone answered.

"Yeah, him," I said. "He's really pissed that the U.S. went into Cambodia. He's a part of some organization called the New Mobilization Committee. He's quoted here saying that 'the U.S. government is committing titanic violence in Vietnam and Cambodia.' "

"If he wanted to see some violence committed," Erickson said, "he should have been here at Dak Pek on the night of twelve April . . . especially up on 203 hill when the bastards were raping and mutilating that little girl, or down in the generator bunker when the sapper was shooting Minh and his wife in the back!"

"The thing I've never understood about these pricks," I said, "is what makes them think they are suddenly experts on this war? What irritates me is that people back home would rather listen to some fucking baby doctor, or a stupid cunt actress, than they would to someone like General Westmoreland. Am I the only one who sees that the goddamned commies are winning this war the same way they won it against the French? Isn't it obvious that they're using their dupes and agitators back in the U.S. to turn the people against us?"

Everyone was looking at me silently. It wasn't the first time I'd gone into a ranting-and-raving fit.

Someone popped the cap on a rusted can of Black Label beer and shoved it over in front of me. "The war's over, and we lost," Young said. "My girl back home ran off with a civilian, and I'm over here attacking rusty steamrollers. So I propose a toast:

> Here's to me in my sober moods, when I sit,
>   ponder, and think.
> Here's to me in my wilder moods, when I sin,
>   gamble, and drink.
> And when my paratroop days are over, and from this
>   life I pass—
> Tell 'em to bury me upside down, so the
>   world can kiss my ass!"

"Yeah, tell someone who gives a shit!" we all said in chorus.

Chapter 20

By the first of August, I'd been in-country for six months and was due some R&R myself. There were several options among places to go for the one-week binge. Many of the married men traveled all the way to Hawaii to meet their wives and kids. A lot of the guys, anxious to get away from the Orient, went to Australia. Just about all the other major, non-Communist cities in Asia also welcomed us free-spending American GIs.

There had never really been any doubt in my mind that I'd be taking my R&R in Bangkok. Besides the nagging business of being in love with the nubile and round-eyed Vicki, I still had many other friends, Thai and American, in Thailand.

I had a problem, though, because to travel to Thailand I'd need a passport and a tourist visa. My government passport, which I'd been using since my first tour to Nam back in '63, had been in the field safe with my money and my gold and was toast. That meant I'd have to waste some time at the embassy in Saigon going through the red-tape hassle of getting the passport replaced.

When the next mail chopper dropped into camp, I left with it, amid gleeful admonishments from the rest of the team not to catch any sort of venereal disease and not to drink too much. I left camp traveling light. Besides my uniform, weapon, and web gear, I carried only my empty Samsonite briefcase—the only personal item I'd brought with me to Dak Pek that had survived the battle of April 12.

As soon as I got to Kontum and was assigned a cot for the night at the B-team, I went over to the SOG compound to look for people I knew. The first person I ran into was Bill Spurgeon. After one look at me, he grinned and said I'd lost a little weight since the last time he'd seen me.

"So," he said, "do you still think the war's over?"

"Oh, it's fucking over," I told him, "it's just that no one bothered to tell the goddamned NVA." Then I launched into a brief synopsis of the six-week battle we'd just been through up at Dak Pek.

Bill signed out one of the jeeps from SOG, and we drove around the town, once again hitting a few of the sleazy joints. The first time Bill had taken me on the tour, six months before, the establishments had seemed pretty bleak. Of course on that round, I'd just come off a forty-five-day leave in Bangkok. Now I was coming off six months at Dak Pek!

Even so, I complained that the war just didn't seem too much fun anymore. Bill answered that in the SOG units, things were still pretty entertaining.

"We got this one nutcase," Bill told me, speaking of one of the American recon team leaders, "who carries an M-79 with the stock cut off so it's just got a pistol grip. He's dyed his bush hat black, and has the brim starched flat, like an old, Spanish vaquero hat.

"He always wears a short, indigenous poncho, and carries his chopped M-79 hung on a sling underneath. The screwball thinks he's Clint Eastwood. I was sitting in a bar the other day when he walks in, stops in the door, and throws back his poncho to show everyone the M-79. He's got this thin cigar in the corner of his mouth, and he says, 'I need a bottle of whiskey, and a woman!' "

I laughed approvingly. "SOG is the only place you can still get away with that shit," I told him.

There was a group of four indigenous waving at us from the side of the road, and Spurgeon came to a screeching halt to give them a ride. When they piled in, I recognized one of them. It was the interpreter, "Bobby," whom I remembered from Camp Vinh Thanh, where I'd been assigned back in 1965.

Bobby had grown up since I'd last seen him. The first time I'd met him, five years earlier, he'd been an orphan, doing odd jobs for the madam of a whorehouse in Qui Nhon. One of our interpreters at Vinh Thanh had just been killed, and our A-team hired Bobby, then only about fifteen years old, as a replacement. Now, I discovered, he was one of the most respected combat interpreters in SOG CCC.

"You know, Sergeant Wade," Bobby told me that day, "if you no take me and give me job at Vinh Thanh, today I just be fucked-up ARVN private. Now I make as much money as ARVN colonel!"

SOG always paid good money for good people.

That night, as we were having a few drinks at the B-team club, there was a brief flurry of incoming 122 rockets. Most of them hit in the city, and only killed civilians, but we still all had to run to our assigned defensive positions, and the attack ruined our evening's entertainment.

The next day I caught a ride on a truck and made the tense ride down the highway that connected Kontum and Pleiku. American engineers had widened and repaved that section of road, and it was supposedly "secured," but that word was always taken lightly anyplace in Vietnam.

I didn't have to spend much time at the C-team in Pleiku, because when I got there I was told a C-130 to Nha Trang was leaving that afternoon. By that evening I had checked into the transit quarters at the SFOB in Nha Trang, and was at the Delta Club drinking a beer. Someone told me Bill Martin was still in-country, apparently on an extension, and told me where to look for him.

I found Martin over at his quarters, watching a big game of poker. There were lots of chips on the table, but no cash in evidence, because gambling for money had been forbidden at the headquarters. They were hell on stamping out sin back there in the rear areas.

"Oh, they're playing for money, all right," Bill told me when I asked him about it. "They keep track of the amounts and pay out later. A couple of these guys are really cleaning up, and a couple of them have been losing their asses. If they don't blow their money on gambling, though, they'll just go into town and spend it on booze and whores. At least you can't catch a dose of clap from a game of poker."

I asked Bill how the VD situation was in Nha Trang, and he advised me to stay away from the whores there. "It's not like it used to be, that's for sure. There's a real epidemic going around," he told me. "One of the cadre over at the Recondo school caught some sort of incurable shit. The glands in his groin all swelled up, and they had him down in the hospital, hooked up to IV tubes, running every antibiotic they could think of into him. He was supposed to go on R&R to meet his wife and kids in Hawaii, but he had to cancel out . . . gave her some excuse about having to go on a big operation or something."

Bill was still flying shotgun on "sniffer" missions. The "sniffer" flights were just what the name implies. In another of those endless U.S. attempts to use high-tech gadgets to locate the enemy, someone had invented a device to sample the chemicals in the air, which could be mounted on a helicopter. Supposedly it could detect the enemy soldiers hiding on the ground by their damned body odor.

Bill told me that a couple of weeks before he had narrowly missed getting zapped. "There was this sergeant from the Mike Force who was about a week away from going home. He needed one more combat flight to earn his Air Medal," Bill said. "I was walking out to get on the chopper one morning, and he came up to me and asked if he could take that mission instead. I said it didn't matter to me, so he went in my place. About two hours later I was over at the club drinking my lunch, and we got the word that the chopper had crashed and killed all aboard. I guess it just wasn't my time yet."

Bill was leaving Vietnam in just a few days, and said he'd be glad to go. He told me he'd already been shot down on two "sniffer" flights. "The pilots fly right at treetop level," he said. "Two or three times the branches have knocked holes in the bottom, Plexiglas windows."

When I left Martin that day, I told him I'd see him back at Fort Bragg. As things turned out, I didn't see him again for almost twelve years.

Flight operations at the Nha Trang airfield were the usual zoo, but I lucked out and caught a C-130 to Saigon the next day. Also by luck, I got a seat next to a Special Forces major whom I remembered from some years earlier when he'd been a lieutenant. When we got to Tan Son Nhut, he offered me a ride with him to the B-team in his waiting jeep, otherwise I'd have been stuck at the airfield for hours trying to catch a lift.

The sun was just setting as we drove out the air-base gate and into the frenetic stream of traffic. I remembered the first trip I'd made to this city, back in '63. That had only been seven years before, but seemed more like twenty or thirty. It had been this same time of day when Bill Martin and I had arrived that first time, on a three-day R&R from Camp Tan Phu. I'd been young and impressionable back then, and had immediately fallen in love with Saigon. Looking around at it in '70, I wondered why.

Getting my new passport turned out to be just about as difficult as I'd expected. The room at the embassy where such matters were taken care of was jammed with American and Vietnamese travelers, all with problems similar to my own. The room was hot, dirty, and had only a few chairs for the twenty or thirty people who waited. There was only one American employee in evidence, with most of the work being handled by two female Vietnamese clerks.

After a wait of several hours, my turn finally came. The bored clerk handed me a fistful of forms to fill out, and to get signed off on by various officers in my chain of command. She told me to come back when the papers were in order. I spent the rest of the day running around Saigon, trying to find the people I had to see, getting more hot, sweaty, and frustrated every minute. By the time all the office buildings closed that afternoon, I still had some blanks on the forms, which meant I'd have to finish the nightmare the next morning.

I still hadn't gotten laid since leaving camp, but I was a little leery about doing so until I got to Thailand. I didn't want to *start* my R&R with a case of clap, for goodness' sake. I did go down to Tu Do Street, just to look around, and that part of Saigon also seemed very different.

Rosy and some of the other regular girls were still manning the bar in the Sporting, and there were several others I remembered down at the Morning Star, but they were beginning to show signs of hard work. I went up the side street to Lyn's bar, but was told she was in Nha Trang for a while, living with some American civilian she'd met.

By the end of the next day I had my temporary passport and visa in hand, and the day after that I caught a commercial flight to Bangkok.

All of us R&R guys, a group of about twenty, were met at Bangkok International by a military representative and taken by bus to the Opera Hotel. "This is the official R&R hotel in Bangkok," a fat REMF master sergeant briefed us. "You don't have to stay here if you don't want to, but it is highly recommended that you do, because this is where we will leave from again in exactly five days. This bus will depart for the airport at 0500 hours, and your asses better be here, ready to get on it. If you miss the bus, you will miss the airplane, and if you miss the airplane, you will be reported as being a deserter in time of war."

Most of the R&R group, being as yet unfamiliar with the

town, sheepishly lined up at the Opera Hotel check-in desk to be assigned rooms. I picked up my single piece of luggage—the briefcase, which now held half a carton of cigarettes and three months' pay—and caught a taxi over to the Raja Hotel instead.

There was no line to stand in at the Raja. The entire staff of the place remembered me from the forty-five-day leave I'd recently spent there, and several taxi drivers, who were lounging around out front, waved in greeting. Hell, I was home.

I gave one of the taxi drivers some money and told him to go buy me a set of civilian clothes.

"What size you want?" he asked.

I looked him over. "Same size you wear," I told him.

"What color you want?" he said.

"Same color you like," I said.

While I waited for him to return with my new outfit, I sat in the coffee shop drinking a Singha. There was a phone at the register, and I tried to call Vicki to tell her I was in town, but got no answer. Frankly, I was a little relieved. At least I could truthfully tell her that I'd tried.

An hour later I was around the corner from the hotel at a place called the Happy-Happy Steam Bath and Massage Parlor, and was getting reacquainted with all my old girlfriends there.

The next morning, feeling hungover and guilt-ridden for not having tried harder to get in touch with Vicki, I tried several more times to call her apartment. It was early enough for her not to have left for work yet, but I still got no answer. Later that afternoon I took a break from my rounds of the joints and stopped by the embassy.

The Marine guard at the embassy gate reluctantly allowed me to enter the building, but only as far as the information desk. With a sneer, the receptionist told me I could leave a message for Miss Munck if I so desired.

Another young PFC Marine had escorted me to the information desk, apparently afraid that such a disreputable-looking character as myself might be dangerous. When he heard me mention Vicki's name, he gave me a sharp look. I found out later that the young PFC had the hots for Miss Munck himself and had recently taken her to the annual Marine ball.

Vicki showed up at the Raja Hotel after work that day, and found me at my usual table by the window in the coffee shop. The gaggle of taxi drivers and prostitutes sitting with me respectfully got up and excused themselves when she walked over to the table.

I stood up, putting on my gentleman act, and pulled a chair out for her. "I tried to call you several times at your old place, but never got an answer," I immediately explained. Vicki said that her parents were back in the States for a visit, and she had been staying at their apartment while they were away.

Vicki was friendly and seemed genuinely glad to see me, but I detected a distracted coolness to her manner. After a few drinks she casually mentioned that she had recently fallen in love with an Australian, the drummer in some fucking rock-and-roll band. She told me the name of the band, and where it was playing, and said I should go see it. "They're really good," she said, "they sound just like the Beatles."

Although hurt by the news, I also felt relieved. Now I could forget romantic bullshit and get back to serious carousing. "Well," I told her, "maybe we can have dinner sometime before I have to go back. . . ."

Vicki agreed and told me that Chuck Floyd, who had been the medic on the team down at Hua Hin, was still in Thailand and was then stationed in Bangkok. Chuck, his wife Cathy, and their infant daughter lived in an apartment not far from Vicki, and she said she would tell them I was in town. "I'll suggest they invite us over for dinner," she volunteered.

Vicki declined the offer of another drink and seemed anxious to get away, so we parted company. She promised to get in touch with me again as soon as she found out something from the Floyds.

"Yeah, sure," I mumbled to myself as Vicki walked outside to her waiting cab. As soon as she was gone, the taxi drivers and whores came back over to my table and sat down.

"She girlfriend-you?" one of the whores asked.

"No," I answered.

"Too bad," one of the drivers said. "She big up here," he told me, lewdly cupping the air in front of his chest.

Two days before my R&R was over, I found a message from Vicki in my box at the hotel, informing me that the dinner at the Floyds' was all set up for that evening. The note gave the time, and included the address of their apartment. Vicki said she would meet me there.

Cathy and Chuck were good hosts. I arrived, already drunk, several hours early, and by the time Vicki showed up, I was in fine shape.

"So what the goddamned F-4s did," I said, as we sat around the table eating the great meal Cathy had prepared, "was drop nape on 'em first, then come right behind that with twenty mike-mike. When I got up to the top of 203 hill the next day, I could see where this one NVA had been set on fire—there were pieces of charred equipment and clothes, and you could still smell the burned flesh. Anyway, then he must have run from the bunker he was in, out into the trench. I guess he was trying to put himself out. That's when the twenty mike-mike got him. Blew big hunks of him up on the side of the trench. It was really neat!"

"So how are things at work, Vicki?" Cathy Floyd said. "And have you heard from your parents since they've been gone?"

". . . So then there was the bastard that kept shooting at us with an RPD, but we dropped a 750-pound bomb on that one, and he blew way up in the air, and . . ."

"Work is the same," Vicki said, "but it's getting pretty boring. I haven't heard anything from Mom and Dad since they got back to New York. . . ."

". . . Blammoo! Blasted this other one with a goddamned

M-79 grapeshot round, and Young told us there wasn't nothing left of him but a big pile of chopped, bloody meat!" I said, finishing my story and looking bleary-eyed around the table.

"This roast is delicious, Cathy," Vicki said.

"Well, thank you, Vicki," Cathy replied. "I was afraid I might have gotten it too rare."

After we ate, I sobered up a little, and Vicki suggested she and I go to a quiet bar for a nightcap. When we got there, Vicki started to cry and told me that she and the Australian had a big fight and were no longer an item. She turned her big, brown eyes on me and said I was the one she really liked the most anyway.

That news pleased me so much that I didn't even feel the collar go back around my neck or the leash being reattached.

We had a pretty good two days together. I met her each of the two evenings at the embassy, when she got off of work. The young Marine guard was obviously jealous, which of course made it all the more fun. I cleaned up my act a little those last days, and stayed almost sober. My last night in town, Vicki took me to her parents' house and cooked dinner for me.

I stayed late, and we talked and necked until the early-morning hours. By this time I was once again hopelessly in love with her and didn't want to leave. I told Vicki I planned to request a transfer back to Thailand if I survived the next six months. Vicki said she was planning to go to England soon to live with a friend there, so there was no obvious future for us.

It was two in the morning when Vicki finally said I'd better leave. She had to be up in about four hours to go to work. When we said good-bye, I was certain it would be forever. I told her I loved her and probably always would, and she said she felt the same way about me, but I don't think I really believed her.

I took a cab to the Raja, changed back into my freshly laundered uniform, checked out, and went to the Opera Hotel to await the arrival of the R&R shuttle bus.

At the Opera, the other guys in my travel group were all

there, most of them standing around outside in the dark, gloomily waiting for the bus. A few of them had their Thai girls with them to say good-bye. It was a depressing scene.

We were all badly hungover, none of us anxious to go back to the war. Each man in that group knew that in the course of the following six months, some of us would be badly wounded or killed. We didn't seem to want to look each other in the eye. No one talked much.

On the jukebox in the nearby coffee shop, someone played the popular Beatles song "Hey, Jude." It's a long tune, and played on and on in the sad darkness. The lyrics seemed directed especially to me.

Chapter 21

Because we had reentered Vietnam on a commercial flight, everyone had to go through a customs inspection. This amused me to no end. What in the world did the Vietnamese think anyone could smuggle into their country that was worse than what was already there? Drugs? Guns? Explosives?

I slid my Samsonite briefcase across the counter and grinned as the Vietnamese customs inspector opened it up. He wrinkled his nose at the smell, and using his pen so as not to have to touch it, poked through the pile of dirty civilian clothes inside. I'd worn the same outfit for a week without bothering to wash it, so I suppose it was pretty rank.

"This all you bring back?" the customs agent asked suspiciously.

"That, and maybe the clap," I told him. "I won't know for sure unless I start to drip."

"Enjoy the remainder of your stay in our country," he told me, reclosing the case and sliding it back across the counter.

Because I was in no particular hurry to get back to Dak Pek, it seemed I had no problem at all catching hops, and before I knew it, I was already once again at Pleiku. As I sat in the C-team club, which overlooked their famous swimming pool, I found out all the latest disasters.

"Jeep got ambushed on the highway to Kontum the other day," a guy from the Mike Force told me as we sipped a cold one. "There were five men from CCC in it. We figure it was about a squad of NVA, and they were pretty damned good. Initiated the ambush with a round from a captured M-79. It hit the middle of the windshield and killed or wounded everyone in the front right then. The jeep went in the ditch, and they opened up on it with AKs and an RPD. One guy survived. He was wounded, but thrown clear when the jeep crashed, and he managed to get away down the road. He said he glanced back one time and saw the assault party from the ambush moving through, killing all the wounded."

I'd been planning to go to Kontum with a convoy the next day, but decided to wait around Pleiku until I could catch a hop on a chopper instead.

When I did get to the B-team at Kontum a day later, I discovered there had also been some excitement out at Dak Pek while I'd been gone. Four or five Americans had been killed in a plane crash.

"What happened, was it shot down?" I asked the S-3.

"No, actually it didn't involve enemy activity at all as far as we can tell," the officer told me. "A group of combat engineers was making an inspection tour of the border camps. They were flying in an Army Otter. The plane landed at Dak Pek, and while the engineers looked around at the new construction, the aircraft crew took on some fuel.

"They started to take off again to leave, and evidently lost power just at liftoff. They crashed right at the end of your runway. The plane blew up and burned. There weren't any survivors."

"It was god-awful," Erickson told me the next day when I got back to camp. "We got down there right after it happened, but there wasn't anything we could do for them. One or two were still alive when we put 'em on the dust-off, but they died at the hospital."

I thought about what it would be like to go through life covered with the horrible, disfiguring scars that bad burns leave. "Maybe it's better that they died," I said.

"Yeah," the medic said, "maybe it is."

That night in the mess hall, everyone on the team wanted to hear about my trip to Bangkok. I told them it had been all right except that I now had one small problem.

"Ho-ho," they all chortled, "Wade's got the clap, Wade's got the Vie-Doggie!"

"No, it's worse than that," I told them.

"You mean you got syph?" Ellis asked.

"Worse," I told them.

"God, what could be worse than syph?" someone asked. By now I had them all hanging on my every word.

"I'm in love," I announced.

When the howls of laughter, jeers, and catcalls finally died away, I added the final punch line: "And she's an *American*!"

"You poor bastard," someone said.

My assistant radio operator, Hull, ended his tour and was replaced by a new buck sergeant (E-5) by the name of Fred Adams. "Everyone usually calls me 'Injun,' " he told us when he was introduced.

Injun Adams looked like what most civilians think of when they picture a Special Forces guy. Injun was part French-Canadian and part American Indian, and real big. Injun was one of those guys whom you loved to go hitting the bars with, because you knew he could whip the shit out of about anyone foolish enough to provoke him.

Adams had been in the Army before, back in the early sixties, and had served a tour in Nam with Special Forces before getting out. " You know how it is," he told me. "I got back to the States and was bored to death. I tried everything: fast cars, motorcycles, bumming around, drinking, women—you name it. When I'd gotten out I thought the war over here was about over. But I kept reading about it and seeing it on TV. The damned war kept going, and I couldn't stand to be missing it, so I reenlisted and here I am back again."

"You probably should have stayed away," I told him. "It isn't as good as it used to be."

"That's what I'm finding out."

Other than the plane crash, things had been pretty quiet in the valley for several weeks. A new operation was in the planning stages, though, and would depart in a few days. I was told that Sergeant Bodt, the engineer sergeant, and I would be accompanying it. The operation would be to the west of camp, the area we had been staying away from since the siege that spring.

We would be going with 201 Company, and the LLDB were sending their XO and one of their senior NCOs. "We have intelligence reports that something might be cooking again over around the border," Britton told us at the operations briefing. Our area of operations for the seven-day patrol covered the foothills to the west and some of the open rolling hills on the valley floor.

"Don't do a lot of moving around," Britton said. "The main thing is to check out and interdict the damned trail networks over there. We got reports lately from both electronic surveillance and from our own agents that there's been movement and activity lately. We don't want another surprise attack like the one in April."

I didn't bother to mention that Erickson and I had been

working the same area just before the April attack and had seen nothing to make us suspicious. The Communists were pretty good at selecting the time and place for engagements, and if they didn't want you to find them, you usually didn't. Sometimes they fucked up, though, and maybe this would be one of those times.

If I remember correctly, the name of the LLDB executive officer who accompanied this operation was Trung. This was the same guy who had spent the night of April 12 buried alive in his bunker, and as I mentioned earlier, he was always a little strange after that experience. Besides being odd, he was also pretty much of a prick, and although I got along pretty well with most of the other LLDB team members, I didn't much like working with him.

The other LLDB man accompanying this operation was their senior weapon NCO, and he wasn't a bad type. He'd been around a long time, had worked with many Americans over the years, and was pretty laid back and easy to get along with. When we left camp in the early-morning dawn, Bodt and I fell in behind the two LLDBs, who were following directly behind the company commander. The Yard carrying the PRC-25 was right behind me, and as we went out the gate I called in a commo check.

There were good points and bad points about patrolling around the open, rolling hills that surrounded camp. The good part was that you were in range of just about every support weapon in camp. You could also easily be seen from the air if there was need for an air strike, and a dust-off could come in and land anyplace if you needed a medevac.

The bad part, of course, was that the enemy could also easily see you from lookouts in the surrounding hills. There was the danger of snipers and also the danger of being hit by a mortar barrage or even a couple of 122s, although the enemy seemed to prefer saving the big stuff for the camp itself.

That first day we didn't move far, only the two or three kilometers to the edge of the valley. We established our perimeter for the night early, at about 1400 hours, in an old, well-used bivouac area that had many predug emplacements. For some reason I got the feeling right off that we'd probably make some heavy enemy contact during the operation. It was more a hunch than anything else, so I didn't say anything about it.

Several of the small security patrols we'd sent out that afternoon to scout around the immediate area reported spotting suspicious-looking characters in the vicinity. "Man stand still under tree, watch camp" was the typical report. Well, I thought, maybe he was just resting there in the shade. Or maybe not. Maybe he was performing target surveillance.

Despite the reports, we spent an uneventful night. The next morning we moved up into the surrounding foothills. Our operation stayed there under the jungle canopy for several days, slowly working its way to the south. We stopped early each afternoon, sent out patrols, and at night laid ambushes on any adjacent trails. Although we made no enemy contact, there were numerous reports of fresh enemy footprints.

With two days left to the patrol, we once again dropped down out of the mountains and made camp in the valley. We were within sight of Dak Pek, and I always felt a little relieved to be out of the close, claustrophobic jungle vegetation. We bivouacked in a comfortable location, on a small hilltop shaded by a few trees.

It was a good tactical location too, for that particular operational mission anyway, because the hill overlooked the intersection of three well-used trails. After a little discussion with the LLDB and the Yard commander, we decided to send one squad to the top of a lower adjacent hill to establish an ambush.

Following the usual procedure, I radioed in our position along with two preselected concentrations for the camp mortars. Although we were once again in the valley, near camp, and only had one more day of the operation left, our Yards were acting jumpy and nervous. Maybe that was simply due to the recent heavy fighting they'd been through, but maybe it wasn't. . . . I was getting the same vibes.

Sergeant Bodt and I built our poncho shelter right behind two of the deeper foxholes and spent the remainder of the afternoon bullshitting about things like women and American food.

"You know what food I really miss the most?" Bodt asked me as we lay in the shade.

"Milk shakes?" I ventured.

"No," he said, "I miss those hot English muffins I used to get down at this restaurant I went to for Sunday morning breakfast. Remember those? Remember how they came out all warm, and the butter would run down your chin when you bit into 'em?"

"Yeah," I said, "I'd forgotten all about them. I liked to put a lot of strawberry jelly or honey on mine. Sometimes I'd eat two or three of the damned things!"

"And the waitress that worked in the place my buddies and I used to go to had these humongous tits. She was an old gal, probably thirty-five at least, but there was just something about her, you know what I mean? Seemed like the top button of her little uniform was always unbuttoned, and she used to lean *way* over when she asked what we wanted!"

"She probably did it on purpose," I sagely advised, "so you'd leave bigger tips."

"Well, it sure as hell worked. Sometimes we'd leave fifty cents for a ten-cent cup of coffee. I found out later she was married and had five kids at home."

"But the English muffins were good, right?"

"Yeah," Bodt said, "the goddamned muffins were wonderful."

The shooting started at about 0100 hours. There was a rattling of automatic-weapons fire from the squad ambush on the nearby hilltop, then the sharp blast of a claymore mine. I was wide-awake and already in the foxhole before I'd consciously analyzed what was happening.

A long burst of automatic-weapons fire ripped overhead, and I ducked down into the foxhole. Fuck, Wade, I thought, get yourself organized! Fearful of an immediate enemy assault, I forced my head up over the edge of the hole so I could see. A trip flare was burning over on the other hill, and there was more firing.

"You okay, Sergeant Wade?" Bodt asked from the hole next to me.

"Yeah," I answered, trying to control my voice and my breathing. "The shit all seems to be coming from the direction of the hill the ambush is on, but keep your eyes on that fucking ravine over to our left. This might be a diversion. I'm going to call camp and get some illume, then have 'em drop a few rounds of HE."

Injun answered the radio immediately. He'd been awake, pulling radio watch, and had already heard the firefight going on. Less than a minute after I requested it, camp had two rounds of 81 illumination floated over us.

Something else exploded near our perimeter, but it was impossible to figure out if it was ours or theirs. More shooting erupted on the other hill, and one of the Yards from our perimeter yelled excitedly to his friends over there. He got a muffled response, which was drowned out by more shooting. Green and red tracers ricocheted high into the night air.

A few feet away, over at the LLDB position, the weapons NCO seemed to be handling things. The XO was huddled down in the bottom of his hole, perfectly happy to let the noncom fight the battle. Another burst snapped and popped just above my head, and I did a little crouching down myself!

I was still worried about an attack from the nearby ravine, because it was an area we couldn't cover with our own direct-fire weapons. Since that danger area had already been reported to camp as one of the mortar concentrations, it was a simple matter to get some rounds on the way in a hurry.

"Delta Papa, this is Delta Papa Oscar, give me three rounds on concentration Alpha, over."

"Rounds on the way," came the immediate reply.

The explosions from the 81 mortar were satisfyingly loud, and I heard approving mutters from some of the nearby Yards. The rounds had landed pretty much where I'd hoped they would, so no adjustment was necessary. After a few minutes, when I hadn't said anything else, camp called me back on the radio.

I told them that their shooting was good and that it didn't look like we'd need any more. A few minutes later I realized that all firing had stopped, and I could just make out the first indications of dawn behind the row of mountains to the east.

As soon as it got light, we sorted things out. Our side had suffered several wounded and one dead, whom we immediately sent back to camp via litter parties. The bad guys had also been hurt, and they'd left a couple of dead. "They come up trail," the ambush squad leader told us, "set off trip flare. We shoot claymore. VC shoot AK. We shoot machine gun."

One of the dead NVA had been badly wounded by a round through the upper stomach. Apparently he'd lain out there, dying, for some time. Either in an attempt to stop the internal bleeding, or to keep from groaning, the wounded man had literally swallowed his neckerchief, leaving just the tip of it sticking out his mouth. One of our troops tried to pull it out, but it wouldn't budge.

"These are some tough motherfuckers we're fighting, buddy," I said to Sergeant Bodt.

"No shit," Bodt agreed.

Chapter 22

We still had one more day to go on that operation, and after breakfast we packed up and moved farther to the north, to a hill that dominated the surrounding terrain. The NVA had used the hill during the recent battle and siege, and we found their telephone wire, still strung out to the various fighting positions. The NVA used a lot of landline communications, either because it was all they had or because they were aware of our electronic surveillance capabilities.

We now knew for sure that there were once again enemy units operating in and around the valley floor. The group that stumbled into our ambush had been a reconnaissance patrol, either looking for us or sent out to check out the camp. I suspected that the increased enemy activity was the prelude to yet another major attack.

We ate our noon meal on top of the large hill and tried to decide our next move. The hill we were on would be easy to defend. It was just about in the middle of the cleared area that stretched from camp back west toward the mountains. If we were holding it, the Communists wouldn't be able to use it again. The problem was that the position was the most obvious one, and since we knew the NVA had also recently used it, they would not only be very familiar with the terrain but also know the layout of the prebuilt fighting positions.

We decided to get tricky.

"We stay here, build poncho shelter, pretend to spend night," the LLDB weapons man said. "Before dark, we move, go other place."

Sounded like a good plan to me, as I already had a bad feeling about trying to spend the night where we were. That afternoon we sent out a few security patrols and lounged around in the shade. We cooked and ate the evening meal there, then just at dusk moved to our real night defensive position.

The location we'd chosen to move to was one of the small, strategic hamlets abandoned during the fighting in April. This position was several kilometers due north of camp, and occupied a small hill beside the old road and the river. The Montagnard defenders had been overrun during the battle, and many of the defensive positions were destroyed. Most of the earthen wall surrounding the small village still stood, however, and many of the bunkers and fighting positions on the perimeter were still intact.

Using what little daylight remained, we immediately began improving the positions as best we could, cleaning out the holes and replacing some of the punji sticks that still studded the outer wall. Bodt and I commandeered one of the better bunkers, which still had part of its overhead cover.

"You think they'll hit us tonight?" Bodt asked me as we settled in.

"It's hard to tell," I answered. Actually, my gut feeling was telling me that something big was definitely in the wind, and the way the troops were acting, I could tell they expected more action. I didn't want to say anything, though. Saying it might make it come true.

Bodt and I divided the guard duty in the usual fashion, each pulling half the night. I had the first shift, which lasted until 0100 hours, and I'd just curled up in the corner of the bunker after waking Bodt when it began.

Most of the enemy fire was coming from the west, with some from the north and south. Along our eastern flank, where the river and the old road ran, things remained quiet. I called camp on the radio and alerted them of the situation, and they told me they were standing by.

This attack seemed more aggressive than a probe, and I thought it might be leading up to a major assault. As usual, my mind was working, trying to figure out the enemy's real intent. They were such cunning bastards, it was never a good idea to immediately react to their first move without thinking things out a little first.

In the case at hand, my first thought was that the enemy would again attempt overrunning the village, as they had a few months earlier. If they were successful, our obvious route of retreat—the road to our east, which led directly back to camp—had been left tantalizingly open. I suspected that if we were forced off our hill and took that way back, we would find a very nasty surprise waiting for us.

There was increased firing from the western side of the perimeter, and much yelling. We took a few rounds of what was either mortar or recoilless-rifle fire. We had two 60mm mortars, and the crews began plunking out rounds of illumination and HE. The LLDB weapons sergeant came running over to where Bodt and I manned our position on the southern side and told us there was a ground assault in progress.

This all fit with what I suspected to be the enemy's real intent, which was to push us off the hill and into a trap. But now I faced the sort of problem so common for Americans out on the Special Forces A-teams.

In the first place, how could I quickly communicate my fears to the LLDB and Yard chain of command? We were in the middle of a firefight, with all the confusion, excitement, and noise this entails. We had a combat interpreter with us, but he didn't speak much better English than the LLDB sergeant, and neither Bodt nor I spoke Vietnamese.

The main problem was that Bodt and I weren't really, *officially* in command of the goddamned operation. Neither was the LLDB weapons sergeant, as far as that goes. Unfortunately, the actual commander of this operation, the LLDB executive officer, was off cowering down in a hole someplace. As it turned out, however, we soon had bigger things to worry about.

Suddenly all hell broke loose around the camp itself. Enemy rockets and mortar rounds exploded inside the camp perimeter, and flares went off in the defensive wire. Sheets of tracers flew in both directions, and the camp 81s opened up with a string of outgoing HE and illumination.

Across the river, on the other side of the valley, I could see that at least one of the other strategic hamlets was also under attack. Now the enemy's real intent became clearer. They weren't just after us. They still wanted to take the whole damned area!

With the camp also busy fighting for its life, we couldn't depend on much support from them, and would now have to defend ourselves the best we could. My mind was in a whirl, trying to figure out all the possibilities. I wondered if Injun had managed to get a call to higher headquarters on the single sideband to let them know what was going on. Were the antennas at camp already shot down again? What if the camp was taken but our operation survived until morning?

I monitored the camp radio traffic on the PRC-25, listening to the excited reports of enemy assaults, calls for fire missions, requests for ammo, and status reports. It sounded like the enemy's ground assaults were being beaten back. During a short lull in the flow of messages, I called in and reported that we were also still under attack, but so far still alive. Captain Britton came on the radio, saying that help was on the way and urging us to hold out.

Most of the incoming at our location had been from the western side of the perimeter, but now we began taking increased fire from the south, which was the side Bodt and I defended, the side of our perimeter that faced the camp.

At first I thought the increased firing might be the beginning of a ground attack, but in a moment or two I figured out what was going on. A group of enemy had moved between our location and the camp. The camp was pouring fire at the enemy, and much of it was going over the intended target and hitting us. God, if it wasn't one thing, it was another.

It occurred to me that the presence of the enemy unit to our south, between us and the camp, verified my previous suspicions that an ambush had been laid for us there. I wondered if we would have to fight our way through that enemy unit when returning to the camp the next morning.

"Camp Dak Pek, this is Spectre," came the voice on the radio. "I've got Blind Bat with me. ETA your location in one mike, need to know location of any friendlies outside your perimeter, over."

"Spectre, this is Dak Pek," Injun answered. "We have friendly troops in defense approximately two kilometers due north of our position, over." He was, of course, talking about us.

"Roger, Camp," the Spectre pilot answered. "We'll drop a few illume, but won't go hot until we identify friendlies."

As soon as Spectre got overhead, two of his parachute flares lit up the valley. Sometimes just the arrival of a gunship overhead and one or two parachute flares was enough to make the enemy break off an attack. In this case it didn't seem to have any effect; the assault continued.

"Camp, this is Spectre," the pilot radioed. "I think I have your friendlies located, need to verify, over."

I keyed the handset. "Spectre, this is operation. I'm signaling with visual now, identify code, over." I pointed my flashlight at the orbiting AC-130 and sent him a series of the letter V. The AC-130s were equipped with night-vision devices, and I knew the weak beam of my small penlight would appear as bright as an arc light.

"I identify three shorts and a long," the pilot told me after a moment.

"That's affirmative, Spectre. Keep any fire outside of the dirt wall and we'll be all right."

Camp had located what seemed to be one of the main enemy

concentrations and vectored the gunship to it. Soon the air was filled with red tracers as the AC-130 opened up, and moments later the eerie roar of the guns reached us. The target area was the same hill our operation had stopped at earlier that day.

With the gunships overhead, I relaxed a little. There was simply no way the enemy could be successful in an attack with all that firepower coming down on their heads. All we really had to do was keep our heads down and hold out until morning, when we could get the fast movers and Sky Raiders in.

Spectre and Blind Bat stayed with us the remainder of the night, illuminating the battle area and occasionally blasting enemy positions they were able to spot. The NVA unit assaulting our operation in the village pulled back, or perhaps moved south to aid the attack on the camp, because not long after the AC-130s arrived, we ceased taking fire.

Things stayed hot and heavy around the camp, however, and I listened to several more radio reports of attempted ground assaults. After Spectre gave them a few squirts, the enemy attacks fizzled, though, and as dawn broke most of the shooting died out.

"The sun is coming up," Spectre told us on the PRC-25. "Time for us to go back to our coffins. Had a lot of fun. Call us again when you need us."

All that night I had been thinking that the voice on Spectre's radio was familiar. It sounded a lot like an Air Force guy I'd had more than a few drinks with when I was stationed at Nakhon Phanon, in Thailand. "When you get back, tell Charlie the bartender hello for me," I told the departing aircraft.

There was a short pause. "Is this Lima Whiskey?" he asked, using my initials. When I verified that it was, he came back with a chuckle. "Small world, ain't it?"

Once again, a pall of smoke hung over our valley, turning the rays of the rising sun a sickly yellow. The camp had repelled all attacks, and apparently none of the strategic hamlets in the valley had been retaken. As in April, however, daylight also brought a new barrage of enemy rockets and mortar rounds crashing into camp.

Now all that remained was to get our operation back home without getting ambushed or mortared to death. From the talk I monitored on the PRC-25, I knew that armed choppers were on the way. The LLDB lieutenant in command of our operation figured it was once again safe to emerge, and we had a short command powwow, trying to decide our next move.

The Vietnamese lieutenant was all for marching right down the damned road, just as I knew he'd be, but the rest of us were able to dissuade him without causing him to lose face. I told him that using the road would indeed give us more cover in case of attack by indirect fire. But I also reminded him there had been an enemy unit between us and camp during the night, and that they might still be there. Of course, since he'd spent the night hunkered down in his hole, he hadn't known that.

"Cobras come from Kontum, Trung-si?" the LLDB weapons man asked me.

I replied that they were on the way and would be overhead in about ten minutes. We decided to wait for them to arrive before moving out. That way, they could give us air cover against waiting NVA infantry, and the only thing we'd have to worry about was getting mortared while we made the two-kilometer march across the rolling, completely open terrain.

I tried to impress on the LLDB lieutenant the need for us to remain very spread out during the march. I was also worried that if the enemy started dropping mortar rounds on us, the troops would more than likely want to hit the dirt. Getting pinned down out there in the open was the worst thing that could happen, and I explained to the LLDB and the Yard commander that if the mortar rounds started falling, we had to keep moving, on the double, through the barrage.

Another problem developed while we were waiting for the

Cobras to arrive. We got a radio message from the LLDB commander back at Dak Pek directing us to make a sweep of the camp perimeter before we came back in. The camp commander, trying to do a good job, wanted us to count goddamned dead NVA bodies!

I didn't think that was such a hot idea. First of all, the longer our operation was exposed in the open, the more time it gave the enemy to react. Also, since we knew the enemy already had mortars and rockets zeroed in on the camp, the closer we got to home, the more likely it would be that they'd shell the piss out of us too.

I got on our radio and relayed all my fears to Britton, and he saw the truth in them. Unfortunately, he was unable to dissuade his counterpart of the idea.

A couple of our Yards had been killed during the night, and five or six wounded. Two of the wounded were litter cases, which would slow us down. After talking it over with the Montagnard company commander, we decided it wouldn't hurt anything to temporarily leave our dead in the village and come back for them later. We briefed the litter parties, ordering them to break off from the main group as soon as we got to camp and go directly to the medical bunker. The rest of us would make the sweep of the perimeter.

As soon as the Cobra gunships arrived, I marked our location with smoke and made radio contact with them. We coordinated our march back to camp with the flight leader, and he assigned two gunships to cover our move while the rest looked for other targets in the valley. The Cobras immediately found a nest of NVA stragglers not far from the camp perimeter and had a turkey shoot wiping out those unfortunates.

We began filing through the break in our perimeter wall, and I was pleased to see that the company's officers and NCOs were doing their jobs and keeping the men well dispersed. Bodt and I took our places in the middle of formation and we began a very scary walk back to camp.

About halfway there we started taking some harassing, small-arms fire from the road, which ran parallel to the route of march, a couple hundred meters off to our left flank. I had to grin to myself as I imagined the leader of the enemy ambush party watching as we evaded his trap. I could practically hear him cursing.

When the rounds started popping around us, the formation hesitated, and I yelled and waved at the LLDB weapons sergeant. "Keep 'em moving, Trung-si! Don't stop!"

Soon we crested the last rolling hill and had the camp perimeter in sight. I saw a man standing on one of the bunkers waving at us, then there were a few shots and the man jumped back down out of sight. I'd been keeping close radio contact with camp and with the choppers during the move, and now I got a call from Frye, who was manning the U.S. 81 mortar. "Okay, Operation," he told us, "we've got you in sight. Lookin' good!"

I had mixed emotions about nearing home. We didn't have to worry too much about an infantry attack anymore, but the closer to the camp we got, the easier it would be for the enemy gunners to make a slight shift of aim and begin hitting us with indirect fire.

We pushed on, and within a few minutes had reached the camp perimeter without incident. The column again hesitated as the litter parties moved through the front gate. Every time we stopped, it increased our chances of getting clobbered, and I ground my teeth at the delay. Once again I waved my arms and yelled at the troops to get moving.

There were plenty of dead bodies to count, but frankly I wasn't paying much attention. Whatever the real number of enemy dead turned out to be, I knew that the LLDB would inflate it by ten or twenty percent anyway. About a third of the way around the wire, we bumped into a wounded NVA soldier who had been left behind. He still wanted to fight, and was quickly dispatched by our point man. The short exchange of fire caused yet another maddening delay, however, and we'd only gone another hundred meters or so when NVA mortar rounds started falling.

By that time we were halfway around the perimeter and at the farthest point from the front gate. The LLDB sergeant looked back at me in alarm. "Fuck this shit," I yelled at him, and gave the hand and arm signal for double-time.

The operation broke into a wild run, completing the remainder of the perimeter sweep in record time. Panting and gasping for breath, we came streaming back in through the front gate, then dove headlong into the nearest trench lines. As soon as we were all under cover, the rounds stopped dropping.

Now, feeling a little embarrassed and trying to regain our dignity, Bodt and I casually walked the rest of the way up the hill toward the American TOC. A few mortar rounds suddenly burst somewhere behind us, however, and we were once again forced to run like hell.

We came crashing through the door to the TOC, by this time actually laughing at ourselves. Several other team members were there, watching us as we dumped our weapons and web gear in a corner.

"So, how was your night?" someone asked. "Get plenty of sleep out there?"

"Ha-fucking-ha," I answered.

Injun walked over and handed me a nearly full bottle of rum. "Have some breakfast?" he offered.

I unscrewed the cap and took a giant swig. It was the best drink of booze I'd ever had in my life.

Chapter 23

We were under siege again, a condition we were becoming accustomed to. Most of our team's new living quarters had been completed by this time, so it wasn't too bad. We just had to be careful when moving around outside, and always be aware of where the nearest bunker, trench, or hole was.

After that second big ground attack on the camp, the NVA pretty much curtailed their nightly probes, and appeared satisfied with simply laying back, shooting rockets and mortars at us, and trying to shoot down aircraft. I think the NVA just wanted to demonstrate that they could keep us bottled up any-time they felt like it, since the large American units had left the valley.

The main trouble with being under siege was that it hindered the coming and going of aircraft. Fixed-wing aircraft couldn't use our paved runway, and choppers didn't like coming in much either. In fact, about the only choppers we saw were the dust-offs, and we requested them only for very serious cases or for Americans and LLDB wounded.

Supplies again started coming in by parachute drop, a means of resupply that was much slower and more time-consuming than simply unloading the stuff on the runway and trucking it up to our newly reconstructed supply building.

Deliveries of nonessentials, like mail, reading material, or the occasional box of goodies, became erratic. Men put off leaving for their scheduled R&R trips because it was too dangerous to attempt getting on the infrequent dust-offs.

Probably the only good thing about being under siege was that it kept the REMF tourists and sightseers away. Our own chain of command still made occasional visits, however, just to show concern, and we appreciated that. Another visitor whom the enemy incoming didn't keep away was the undauntable Martha Raye.

Martha Raye, who had taken it upon herself to adopt Special Forces as her own, was by that time considered the unofficial Mother of the Regiment. She made many visits to Vietnam, entertaining for free in our clubs and visiting as many of the outlying A-camps as she could get to.

She arrived at Dak Pek without any prior notice while we were enduring this second siege. Besides being an entertainer, Martha was also an Army nurse, and held the rank of colonel. She thus had an easier time catching hops than some of the other civilians who floated around the country.

One afternoon a couple of dust-off choppers flew up the valley, quickly touched down between enemy incoming, dropped off three passengers, then departed.

"Who the hell's that?" the captain asked me, poking his head in the commo bunker.

"Beats the shit out of me, sir," I answered. "They didn't call in."

The visitors turned out to be Colonel Raye and her small entourage. She was accompanied by another nurse, a pretty, young captain, and a sergeant major from the headquarters in Nha Trang.

"Got any vodka?" Colonel Raye asked, making herself comfortable at our mess hall table.

She stayed, bullshitting with us, for about an hour, then the choppers radioed that they were on the way back to get her. That was the first and only time I ever had the chance to meet Martha Raye while I was in Vietnam, and I've always been glad I got the chance. Maggie was a good ol' gal, and Special Forces men still miss her.

My twenty-eighth birthday came and went, the fourth one I'd spent in Vietnam. A birthday in combat meant a little more than it did in normal circumstances, because I was always a little surprised and delighted that I'd survived that long. A birthday also brought a nagging worry that it could well be the last.

Around the first of September a new team sergeant was assigned. The previous team sergeant, Smith, had been gone for several weeks by the time headquarters found someone to replace him. At that stage in the war, Special Forces was drawing down, no longer receiving many replacements for guys ending tours and leaving country, and all the A-teams were short of personnel.

I'd been pulling double duty as both team sergeant and radio supervisor, and had given up hope of getting any help until we turned over the camp to the ARVN, so I was particularly happy to hear that a new man was on the way. This replacement turned out to be SFC Clyde Hashaw, who had the distinction of being the last officially assigned team sergeant of Camp Dak Pek.

Hashaw and I got along well. Clyde already had the proper mind-set for duty at a place like Dak Pek, having previously spent time at Camp Polei Kleng, but because of the poor morale at our camp, and in the entire 5th Group, taking over the job of team sergeant just then probably wasn't easy.

It also must have been a little difficult for Captain Britton and his XO, Lieutenant Scott, those final months at Dak Pek. Hashaw and I were the senior NCOs on the team, and we both had the same attitude concerning combat nonessentials, one of which was uniform regulation.

Since the beginning of the war, the regular Army in Vietnam had been griping about the weird uniforms Special Forces men wore. At first they didn't think we should wear camouflage, then they didn't think we should wear Montagnard jewelry with the uniforms, and on and on. Being REMFs themselves, they couldn't understand why we couldn't keep our boots spit-shined out at the A-teams and why we didn't wear underwear. After Abrams took over, things got worse, and our own Special Forces officers were finally browbeaten into trying to enforce the REMFs' silly rules.

Those of us on the team who had been there since the battle in April still only had one or two sets of faded American jungle fatigues, and those had no patches or insignia on them. We definitely looked like rag-bags. Mostly we just put on whatever clothing was handy, mixing camouflage with OD and jungle sweaters with the occasional civilian shirt or jacket. Sergeant Hashaw didn't like to wear a shirt at all, preferring to work on his suntan. I'm sure we caused our officers a good deal of embarrassment, especially after things quieted down again and the visitors from higher headquarters once more got up the nerve to come see us.

I suppose I was a special problem to the team's officers, because by that stage in my career I was getting the reputation of being somewhat of a character. In fact, at the very beginning of my tour at Dak Pek, I'd picked up the nickname of "Crazy," a moniker I did nothing to discourage.

After several weeks, the second siege basically just petered out. The number of incoming rounds gradually decreased to only one or two a week, and other intel indicated that the majority of the enemy had again left the AO, for the time being. I suspected they had simply run out of rockets.

"I guess I'll take Crazy with me," Hashaw told the captain as we stood around the map, planning the next operation. It was to be Hashaw's first patrol at Dak Pek.

Captain Britton didn't much like the idea, because it meant that both his senior NCOs would be out of camp at the same time. "Crazy's the only one here besides Erickson and Young who's been over to that eastern AO before, and they both need a break. Sergeant Fry can handle the team sergeant duties while we're gone."

After a while Captain Britton reluctantly agreed, probably secretly glad to get rid of us both for a week. In fact, after accompanying Hashaw on his first operation at Dak Pek, we teamed up on all the others too. I never did know if the team sergeant liked my company or was simply afraid I'd piss someone off if I was left back at camp on my own.

"It's hard to tell if the enemy have actually pulled out of the AO again or not," Britton said. "I want you guys to check the tops of these hills over here on the eastern side of the mountain. That's where they usually shoot the rockets from. Maybe you can find one of the launch sites and ambush the turds when they move in to set up."

The captain rather casually indicated the tops of four very tall, very steep hills. More damned mountain climbing, I thought, and inwardly groaned. I made a note to myself to travel especially light. Maybe I could con my Yard radio bearer into carrying some of my ammo for me too.

Trying to break our usual pattern of starting operations at first light, we left camp the next afternoon and traveled only as far as the outskirts of a large fortified village that sat at the base of the mountains. There we camped, hoping that the watching enemy would think we were simply performing a medical patrol. The village chief loaned us a member of his village defense force who knew the area we were going into and who could act as a guide, and early the next morning, before it got light, we quietly moved up into the mountains.

It was early autumn by then, and the weather around Dak Pek had begun to subtly change, becoming cooler and wetter. Or maybe the changes were only my imagination playing tricks on me. The next thing you knew, I'd be expecting the Yards to fall out for football practice. Still, as we began to ascend the mist-shrouded mountains, I was thankful for the jungle sweater and was beginning to wish I'd brought a field jacket.

After humping over and around a few of the lower hills, we came to the large rope-and-vine suspension bridge I'd crossed on my previous operation in this area.

"Holy shit!" Hashaw whispered to me when he first saw it. "I thought these things were only in Jungle Jim movies."

"Humgawaa!" I answered.

Either the NVA or our own Yards had recently removed most of the planks on the bridge, so we had a short wait while a labor detail rebuilt it. We didn't want to spend a lot of time on these repairs, and when the bridge was just usable, we cautiously crossed over the roaring river, which flowed around jagged rocks thirty or forty feet below. To my relief, we didn't get shot at and no one fell off the treacherous contraption. After a short break on the other side, we began climbing the first really tall hill.

By that afternoon, having made no enemy contact, we reached the summit and established our night bivouac. It was not one of the more popular bivouac locations, and we found no old fox-holes to use. Having only a couple of entrenching tools among us, it took most of the afternoon to dig in. I gave my Yard radio bearer two flashlight batteries and a C-ration candy bar to dig my hole for me.

There was a great view of camp and of the rest of the valley from that position, and as I watched the Yard busily working on my fighting position, I sprawled with my back to a tree, wishing I'd brought a camera to capture the scenic panorama.

Except for being scared, I liked being out of camp and in the jungle. The only time I felt really normal anymore was in the field, on operation. By this time in the war, I'd degenerated into such an uncouth, uncivilized animal that even the casual lifestyle of an A-team camp seemed too restricting and full of stupid rules and regulations. I was already beginning to dread the thought of returning to Fort Bragg and the peacetime Army.

Hashaw had been over having a talk with the LLDB and the Yard commander, and now rejoined me. "Hey, Crazy, what did you have to give that poor bastard to dig your hole?" he asked. When I told him, Hashaw began digging around in his own ruck, looking for something to trade. He eventually found an extra penlight, which was eagerly snapped up by one of the LLDB's many flunkies, and the Yard immediately began work on the team sergeant's hole.

"This Jai tribe is pretty good at digging," Hashaw mentioned to me later as we made a round of the perimeter.

"It's their best trait," I told him. "I haven't been too impressed with their fighting ability, though. When we got overrun in April, there was one whole company of them who wouldn't fire their weapons."

"Oh, that's nice to know," he said as we prepared to spend our first night in the enemy-controlled area. "Now I'm beginning to wish I'd stayed at Polei Kleng."

"Wait till I tell you how they do their fishing," I said.

As it turned out, we didn't make any significant enemy contact on that operation. Sometimes it was like that, and you just had "another walk in the sun." The hardest part of the patrol had been climbing to the tops of those damned mountains. On the side of one tall, jungle-covered hill we actually did run across what appeared to be an old enemy rocket-launch area, but it had been abandoned for some time and was probably left over from the battle six months before, in April.

On the last day of the operation, when we'd already descended into the valley, the lead platoon opened up on something, causing a good deal of excitement. They claimed they'd seen a squad of NVA, but a later search of the area produced no evidence of the enemy, and I figured they started shooting just for the fun of it, maybe out of boredom.

Chapter 24

When a man finished a year tour in Vietnam, he was supposedly given his choice of next duty assignment. The more I got to thinking about going back to Fort Bragg, the less enthused I got. I was smart enough to know that with my current attitude, it would be very difficult for me to fit myself back into the normal, garrison-duty nonsense that was the norm around Bragg. I figured that if I went back there, it would only be a matter of time before I messed up or pissed off the wrong person and got myself busted back down to private.

About the middle of October, I received a blank form from personnel at Nha Trang. There was an instruction sheet attached, telling me how to fill out the form and request my next assignment. I was told to put down a primary and two alternate duty stations, but the sheet said that most people got their first choice.

I actually didn't want to go back to the United States at all, but because I'd been in Asia so long, I knew my chances of staying overseas were slim. I decided to try the Language School Ploy, which had been popularized by the famous Neuhaus twins.

The Army didn't like to have its men homestead in overseas assignments, so every few years one was required to have a permanent change of station (PCS) back to the continental U.S. The Language School Ploy amounted to spending a mandatory PCS at the Army Language School in Monterey, California. Most of the language courses were only six months to a year in duration, so you wouldn't have to be back in the United States for very long. The trick was to study a language that was spoken in the overseas area you wanted to be reassigned to.

Back in those days, if a man had successfully completed one of the courses at Monterey, he was just about assured of being allowed to take another. Since I'd previously completed the Thai course, and since I had reassignment priority due to being a Vietnam returnee, I figured that getting back to the Language School was a sure thing.

I carefully filled out the reassignment request form. As first choice, I requested to attend the one-year Mandarin Chinese course. My second choice was to go back to 46th Company in Thailand, and my third choice was the 8th Special Forces Group in Panama.

That night, as I lay on my canvas cot, I began thinking about my future. With the war ending, it looked like I might actually have one to plan. All I had to do, I decided, was survive the next few months and then make it through the Chinese course. With two Asiatic languages on my Army record, and with my prior background in the Asian theater of operations, I didn't see how the Army could logically station me anywhere else. Oh, the stupid rules might require a brief return to the States now and then, but I could use the Language School Ploy to get around that, and learn even more Asian languages.

In ten years I'd be eligible to retire. Then it would be no problem to get a job with an American company or, maybe, with some government agency, and just stay in Asia forever. If South Vietnam managed to survive until then, I could return to live in Saigon, the way Lyn and I had talked about all those years ago. If not, there was always Thailand, or maybe Taiwan. Yes, I decided, my future was bright indeed.

The personnel section at Nha Trang was very efficient, and within a matter of weeks I had my reassignment orders. The orders told me to report to the 6th Special Forces Group, Fort Bragg, North Carolina.

* * *

"Sir, I need to go to Nha Trang, right-fucking-now!" I announced, storming into the TOC. Britton and Hashaw were sitting at the table going over some intel reports.

"What do you want to go back there for, Crazy?" Hashaw asked.

"I want to kill some goddamned clerks," I said.

"You want to do what?" Britton asked.

"Okay, I'll just hurt 'em a lot," I answered.

After getting me settled down and making me promise not to do anything rash, they gave me permission to make the trip to headquarters. The next day I caught a ride on a chopper and began the trip back to the rear area.

At Kontum, I discovered that Spurgeon and just about everyone else I knew in SOG CCC had already transferred out. Spurgeon was on his way back to Thailand, someone told me, and this pissed me off even more. Why could he go back but not me?

I didn't stick around the B-team long, but managed to catch a ride on a Caribou the next morning that took me straight to the headquarters. I spent one day there, trying to argue about my re-assignment orders, but could find no one who particularly gave a shit about my problem. The entire 5th Group would be rotating back to the States in a matter of months, and the administration had much more important things to worry about than where some ragged-assed boony rat wanted to go.

"What are you bitching about?" a sergeant major asked me. "At least you got orders to a Special Forces unit. They've already started to gut Special Forces, and a lot of the guys are getting orders for fucking leg *infantry* outfits!"

Everywhere I looked around Nha Trang I could see signs that the 5th was already beginning to pack up. Bill Martin had gone back to the States, and I couldn't find anyone else I knew. Even over at Delta and the Mike Force things appeared to be winding down. It was over, and we'd lost.

I gave up and went back to Kontum the next day. I had a three-day layover there while waiting for the next milk run up the valley to the A-teams, and spent all my time in the club, getting drunk. The second day I was there I stood in an awards ceremony with a few other men, and medals were pinned on. Those of us in the formation who were from the A-teams got Purple Hearts and Bronze Stars. Guys from the B-teams and C-teams got Silver Stars.

When this formation was dismissed, one of the A-team men standing next to me in formation ripped off the Bronze Star he'd just been awarded, threw it on the ground, and stomped on it. He and I went to the club and drowned our sorrows together. I was sitting on a bar stool, and got so drunk that I passed out, fell off backward, and landed on my head. Luckily, the cement floor was undamaged, so no one cared.

The next day I was ordered to report to the B-team signal officer, and he told me they needed a senior radio operator at the C-team in Pleiku, and asked if I'd like to transfer there for the few remaining months I had left in the country. He thought he was doing me a favor. I told him, quite honestly, that I didn't think I could last even a few days back at the C-team without getting myself in trouble, and was allowed to return to Dak Pek to finish my tour.

"Well, you get everything straightened out back at headquarters?" Injun asked me when I slouched into the commo bunker the next afternoon.

"Yeah," I said. "I told those bastards I didn't want to go back to Bragg, and they told me to tell someone who gives a shit."

"I wonder how they got such a poor attitude?" Injun said.

I asked him if he could handle the radio for the nightly sitrep, and when he said it was no problem, I told him I'd be in the mess hall, getting drunk and throwing knives into the wall.

"You know, Crazy, you really taught me something," Injun said.

"What's that?" I asked.

"I never saw anyone throw a round-pointed table knife hard enough to drive it clear through a half-inch piece of plywood before. How in the hell do you do that?"

"Beats the shit out of me," I told him. "I can only do it when I'm drunk."

It was hard for both the U.S. and the Vietnamese Special Forces teams to get used to the idea that the Americans would soon be leaving. We had been operating under the same set of rules and playing the same damned games for over eight years, but now everything was changing.

One day that fall, a month or two before we were scheduled to turn everything over to the ARVN, the LLDB radio operator came to our commo bunker. We'd just received a resupply, and there were five cases of new PRC-25 batteries and three cases of flashlight batteries stacked in the corner.

"You give LLDB new battery?" my counterpart asked.

I had been hearing this same request, and had thus been forced to dole out batteries—many of which ended up in the black market—since my first tour to Vietnam in 1963. It now dawned on me that in weeks the young LLDB sergeant would be in charge of all the commo supplies and it would be his turn to deal with these requests. It was time he learned how to do it.

I had two opened cases under the commo table, and figured that would probably be all the batteries the American team would need until we left. "Take them all," I told him. "In a few months you'll have them anyway."

At first he thought I was angry and was just being sarcastic. Then the truth of the matter hit him. I'll never forget the look that came over his face; he actually seemed a little sad.

Chapter 25

Every time there was a big battle in Vietnam that resulted in a large number of American casualties, it caused a new antiwar uproar back in the States. That was one part of the antiwar movement that I kind of sympathized with, particularly in those closing days of U.S. involvement. It's one thing to fight hard and take a lot of friendly KIA in the beginning or middle of a war; it's quite another thing to get a bunch of people killed toward the end. The popular saying was: "No one wants to be the last American killed in Vietnam."

For the first time in the war, the higher-ups weren't pushing American troops to perform "aggressive operations." In fact, the word was definitely out to minimize U.S. casualties. At Dak Pek and the other A-team camps, we began sending out more patrols and combat operations with no accompanying U.S. personnel.

It was November by that time, and we were getting near the holiday season. The morale at Dak Pek and everywhere else in II Corps was so terrible that no one really gave a damn about trying to get into a festive mood.

We'd already received word that the camp would be turned over to the regular Vietnamese Army on or about December 20. Our Strike Force would be converted to a border ranger battalion, and two or three American Ranger advisers would take the place of our Special Forces detachment. We'd been told that the ranger advisers would not be allowed to accompany combat operations at all but only coordinate things, such as air support, from the camp. As soon as it was deemed feasible, the advisers would also be pulled out and the Viets would be completely on their own.

Sergeant Hashaw and I went on the last U.S.-accompanied combat operation run at Dak Pek.

"I'm getting too damned short for this kind of bullshit," Hashaw told me as we trudged out the front gate. "I'm due to rotate in about two weeks."

We were with a combat patrol of company strength and going north, close to the border between our II Corps and the southern boundary of I Corps. It was an area that often got overlooked because each corps thought the other was taking care of it. The last time any friendlies had been as far north as we were going had been when Mike Force worked the area about nine months before.

The abandoned roadway wound up the valley floor, following the side of the river, and eventually turned to the west and into Laos. A branch of the Ho Chi Minh trail also angled off its main, north-south route and followed that natural path into Vietnam. Oddly enough, the northern area of our AO never seemed very threatening, nor even of much interest to us at Dak Pek, although I suppose it should have.

The plan for the operation wasn't very complicated. We intended to sweep north up the valley, keeping to the western edge, then turn around and come back down the other side, working the eastern foothills. During the operation briefing, Hashaw and I had made it clear to the LLDB that we were going along simply as observers, that except for calling in needed American fire support, we would take no active role in running things.

We'd been out the gate and moving on our route of march for about five minutes when the LLDB sergeant walked back to Hashaw and me. He had his map out.

"We go here?" the sergeant asked Hashaw, pointing with his finger to a small draw that angled off to the west. It was obviously a test.

"Okay with us," Hashaw told him. "You guys are in charge; we're just along for the exercise." The LLDB sergeant nodded and walked off.

"What the hell do they want to go up that draw for?" I asked Hashaw when the LLDB was out of earshot. "It looks like ambush city in there to me."

"I don't know," Hashaw answered, "maybe they're just trying to do a good job and impress us with their bravery."

"I wish they'd save their damned heroics until we're out of here," I said. "My bravery days are a thing of the past."

"Amen to that," the team sergeant said.

We pushed up the draw for only half a kilometer or so, then stopped and established a perimeter. The LLDB and the Montagnard leaders had a short discussion about what to do next. Hashaw and I sat in on the meeting but did not say anything. Their plan was to establish a couple of ambushes, eat the noon meal where we were, then go back out to the main valley and continue north for another kilometer or so before stopping for the night. This all sounded pretty sensible to Hashaw and me.

"Maybe after eight years of training they've finally figured out what to do," Hashaw said.

"I think they probably knew all along," I said. "The Yards have been fighting each other and using these same tactics for a thousand years or so. It's the modern stuff they had to learn, like how to integrate the radios, artillery, and air support."

"That, and the part about not fishing with hand grenades or shooting monkeys out of trees while on patrol, or running away before someone gives the order," Hashaw added.

"Minor shit," I said with a smile.

All the troops seemed to be on especially good behavior, like students trying hard to demonstrate their abilities to the teacher.

Hashaw and I wandered around the perimeter to check everything out, and things looked just the way they should. "Straight out of Fort Benning," I told Hashaw. He agreed.

We made no enemy contact up there in the draw, and at about 1330 hours we resumed the march. Within half an hour or so we again walked out into the main valley.

At 1600 hours we came to the small fortified village that was the northernmost strategic hamlet in our AO. Strangely, unlike many of the others, this rather isolated outpost hadn't been overrun during the big battle in April. We stopped on a shady hill outside the village's earth walls, and the LLDB and Yard commander went to talk to the village chief.

"I suppose I should take the interpreter and go see what they're talking about," Hashaw said. "I may be missing some hot intel."

"You're just afraid you're missing a rice wine session or think you might see some half-naked teenage chicks," I told him.

"Well, of course there's that too," he said, then wandered off to find the interpreter.

They were gone about an hour, during which time I occupied myself with attaching a new feather to my bush hat and whittling on a stick. When that got boring, I killed a few ants.

"Well, how did it go?" I asked Hashaw when they all returned. "Learn anything new?"

"No, same old shit," Hashaw told me. "The village chief says there's ten or twenty enemy infantry regiments, two armor divisions, and seven artillery units, all hiding someplace just across the border in Laos. He says the Americans should put in some B-52 strikes, and maybe a nuke or two. Wanted to know if we had some poisonous gas we could let him have for village defense."

"Did he offer you any rice wine? Did you see any bare-breasted babes?" I asked.

"Actually, yes and yes," Hashaw said. "The damned LLDB screwed me on both of them, though. He told the old Yard that we never drank anymore while on operations because the camp was soon going to be part of the regular Army. Then he yelled at the chief's fifteen-year-old daughter to go cover up her chest."

"I've noticed that bare tits seem to somehow offend the Vietnamese morality," I said. "Did you ever notice how prudish the Viets are?" Then I continued, trying to sound like a college professor. "Apparently, the lowland Vietnamese do not understand that the Montagnard women allow their breasts to show because it is part of their age-old culture."

"I thought the young ones let 'em show to entice a husband," the team sergeant said.

"I don't know about that," I answered, "but it sure gives *me* a hard-on!"

"I did get a couple of Yard bracelets," Hashaw said, changing the subject. He held out his arm and showed them to me. "Now I'm just like John Wayne."

"I'll bet those bare tits gave the Duke a boner too," I said.

That night, after we established our defense, Hashaw and I made it a point not to go with the company commander when he made his rounds of the perimeter. I did make sure to call camp, though, and give them the coordinates of two possible danger areas. I wasn't quite ready to let the indigenous start handling that part of the show yet, and I probably never would be.

We spent a quiet night there beside the little village, and the next morning before we left, many of our troops bartered and bought numerous items of fresh food from the inhabitants. A couple of our men had family members in that group of villagers, so I suspect it was hard for them to break away. We got a later start than usual, not moving out until almost 1000 hours.

As we pushed on north, the terrain began looking a little more wild and we ceased seeing signs of habitation. A change came over our troops as we ventured into that unfamiliar territory. The farther north we went, the slower we moved, carefully clearing danger areas such as stream and trail crossings.

We were following a trail that wound through the jungle-covered foothills and gave us some concealment. Although I'd been expecting something to break loose at any time, I'd let my mind drift off while my body slogged along on automatic pilot. When our point squad suddenly opened up, I was jerked back to reality.

A few stray rounds popped through the tree limbs overhead, and before I realized it I was already crouched down, out of the line of fire, in a low spot of ground that I had no conscious recollection of moving to. I'd gone from half awake to fully alert in a microsecond as my pounding heart pumped a sudden flood of adrenaline.

There was another burst of shooting from up front somewhere, and then the usual crumps of grenades and M-79 rounds. Someone started yelling in Vietnamese for a medic, and one of the Yards left the command group and ran forward with an aid bag.

"Maybe we ought to go up and see what's happening," Hashaw said.

"Let's let them handle it," I answered, remembering once more what had happened to my friend Spencer. "They have to start doing things by themselves. Besides," I added, "you're getting short and I'm too scared."

"That's the reason I always take you with me on operations, Crazy," Hashaw said. "Murphy's Law says you should never share a foxhole with a man braver than you are!"

The Yard radio bearer came crawling up next to me. "You call camp, Trung-si?" he asked, offering me the handset. I took it and talked to Injun, telling him that we were in contact with an enemy unit of unknown size, and asking him to have the camp mortars stand by for a possible fire mission.

There was a short pause in the shooting, then another loud explosion that scared me because I couldn't identify what had caused it. "What the fuck was that?" Hashaw asked. When I told him I didn't know either, the team sergeant cursed and crawled away to look for the LLDB or the Montagnard commander.

The shooting abruptly stopped again, and the silence was broken only by several questioning cries in Vietnamese. Someone barked a command, and it got quiet again. I became aware of the sweat running down my face and of a mosquito buzzing around my right ear. I'd bumped my knee on a rock when diving for cover, and I was starting to feel the pain. I'd cracked it pretty hard, and I vaguely wondered if it would stiffen up on me, hindering my ability to walk.

A wave of weariness swept over me. I suddenly felt as if I had been doing that kind of thing forever. I felt as if my life would continue like this, on and on, without end. It was quite an odd sensation, almost a mystical vision, and I sensed that what was happening involved the repayment of some debt owed from a previous existence.

Hashaw came back, bringing the LLDB sergeant with him. "We've got one wounded," Hashaw said. "Apparently we hit some kind of small ambush. It looks like the enemy are pulling back, and we think they're probably going up this ravine here," he said, taking the map from the Vietnamese sergeant and pointing it out to me. "Call camp and have 'em put a couple of 81 rounds at the following coordinates . . ." He read them off to me.

I called in the fire mission, and in short order we heard the concussion of the rounds going off in the nearby ravine. When the fire mission was over, camp wanted a situation report.

"They want a sitrep," I told the team sergeant. "Any confirmed enemy casualties?"

"Naw," he said, shaking his head. "Just tell them we have one friendly WIA, and that we'll get back with them about what we'll do with him. Tell them we're continuing the operation as planned."

The wounded Yard was a litter case. We didn't feel he was critical enough to call in dust-off, and, anyway, it was hard to get a helicopter evacuation for a Montagnard. It was decided to send the wounded man back to camp with a detached squad whose men would act as litter bearers and security. We told the litter party to go out into the middle of the valley, where it was safer, and then head for the strategic village where we'd spent the night. We figured the village chief could furnish a few of his men for added security, and that they could all get back to camp safely.

Following a different trail from the one we'd been on, the rest of us continued north. I never did find out what caused that scary explosion.

That was the only excitement we had on the operation, although once we got to the northern end of our AO, things remained pretty hairy. Hashaw and I continued to stay out of the way and let the Vietnamese LLDB and the Montagnards run things, and they did a creditable job. Their demonstrated proficiency gave me new hope that after we Americans left, the ARVN might actually be able to hold out on their own.

That was the last combat patrol I went on in the war.

Chapter 26

By the end of November 1970, we had reached and even surpassed the point of readiness that Camp Dak Pek had been at prior to being overrun. The Montagnard school had been rebuilt, along with the supply building. All of our troops had been issued new sets of camouflage fatigues, and all carried the latest weapons and equipment.

To make the conversion to ARVN control a little more palatable, there would be many promotions once the conversion took place. The LLDB detachment commander, a captain, would be promoted to major and become the battalion commander. The NCOs on the LLDB team would get commissions to lieutenant and become the battalion staff. Likewise, the Montagnard company commanders, platoon leaders, and so on, would all be given commissions in the regular ARVN, something that was unthinkable in years past.

Our troops were putting on a good show of being confident and optimistic about their future at Dak Pek. However, behind all their bravado, there still lurked the dark truth that the Americans were cutting and running. And the NVA weren't.

Men on our detachment continued to rotate out, and as they departed, they were not replaced. Sergeant Hashaw completed his year tour and went home. As the ranking NCO, I took over as team sergeant. Captain Britton went home, and Lieutenant Scott, newly promoted to captain, took over as team leader.

As my own tour's end and return to the States neared, I became more and more confused and unsettled. Because it had been completely taken over by the bureaucrats, REMFs, and politicians, the war was not much fun anymore. Also, it seemed I was pushing the envelope as far as my luck went. Over the course of the war, I had lived through some very close calls, and I felt as if the odds were against me. On the other hand, I did not want to return to the U.S. either.

One day, the LLDB detachment commander got me off to the side and asked me to stay at Dak Pek for another year. I reminded him that Special Forces was leaving, and he said that if I agreed to stay, he could pull strings and arrange it.

"When other Americans go home, then be like when you come Vietnam first time," the little Viet captain said. "I be in charge camp, and we do what we want. I take you to Saigon, introduce you to my wife. We go Vietnamese bar, and I fix you up with number-one girlfriend!" I realized for the first time how much this man liked me, and also how much he appreciated my abilities. I told him, quite honestly, that I would think it over and let him know.

Life around camp got really weird those final weeks before the conversion. We'd been issued a new movie projector to replace the one destroyed in April. The projector was supposedly for the purpose of showing the troops propaganda movies, but occasionally we also received fairly recent Hollywood films. One of the movies that came in was my favorite western, *The Wild Bunch*. We showed this one in our team mess hall, and invited the LLDB team to come watch it with us.

As we watched the movie, we all drank beer, and a couple of the LLDB NCOs drank too much. The overwhelming, graphic violence of the movie greatly excited the two men, and as soon as the movie ended, they went outside to have a damn quick draw contest . . . for real! Standing about thirty feet apart, each one went for his .45-caliber M-1911 auto. Each man emptied his gun at the other, but they both missed with all seven shots. After the duel, they shook hands, embraced, and were buddies again. As I say, things were definitely strange during those final weeks.

By the time our ranger replacements arrived at camp, only a few of us from the old team were still there. Several high-ranking officers arrived one morning and we had a formation of all the troops for the official conversion ceremony.

The little Yards looked really impressive in their clean new camouflage uniforms, and all of them were doing their damnedest to look like real soldiers. After the promotions were passed out, several of the troops were given awards for past bravery. I felt proud for them. I felt proud for U.S. Special Forces too, for developing a ragtag bunch of irregulars into a creditable regular unit.

A few hours after the ceremony, the LLDB commander—now a major and the battalion commander—asked me if I had made my decision yet about staying with him. I told him I didn't think it would work out, and that I would feel out of place in the new order of things. He said he understood, and we shook hands. The next day, Ellis and I got on a Caribou and left Dak Pek for good.

I still had about six weeks to serve in Vietnam until my rotation date. That was not enough time to start a new permanent assignment, so I was told to hang around the C-detachment in Pleiku until someone decided what to do with me.

Things were absolutely dreary around the C-detachment headquarters. Special Forces units had been at Pleiku since the very beginning of American involvement in Vietnam. We had gradually turned our compound there into a quite comfortable place. Almost all the building materials had been scrounged, begged, or stolen, and we'd used our own labor and sweat to do the actual construction. There was even a swimming pool! The compound was the envy of all the other units in II Corps, including the well-supplied and -equipped 1st Cav.

By the middle of December 1970, however, the old homestead was already getting that abandoned ghost-town look to it. There weren't many Special Forces men left; the C-team was operating with a bare skeleton crew until all the A-team camps had either closed out or were officially turned over to the Vietnamese.

A large Christmas tree stood in the club. God knows where things like that came from, maybe from the USO. In any case, the tree stood absolutely bare for several days, no one in the mood to bother decorating it. One night I and a couple of other drunk cynics hung a few empty beer cans on it, and a sign that read "Ranger." This last was in reference to the newly authorized camouflage uniforms our ranger replacements wore. The tree gradually withered, turned brown, and became a fire hazard. It was tossed out several days before Christmas.

While I was hanging around the C-detachment waiting for someone to tell me what to do next, I got wind of a new unit being formed. Apparently, after the 5th Group officially departed from Vietnam, there would be a few guys left to help the

Vietnamese develop their own clandestine SOG-type operations. Volunteers were being sought for the unit, and since I had
past experience with those kinds of operations and also had the
requisite Top Secret security clearance, I was asked to join.

Injun was with me at Pleiku, also waiting for a reassignment,
and he told me he'd volunteered for the duty. As usual, there
were several catches. The first problem was that to get assigned
there myself, I would have to request a year extension in Vietnam. Another problem was that no one seemed to know exactly
whom the unit would work under or for. With the rest of the
5th Special Forces Group gone, the remaining men would be
under complete control of the regular Army generals, who hated
our guts. It just didn't sound like a very good deal to me, and I
decided against it.

One day, while I was killing time, I read a book about the war
that was then still raging in Rhodesia. It interested me greatly,
mainly because this was still an ongoing struggle with no end
yet in sight. It was obviously a lost cause, just as the war I was
preparing to leave appeared to be, but I've always been a sucker
for lost causes.

When the C-detachment ceased operations, I left with them,
and we all went back to the headquarters in Nha Trang. If things
had seemed gloomy around Pleiku, it was even worse around
the SFOB. This feeling of gloom and despair may seem odd to
civilians or to men who fought the war with other units, who
might think we should have experienced feelings of happiness
and rejoicing because we were going home. But that was not
the case at all in Special Forces. I think we felt the same way the
Foreign Legion did as they prepared to leave Algeria.

There was no job for me at Nha Trang either. I was told to just
hang around and stay out of trouble for a couple of days until
they decided what to do with me. I was handed a long list of
new rules and regulations to abide by while I was there, and

warned that the rules were being strictly enforced. I glanced through the items, deemed them all to be bullshit, and tossed the list in the trash.

Although everyone told me that the city of Nha Trang was overcrowded and no longer any fun at all, on that first evening back I decided to go in and look things over. It would probably be my last chance to see the place, and the town held several pleasant memories from the times I'd been there back in better days. Also, Martin had told me he'd seen Lyn in town, and I thought I'd try to find her and have a look at the fat-cat civilian she was supposed to be living with.

The headquarters ran a shuttle into town that left the back gate every hour. At the gate guard shack there was a log to sign, indicating the time you left and came back. It was 1900 hours by the time I got ready to go, and the headquarters had ordered that all troops were to be back inside the compound by something like 2200 hours, so I didn't have much time.

All this seemed like absurd nonsense to me. Christ, by then I'd been living in Vietnam and other parts of Asia for most of my adult life, and felt like I'd kind of grown up in Nha Trang. I was no longer a stupid, wild kid; I was a twenty-eight-year-old sergeant first class! I'd just about changed my mind about going to town at all when a couple of guys I knew from somewhere showed up, and I got on the shuttle truck with them.

When the PFC driver let us off in the center of town, he warned us that the last trip back to the compound left at 2150 hours sharp, and if we missed it, we'd have to get back the best way we could.

Downtown Nha Trang was just as miserable as I'd been warned. It swarmed with GIs, reminding me a little of Times Square on New Year's Eve. There was standing room only in every bar, and all the drinks were way overpriced. So were the available women.

I went looking for Lyn and actually found a bartender who

knew who she was. Unfortunately, he said that her civilian boy-friend had returned to the United States and that Lyn had gone back to managing her old bar in Saigon.

Time was already getting short, and I wanted to get back to catch that damned shuttle run. But as I was having a final drink, I felt female flesh rub up against me, and looked over into the smiling face of a girl I remembered from clear back in 1965. She remembered me too, and it was so good to see someone from the old days that I bought her a drink. She whispered in my ear that her room was across the street, and that she would only charge me the old rate.

You've probably already figured out the rest. By the time I left her room, I'd already missed the last shuttle back to the headquarters compound. I frantically tried to get a cab, but every-one else was trying to get off the streets too, and the taxis were all full. I finally caught a ride with some drunks in an overcrowded jeep, but by the time I signed in at the gate, the guard had closed out the log and I was three minutes late.

The headquarters detachment in Nha Trang held morning formations, something I hadn't had to endure since I'd last been at Fort Bragg four years before. At the close of the formation, several names were read off, including mine, and we were told to report to the orderly room immediately after we were dis-missed. This brought smirks and snickers from a few REMF clerks in the formation.

I wasn't actually very worried. Hell, I didn't think I'd gotten in any real trouble. After all, I'd only missed the sign-in time by three damn minutes. I figured I'd get the usual ass-chewing, and I'd endured plenty of those before. It turned out, however, that the headquarters *did* think it was an important infraction of an important rule, and I was actually given a goddamned Article 15 for this minor fuckup.

Now, those readers who've been in the military know that an Article 15 isn't really a big deal either. And my punishment turned out to be only a fifteen-dollar fine and a couple of days' extra duty. It was the principle of the thing that got me, though. That and the fact that this was the only Article 15 I'd ever received in my career. Coming as it did, when I was in a very sour mood anyway, the incident caused me to do something I've regretted ever since.

"I've got a fucking expiration of service date coming up in one month," I told the personnel clerk the next morning. "I'm getting out. Change these goddamned Fort Bragg orders into discharge orders!"

The clerk, a PFC, looked at me like I was crazy—a pretty good assumption, actually—and went off to look for his supervisor. The NCO in charge of the personnel section, a sergeant first class whom I'd had some drinks with, came up to the desk. "Are you serious about this, Wade?" he asked. "Don't bullshit us and make us change all the damned paperwork, and then change your mind tomorrow and want us to redo it again."

"I'm serious as a heart attack, Sarge," I told him, quieting down a little. "I want out of this chickenshit outfit."

"But you're an E-7," the PFC clerk said. "E-7s are supposed to be lifers, and lifers don't get out!"

When I just glared at him, he shrugged his shoulders and went to work typing my request. The admin NCO shook his head and walked off.

Word got around about what I was doing, but no one particularly gave a good shit. Because I was requesting a discharge, I had to go be interviewed by the reenlistment NCO, but that was only a formality. In fact, when I told the re-up NCO, who was a master sergeant, how I felt, he agreed with me.

"Frankly, Wade, I understand perfectly. If I didn't have eighteen and a half years in already, I'd get out too." He paused and looked out the window. "Things are going to get really sorry in the Army now that this war is over, you can count on that!"

The signal officer asked me if I wanted to pull a few shifts with the base station until I went home, and I told him I never wanted to work on another goddamned radio for the rest of my life. After a day or two I was assigned as permanent sergeant of the guard and began working one night on and one night off until it was time for me to leave.

I had previously been scheduled to leave with the main body of the 5th Group when they rotated home. Because I was getting out of the Army, however, I'd be leaving by myself a few weeks earlier. I was already being treated like an outsider.

The headquarters in Nha Trang ran guard duty just as if they were already back at Bragg. The nightly guard detail had to first stand an inspection in ranks, then be broken down into the three shifts. The guards weren't responsible for security from enemy attack, but for local, bullshit security, like making sure no one broke into the supply room, or tried to burn down the orderly room . . . or came back from town late.

I had a major case of short-timer attitude by then, and let everyone know it.

"Good evening, Sergeant Wade," the sergeant major said each afternoon when I reported for guard duty.

"Fuck the Army," I'd grumble, sometimes even flashing the hated peace sign.

"What are you going to do when you get out?" many of the guys asked. "I've heard that the civilians are putting locks on the garbage cans, so you'll probably starve."

"Just so long as they don't put locks on the beer joints," I answered.

Chapter 27

Two days before I was to leave Vietnam for good, I caught a ride on the daily milk run and flew down to Saigon. I could only spend one day there, but I felt I needed to say good-bye.

I got off the C-130 at Tan Son Nhut and caught a cab straight to Tu Do Street. Lyn was in her bar, and she came right over to wait on me. I asked her how her family had been, and immediately wished I hadn't. Lyn's face suddenly grew very somber, and she told me her younger brother, an officer in the ARVN, had been killed the month before.

"Mama never smile now," Lyn said. "She feel very cry all time . . . no eat."

It was noon, and Lyn said we could go to her place for lunch. We took a cab to where she was living. It was quite a distance from her old apartment, and was in a poorer part of town. She held my hand as the driver bluffed his way through the heavy traffic. It was scorchingly hot that day, dry and dusty. We didn't talk much.

Her new living quarters weren't as nice as any of the other places she had taken me to over the years. There were two rooms, one barely large enough to hold the small bed and the wardrobe. The other room, the bath, had no shower, only a toilet and a large crock of water in one corner. There were buckets and a drain in the floor.

It was cooler in the room than outside, but not much. Lyn turned on a small fan, and we left the bamboo blinds drawn and

217

the electric lights off in order to keep the room from getting any warmer.

A table and a couple of wooden folding chairs sat in front of the window. Lyn asked me to sit while she went to the door and called to someone in Vietnamese. In a few minutes the old maid, whom I recognized from years before, came in with beer, ice, some fish cakes, and rice.

Several rays of sunlight slipped through the window blinds and fell on the table as we had our lunch and drank the beer. I told her she was looking very good, and asked her how business had been.

"Number-ten," she told me. "All GI go home now." The ones still there didn't spend their money the way they used to, she said. "Very hard time now, Saigon."

We shared some fruit, and then she gave me a serious look. "You look too sad. You homesick, have trouble Army, what?"

I tried to explain things to her the best I could. I told her about the war being lost, and said that many of my friends had been killed. I explained that most of the other Americans I knew were leaving or had already gone, and I said that I was finally abandoning Vietnam too. I also told her I felt very confused and was afraid of the future.

Lyn seemed to comprehend it all. She nodded several times as I talked. "Lyn understand," she said, and appeared very sad.

But being the way she was, Lyn would not let me dwell on it. Always practical and direct, she grabbed my hand. "Come," she said, pulling me to my feet. "We take bath, get cool, then take nap." And she winked at me.

We undressed and took turns pouring buckets of the cold water over each other. Soon we were giggling and jumping around like children, the earlier gloom almost forgotten. We dried each other and then lay on the hard Vietnamese bed.

After making love, we collapsed next to each other, sweating and staring at the ceiling.

"First time you come Saigon, I still work other bar," Lyn said after quite a while. "That *long* time ago," she added, and suddenly sat up cross-legged on the bed.

She reached down and stroked my face. "You remember?"

I told her I did.

"We young then," she said, and paused, seeming to think about it for a moment. "Now we old," she said with finality.

A few minutes later she got out of bed and quickly dressed, talking as she did so. She said I could stay as long as I wanted, but she had to go back to work. She told me I could leave the door key with the old woman.

"You come back again tonight when bar close, okay?" she said. "We play card, and I cook steak for you. We talk about the before times."

"The past."

"The past," she repeated.

Before she left to go back into the gritty, Saigon afternoon, Lyn knelt at the edge of the bed. She took my face between the palms of her hands and kissed me on the lips.

At the door she turned one last time. "Bye-bye," she whispered. She smiled, and then she was gone.

Later that day I ran into a few old friends and got roaring drunk. I never made it back to see Lyn again that night, or ever again.

Returning Home

There was no war here. Then I realized it was over for me. But I did not have the feeling that it was really over. I had the feeling of a boy who thinks of what is happening at a certain hour at the schoolhouse from which he has played truant.

—HEMINGWAY, *A Farewell to Arms*

> Me that 'ave been what I've been—
> Me that 'ave gone where I've gone—
> Me that 'ave seen what I've seen—
>   'Ow can I ever take on
> With awful old England again . . .
>   Me that 'ave been what I've been?
>
>   —KIPLING, "Chant-Pagan"

Chapter 28

We flew home on a chartered civilian flight and landed at night, in a cold, drizzling rain. The plane taxied over to a nearly deserted corner of Seattle International, far away from the civilian terminal, and dumped us off at a dingy building the military used for the in-processing of Vietnam returnees.

We deplaned and sloshed through puddles toward that dreary building, all of us shivering in our short-sleeve khaki uniforms. There were no cheering crowds or bands playing to welcome us home but, on the other hand, there weren't any screaming, spitting, excrement-throwing, antiwar demonstrators either.

All of us had been forced to endure three or four shakedown inspections before boarding the plane to leave Vietnam. When the plane landed in Alaska to refuel, we'd been ordered to get off while customs inspectors got on with drug-sniffing dogs. Now we stood in line while our bags were again pawed through by U.S. Customs. When my turn finally came, I handed the man my Samsonite briefcase, which held three unopened packs of cigarettes. These items represented my worldly possessions.

"This is all your luggage, Sarge?" the inspector asked, glancing inside.

"Yeah," I told him, "I like to travel light."

I was told to move on through. Apparently I looked too old to be a druggie anyway.

Next we were divided into two groups. Those who were staying in the Army went to one group, and were immediately released to go on leave. The second group, we quitters, was herded on buses and driven out to Fort Lewis for immediate discharge.

Most of the men in that group were PFCs and spec fours, with a scattering of young buck sergeants, and one staff sergeant. I was the only senior NCO, and the others of the group refused to talk to me, treating me as if I were some sort of undercover spy for the Army establishment. When we got to the repo depot, we learned we would be processed out of the Army that very night, something that gladdened us all.

The repo-depot people didn't know what to do with me, having never discharged a sergeant first class before. Finally, I was placed with a small group of warrant officers and junior commissioned officers who were also leaving the Army.

In an attempt to keep up with the hordes of Vietnam returnees, the repo depot ran twenty-four hours a day, seven days a week. Most of the clerks doing the work were draftees, thankful that they were spending their two years safely in the U.S. Most of the men they were out-processing were also young draftees, many of them with definite attitude problems. The clerks weren't very interested in doing a good job, and the guys being discharged were interested only in getting the hell out. Because of that, many men, including yours truly, later discovered important errors in their official record of military service.

It was 0300 hours in the morning when I processed out of the Army. As individuals, we slowly moved from one bored, yawning, hungover clerk to the next. The last station was Finance, where we were given our final separation pay. I received five hundred dollars in cash and another thousand or so in a government check. After we were paid, our military ID cards were collected and we were finally handed our discharge papers.

It was just getting light, and I heard Reveille being played over the speakers. "This will be the last time we'll ever hear that," I said to a young former warrant officer who was standing next to me counting his money. He just grunted and walked away.

Around Fort Lewis the troops began getting up. I hadn't had anything to eat in over twenty-four hours, and the only place open was the mess hall. I still had on my uniform, but when I went through the door, the headcount asked to see my ID card, and of course I no longer had one.

"Sorry, Sarge, no ID, no eat. Them's the rules. Gimme the next five men in line!"

As soon as the post exchange opened, I went over and bought some civilian attire. Then I went across the street to the nearest barracks and changed clothes in the empty latrine.

The civilian clothing felt oddly soft, lightweight, and somehow insubstantial. I looked at my uniform shirt, which I'd draped over a sink. It glittered with awards and decorations. The first time I'd returned from Vietnam, eight years before, I'd worn only one ribbon, parachute wings, and the Combat Infantry Badge. Now I was returning for the fifth time, and there were several rows of ribbons.

I carefully took the ribbons and badges off the khakis and placed them in my briefcase. Then I stuffed the dirty uniform in a trash can.

"FTA," I mumbled to myself in the quiet, deserted latrine. The defiant phrase didn't come out with much conviction, though. Carrying my briefcase, I went out into the gray, freezing drizzle and caught a taxi back to the civilian airport in Seattle.

As odd as it sounds, I didn't even start thinking about where I was going until the cab was halfway to Seattle. In combat you get used to living one day at a time, and I actually hadn't planned so far ahead yet. The logical place to go was home, but I no longer had one. Unfortunately, my family had broken up while I'd been gone, all of them leaving Tucson, where I'd grown up. My older sister was married and teaching school in Japan, my father was living in Mexico, and my mother had moved to Houston.

I decided to go to San Francisco for a few days. I'd always

liked that city, hippies and all. Also, for the past several years, all my Army pay had been deposited in the Bank of America, and their main office was there. I needed to check on my account, because I hadn't been getting very regular bank statements at Dak Pek. I also wanted to cash the large check the Army had just handed me.

"What terminal do you want to go to?" the driver asked as he turned off the freeway and onto the airport exit ramp.

"Doesn't matter," I told him. "Go to the biggest one." He pulled over next to a sign that read, DEPARTING FLIGHTS ONLY, and I walked inside the busy building.

The place swarmed with American travelers. The first thing I noticed about them was how fat they looked. Everyone in Vietnam, of whatever nationality, soon became very lean. In America, everyone was fat, pale, and soft.

The second thing I noticed about my fellow Americans was the ridiculous way they were dressed. New styles had developed while I'd been overseas, and I wasn't prepared for them. I actually began to laugh out loud, because the people around me were dressed like clowns. The men were wearing bell-bottom pants. Their suits had wide lapels, and they wore giant neckties to match. There was a profusion of garish plaids, mixed with stripes and psychedelic prints. Besides all of this, men had long hair and sported absurd sideburns.

Thankfully, the American women didn't look quite as stupid as the men. Except for the really old, and the fat, most of them looked pretty good in micromini skirts. Some, however, were wearing long, frumpy things, apparently made from flour sacks, which were known as "granny dresses."

The third thing I noticed about the American population was the way they looked at me. Their glances held suspicion, fear, and loathing. At first I couldn't figure that out, because I was no longer wearing my uniform. It soon dawned on me that with my short hair and skinny, suntanned body, I appeared as alien to them as they appeared to me. Uniform or no, the civilians still knew what I was and where I'd been. In a flash of insight, I understood that this was what black Americans went through all their lives. It would be interesting to relate this with some of my black Army buddies, I thought, but then it suddenly occurred to me that I no longer had any Army buddies, black or otherwise.

I'd had enough of being pushed around and being treated like a second-class citizen while in the Army, so decided to spend some extra money and fly first-class. I paid for the ticket with cash, and the agent at the counter made it a point to suspiciously check each large bill as if it might be counterfeit.

After I'd boarded the plane and taken my assigned seat in the forward cabin, a very fat musician got on. I could tell he was a musician because he was carrying his bass fiddle with him. He wanted his instrument to ride next to him in an empty seat. Unfortunately, there were no other empty seats in first-class.

The musician and the flight attendant, a young man with stylishly long hair, had a discussion about the situation, and as the attendant glanced around the cabin, looking for an empty seat, he spied me sitting there. I'm sure the attendant took me for a GI, flying on a "space-available" ticket, and figured I could be banished back to the rear of the plane with the rest of the riffraff. Getting rid of me would be a solution to his problem.

The flight attendant marched up the aisle to my seat and officiously demanded to see my ticket. After carefully inspecting it and finding it legitimate, he gave me a surprised snort and went back to talk to the musician.

Other arrangements were eventually made for the bass fiddle, and the rest of my flight was quite pleasant, even though the attendant didn't give me the kind of fawning service he gave the rest of the *real* first-class passengers.

"Where to, bud?" the taxi driver asked me when I reached San Francisco.

"I don't know," I said. "Take me to a hotel downtown, something medium-priced."

"Ain't ya got a reservation someplace?" the driver asked.

When I told him I didn't, he gave me a strange look. "Okay, I'll see what I can find."

The driver cruised around a little, running up the meter, but I didn't care. I was enjoying the scenic tour anyway, having fun seeing how much things had changed in the city since I'd been there last. There were still plenty of hippies hanging around on the streets, I noticed, although I'd heard that crap was just about finished.

After a while we pulled up in front of a fairly decent-looking hotel. "This place usually has some rooms," the driver told me. "They got some convention people staying here, but I don't think they're full up." He told me how much I owed him.

"Can you wait out front here for me until I find out for sure if they have a room?" I asked the driver.

"Sure, bud, I can wait, but ya gotta pay me what ya owe me before ya get outta the cab."

I paid the driver, picked up my briefcase, and walked into the lobby. "I'd like a room," I told the desk clerk, "a single."

"Name on the reservation, sir?" the deskman asked brightly. I told him I didn't have a reservation, and the clerk's phony smile faded a little. "Ah, I'll have to see if we have anything available," he told me, turning to look at the key boxes behind him. At least half of them held keys. "You're in luck," he said, turning back around. "We have one room left, but it's a triple. . . . We'll be able to let you only pay for the double occupancy rate, though, seeing as how you're by yourself."

I told him I'd take it, but said I had to go back out to release my cab.

"Goodness," the desk clerk said when I came back, "I hope you didn't forget your luggage in the cab."

"This is all the luggage I have," I said, showing him the briefcase.

"Oh, I see . . ." the clerk said, mouth twisting into a disapproving frown.

I began filling out the registration card. "How many days will you be staying with us, sir?" the clerk asked.

"I don't know," I said without looking up. "I'll be here at least two or three. Depends on if I'm having fun or not."

There was a short pause. "And what credit card will you be using, sir?" the desk clerk asked.

"I don't have one," I said, finishing the card and sliding it over toward him. "I'll be paying cash . . . in advance, of course," I quickly added when I saw his frown deepen.

The clerk picked up the reservation card and looked it over. "Your current residence is Dak Pek, Vietnam?" he asked.

"Actually," I said, "that's my last residence. I don't have a residence right now, I'm just sort of drifting around." He just looked at me. "You know, like one of those hippies!"

I paid him for two days, told him I'd let him know if I'd be there longer, took my key, and went up to my room. Seeing as how it was right next to the elevator, it was easy to find.

I unlocked the door, went in, and flipped on the dim, overhead light. The room was very small, and completely filled with two beds, and the roll-away, which was folded up in a corner. The single, grimy window looked out into an air shaft.

I tossed my briefcase on one bed and sat down on the other. "Well, here I am, home again in America!" I said to the walls.

Clunk, bong! The room trembled a little, and I thought at first it was one of the notorious San Francisco earthquakes. I heard loud, drunk voices outside in the hall, and realized it had only been the noise of the elevator. "Best room in the house," I said, still talking to the walls. "I guess nothing is too good for America's returning war heroes."

By that time I couldn't even remember when I'd last eaten, but for some reason, I really wasn't hungry anymore. I'd spotted a liquor store on a nearby corner when I'd arrived, and took the elevator back downstairs. As I walked through the lobby, I noticed the house detective giving me the once-over.

The sun had just gone down. The civilians were still out milling around the sidewalks, returning to their homes and families after a hard day on the job. I realized that I had none of these things to worry about, and vaguely wondered if this should make me happy or sad. I bought a quart of scotch and carried it back up to my room.

After a few drinks I took a shower and lay down naked on the bed. It was the first time I'd lain on clean fresh sheets for a long time, and I wallowed around on them, soaking up the sensation.

It had also been a very long time since I'd been able to lie in bed with absolutely no fear of incoming rockets, mortars, or murderous sappers bursting through the door. Even stranger than that, however, was the knowledge the I'd *never* have to worry about those things again. The war was truly over for me. I'd actually survived, and there I was. Was it all just a good dream I'd soon wake up from, finding myself back in my stinking cot at Dak Pek?

Sometime during the night the noise and the vibration of the elevator woke me. There was a brief moment when I didn't know where I was, and I started to roll off the bed onto the floor where I'd be safe. When I realized it was only the elevator, and heard the murmuring of voices in the hall, it reassured me rather than made me angry. Closing my eyes, I went back to sleep with a smile still on my face.

The next morning was bright and clear in San Francisco, and seeing as how it was Saturday, and the bank was closed for the weekend anyway, I decided to just goof off for a couple of days. The first thing I needed was some new clothes, and I wandered around all morning, hitting several shops, trying to find something I could wear that didn't look too bizarre.

"But, sir," the prissy clerk in the men's store told me, "bell-bottoms are really the *style* now. Where have you been, on another *planet* or something?"

"I just got out of the state penitentiary," I told him.

"I knew from your hair that it was either that or you were one of our darling Marines," he said, winking at me.

I finally found some pants that didn't bell too much, a few shirts that were almost one color, and some shoes that looked halfway normal, and started walking back toward the hotel.

On the way there I was accosted by a female beggar, the first street beggar I'd ever seen in America. This was another phenomenon that had begun while I'd been overseas.

"Got any spare change?" the chick asked me.

She was wearing one of those granny dresses, wire-rim glasses with blue lenses, and love beads. She was a big, strong, healthy-looking babe, and with her bare feet, reminded me much more of an Iowa farm girl than a hippie.

I thought I hadn't heard her correctly, the phrase still being new back then. I made her repeat herself.

"I said, you got any spare change? I know you do, because I can hear it rattling in your pocket!"

"Lady," I told her, "I've never had any *spare* change in my life."

As I walked away I heard her hawk and spit. "I know what you are, you fucking baby-killer," she yelled after me. "Baby-burning, warmongering, motherfucker!"

I'd become used to seeing beggars in other countries I'd lived in, and usually gave each of them something. The thing was, in poor third-world countries, the people who resorted to begging on the street really needed it. They were almost always physically disabled, usually lacking body parts, or they were blind. In some cases they were just barely alive. Not only that, but begging was all they had to survive, there being no social welfare net for them to fall into.

This American beggar had appalled me. She was fit, and sound of mind and body. Hell, she looked strong enough to get a job as a goddamned stevedore if she wanted. More than likely, she also had a well-off mommy and daddy to go running back to when all of that hippie business got boring.

After dropping off my new clothes in the room, I wandered down to check on the hotel bar. It was almost noon, and time to start some serious drinking.

I was hoping I'd find a few women hanging out in the bar, but I guess it wasn't that type of place. There were only a couple of good-old-boys from the convention, and a Navy petty officer. The Navy man was bravely wearing his uniform, something most U.S. servicemen had by this time stopped doing when off duty, because of all the antimilitary sentiment. I instinctively checked his decorations, and recognized a number of Vietnam service ribbons.

I sat a few seats from him at the almost empty bar and ordered a beer. After a while I struck up a conversation with him.

"Just back from Nam?" I asked.

"Yeah," he said, looking over at me. "You too?"

"Yeah," I answered, not really surprised that he knew.

"Marines?" he asked.

"No, Army," I told him, momentarily forgetting that I no longer was actually a part of it.

We talked through a couple of drinks, discussing the various good and bad points of our individual services, and after the guys from the convention left, the bartender came over and joined in. The bartender was older than we were, and had been in the Air Force during the Korean War. It was about three in the afternoon by this time and things were pretty mellow.

The street door was opened and we were joined by a fourth man. He was a black guy, dressed in a conservative, three-piece business suit. The only thing odd about him was that he was carrying a suitcase. He sat by himself at the end of the bar and ordered a scotch and soda.

The three of us continued the conversation we'd been having

about Zumwalt, the Navy's new commander, and the black guy ignored us, quietly nursing his drink. About half an hour went by, with the black businessman not saying anything to anyone. Then he suddenly stood up and, with no warning, threw his half-filled glass of whiskey as hard as he could at the mirror behind the bar.

The mirror and several full bottles of whiskey shattered and went crashing to the floor. We all looked at the black guy in stunned shock, wondering what the hell was happening. My adrenaline had kicked in and I could feel my heart racing, but I didn't know what to do.

The black man turned and looked at us. "I need help," he said, then picked up his suitcase and walked out.

A while later, once we'd settled back down, had a few more drinks, and the bartender had swept up the mess, I asked him if this kind of shit went on frequently.

"Actually, this is the first time something like this has ever happened in here," he said. "It's a pretty quiet place. But things like this are going on more and more around this town, and around the whole damned country."

"Welcome home," the Navy guy said, lifting his glass to me in toast.

"*Salud,*" I answered.

The Navy chief and I drank together in the hotel bar all that afternoon. When evening came, hoping to find some women to pick up, we wandered out onto the street, looking for a more disreputable place to go. There were several sleazy joints in the neighborhood, and we eventually hit them all. Things got a little blurry around midnight, and the Navy guy might have scored, because he disappeared and I never saw him again. None of the women wanted anything to do with me, however, and when the bars closed at two that morning, I staggered back to my hotel room alone.

* * *

I woke the next morning with the usual foul hangover. I was sick for a while in the bathroom, but after taking a shower and brushing my teeth, I felt a little better. At least I remembered the entire evening and there were no scary blank spots.

The weather was still nice outside, and I decided to walk around town for a while. It was Sunday morning and church bells were playing somewhere. I started off in the direction of North Beach, which lay several hills away. A year in the Central Highlands had gotten my legs in good shape, and even with my lingering hangover, I made the trek with no difficulty.

The North Beach area, where Kerouac and the boys had once listened to jazz, drunk wine, and written beat poetry, now was mostly filled with topless bars and porno theaters. City Lights Bookstore still stood on its corner, but seemed out of place. Kerouac had been dead for two years, and the beats had meta-morphosed into the hippies. Now that movement was also on the way out, leaving nothing behind but the sleaze.

At the base of Coit Tower, I ran across four young hippies, two boys and two girls, and they sat in the lotus position with closed eyes, pretending to meditate. As I approached I could smell the marijuana smoke that clung to their clothing and their hair. One of the boys opened his eyes when he heard my footsteps.

"Got a spare quarter, mister?" he asked as I started past.

"All the Buddhist monks I've ever seen have shaved heads," I told him. "Go shave off that long, greasy hair, get yourself a beggar bowl, and I might give you some leftover rice."

"Up yours, dad," he said.

"All life is suffering, my son," I told him. "It's time you started doing some of it."

In response, he flipped me the finger and closed his eyes again.

I continued my walk, heading downhill to Fisherman's Wharf. Church was letting out by then, and I passed several smiling family groups. I smiled back at them, but they ignored me.

While sitting in a bar down on the wharf, I tried to pick up a college girl I'd caught looking at me several times. She only wanted to talk about the war in Vietnam, though, and when I tried to tell her what I thought about it, she lost interest in me and went away. I guess she'd wanted me to break down and cry.

I stopped in several more bars on the way back to the hotel, one of them turning out to be a lesbian joint, and was thankful when I got back to my room with my balls still safely hanging in place.

Bong! The elevator woke me up the next morning. The quart of whiskey was all gone and the empty bottle lay on the floor next to the bed. I didn't feel very well at all, and it took me a couple of hours to get my act together enough even to leave the room.

As I walked past the front desk, the clerk called to me, and I went over to see what he wanted. "You're only paid up through noon today," he said. "Will you be staying longer?"

I dug out my wallet and paid him for two more days. By this time my five hundred in cash was almost gone, and I was glad that it was Monday and the bank would be open. The main office of BOA was a mile or two from the hotel, and I walked there, hoping the exercise would help cure my still-dreadful hangover. It didn't.

There was a short line at the teller's window. "I'd like to find out the exact balance of this checking account," I told the cute little girl behind the counter, "and I need to cash this government check." I slid the check and a paper with my account number written on it over to her.

"Very well, Mr. Wade," she said, getting the name off the check, "we'll need two pieces of photo identification."

I handed her my passport. "This is all I have," I told her.

Her attitude immediately changed, becoming hard and suspicious. "I'm sorry, sir, our new policy is that you must have *two* pieces of *photo* identification."

"It's all I have," I told her, beginning to get a little upset. "I've been out of the country. I just got out of the Army."

"A driver's license will do, sir, as long as it has your picture on it."

I no longer had a driver's license; it had expired several years before and I'd thrown it away. I tried to explain this to her, but she only shrugged.

"I'm sorry, sir, I have to follow the rules," she said, glancing at the bank guard, who was easing over toward us.

"Look, dammit," I said, talking louder, "that's a goddamned official U.S. passport. It has my photo in it. I can use it to travel all over the world. I've got over twelve thousand dollars in your bank, and now I need some of it!"

A well-dressed man who appeared to be in his late twenties materialized at the teller's side. "I'm Mr. Jones, the assistant manager. Do we have a problem here?"

We regarded each other silently for just a moment, and a wave of understanding passed between us. We were natural enemies. This man had stayed safely home, gone to college, and was now an ambitious young executive with the world at his feet. I'd gone away to war, but now I, and others like me, were coming back, and we would be in competition with him for a slice of the pie.

I explained my problem to him, but he informed me that, regretfully, there was nothing he could do to help me. When I told him the amount of money I had on deposit, which in 1971 was a large hunk of dough, I could tell he thought I was lying. I also sensed that he was getting great secret enjoyment from demonstrating his power over me. I wished the tables were turned and we were on patrol together in Vietnam.

"I'll be back," I told them ominously, then did an about-face and marched away. The bank guard followed me to the door and watched me until I was out of sight.

Actually, I was scared shitless and had no idea what to do. I'd only been back two days, and was already caught in this goddamned net of stupid civilian bureaucracy. I looked through the phone book and called a number listed under Veterans Administration that claimed to be a helpline for Vietnam returnees. They told me there was nothing they could do for me, and made it obvious they thought I was trying to pull some sort of scam.

I bought some more whiskey and took it back to my room. Sitting there, staring out the window at the blank walls of the air shaft, it suddenly occurred to me that I hadn't even called my mother yet to tell her I was safely back in the U.S. I immediately did so, having to go through the hotel operator, who reluctantly agreed to put the call on my room bill, and the phone was answered on the second ring.

I told my mother I was safely home from the war once again, and she asked me if I'd be coming through Houston to visit her on the way to my next duty station.

"I'm not in the Army anymore," I told her. "I got out."

"Oh . . ." she said, and I could tell from her voice that she thought I'd gotten in some sort of trouble and been *kicked* out.

"Don't worry, Mom, nothing happened. I just got sick of it, that's all."

"But what will you do now?" she asked, worried. "What will you do for a living?"

"Jeez, Mom, I'm not even thirty years old yet. I'll get a job somewhere. Hell, I'd thought you'd be relieved to hear I wouldn't have to go back to Vietnam anymore."

"Oh, I am, Leigh, but you've been in so long already, and now the war is almost over . . ."

Same sensible Mom.

"I do have another, small problem, though," I said, and could hear the sharp intake of her breath at the other end.

I filled her in on what was happening at the bank, and of course it was all beyond her. This kind of thing just wasn't something my mother knew or cared anything about. Mom turned the problem over to my aunt, who had been trying to take the phone from her since I'd called.

"What do you mean the weasely bastards won't give you any of your money, darlin'?" my aunt boomed in her aggressive Texan accent. "They'd better, by God, take care of my little nephew, or there'll be hell to pay!"

We talked awhile and came up with a plan. My aunt, who'd lived in Houston a long time, knew many important people in the city. One of these friends was the president of the largest bank in Texas, and my aunt wasn't hesitant at all about asking him for a favor. "Why, he just loves your auntie, honey, and he'll do about anything I ask," she told me, the tone of her voice implying lots more than she said.

The plan was for my aunt to go to her banker's office at a certain time the next day, while I went back to Bank of America. Then she and the Texas banker would call "that prick of a bank manager in Frisco" and vouch for me on the phone.

It worked even better than I could have hoped, and when I walked up to the BOA manager's desk at the appointed time the next morning, he was already sitting at attention, saying, "Yessir, yessir, I understand, sir, yes, yes . . . oh, here he is now!" The yuppie turned to me, all phony smiles and graciousness. "I was just talking to your aunt's good friend at his bank in Texas," he told me, handing me the phone.

Everything was soon straightened out, and I had a big wad of cash in my pocket again. The manager at BOA checked my account for me, and I found out that I had even more money in it than I'd thought. "Aww hope you'll feel free to put your money in my bank, son, if you end up movin' to Houston," my aunt's friend, the Texas banker, told me. "An' thank you for your service to our country."

Chapter 29

Houston is where I did end up, after a roundabout route that took me through Las Vegas. The main reason was that Houston was the only place in the U.S. where I knew I could get my damned checks cashed. Besides, the president of that bank was the only civilian who had said anything nice to me since I'd come home.

My mother, aunt, and eighty-five-year-old grandmother all lived together in a house in Bellaire. Granny was getting senile, my aunt was bossy and mean—although I was her favorite, and she was nicer to me than others—and my mother was depressed due to the recent divorce from my father. Mom also was developing a drinking problem, something I recognized right off. Funny how you can see these things in other people but not in yourself.

At their insistence, I moved in with the three of them, but I could tell right away it would have to be a short-term arrangement. My aunt and grandmother were big drinkers too, and the four of us spent each afternoon sitting out on the screened back porch, boozing it up.

The women laid so many guilt trips on me, I was having a hard time sorting them out. I was supposed to feel guilty about joining the Army after high school, and not going on to college the way my older sister had. ("Your sister is such a bright girl. She's really got a future ahead of her, that one does!")

Next, I was supposed to feel guilty about deciding to stay in the Army longer than my first enlistment, and about spending so much time fighting the war. ("We've all been worried sick for years. You should be ashamed of yourself for putting your poor mother through such misery!")

And finally I was supposed to feel guilty because now I'd gotten out! ("What do you mean, you got out because you were pissed off? That's a stupid reason. I think you made a big mistake . . . good jobs don't grow on trees, you know!")

I didn't feel guilty about any of it. I hadn't gotten to that point yet. Hell, I was still trying to figure out *why* I'd done all of it.

Each evening, after four or five hours of cocktails on the porch, the four of us would retire to the living room and watch the news. I'd hardly watched TV at all during the last ten years, and this was the first time I'd ever viewed the war from this perspective.

I considered the news commentary to be very left-wing and biased in favor of the enemy. The actual combat footage had a strange effect on me, causing my heart to race and making me think I was there again, doing it. I was having the same reflex reaction that old warhorses used to have when they heard bugles, gunfire, or smelled cordite.

After the evening news, we'd watch the nightly offering of dramas. It seemed like at least one of these shows always featured a drug-addicted, kill-crazed, insane Vietnam vet. That was the popular stereotype for us Viet vets in those days. Hell, no wonder everyone was suspicious and scared of us.

After two or three weeks with my three relatives, I began receiving hints that it was perhaps time I began looking for a job.

"Now, Leigh," Granny told me, "I know things were terrible over there in that horrible war, in that horrible country, and having to live with those horrible *Asians*, but you've had a nice little rest now, and it's time to start thinking about your *future*."

"I've been looking at the want ads, Grandma, but I haven't found anything that looks very exciting—"

"Exciting? Jobs aren't supposed to be *exciting*, they're sup-

posed to bring in money, so you can buy things, and be pros-
perous, and *respectable*. Work isn't supposed to be fun! You've
got to put your nose to the grindstone and make your mark in
the world."

And so on . . .

I decided that what I really needed was a change of scenery,
not a job. I called an old high school friend, Jack, who was still
living back in Tuscon, and he invited me out for an open-ended
visit. "You can stay with my girlfriend and me," he grandly offered. "It's a small place, but you can sleep on the floor next to
the stove." I asked him if his girlfriend wouldn't mind, and he
assured me it would be all right. "Don't worry," he said, "she's a
Mexican and comes from a huge family, and she's used to lots
of people hanging around."

It was good to see Jack again, and for the first few days things
worked out just like he'd said. Jack and I had joined the Army at
about the same time, but he'd served only three years, then
gotten out. He told me he'd just recently graduated from college
with a B.A. in English, and had decided to be a poet.

"A fucking *poet*?" I asked him as we drove to his house from
the airport. "Can you make a living doing that?"

"No, but it's what I want to do. My girlfriend has a good job
as a nurse, and she has faith in me. I write four hours every
morning, and then do the housework and all of that. It works out
just fine." He looked over at me. "You'll see!"

His girlfriend was gracious, just as Jack had promised, and I
tried to stay out of the way. Every morning we'd all get up together, and after the girl fixed us breakfast, she'd leave for work,
taking the only car. While my friend sat at the typewriter, com-
posing, I'd sit out on the porch and drink tequila.

At noon, Jack would quit for the day, and he'd start drinking
with me. If he'd produced a finished work, we'd walk to the
post office and Jack would mail it off to one of the literary magazines he submitted to. His poems had actually been accepted

several times, and although he was paid in free copies only, it made him feel good.

By the time the girlfriend got home from work, Jack and I would already be pretty drunk. Then, while she cooked supper, we'd sit on the porch and get drunker. The girl put up with this without complaint . . . for about two weeks.

". . . goddamned, weirdo, alcoholic friend of yours . . . get rid of him . . . him or me, you understand?" I'd walked down to the store by myself one afternoon to get some more beer, and caught just a little bit of her screaming tirade as I came back across the front yard.

"I'm back with the beer," I yelled cheerfully through the open screen door. I heard her storm into the bathroom and slam the door. There was the sound of crying.

"I guess you heard," Jack said, joining me on the porch.

I nodded.

"You better move out, or we'll both be without a place to live."

The next day I got on a plane and flew back to Houston.

Chapter 30

I moved into an apartment by myself that was only a few blocks away from my grandmother's house. The apartment manager wouldn't rent to me at first because I had no job, and no background she could check, but mainly because I was recently back from Vietnam. Only after I agreed to put up several substantial deposits and brought my aunt over to vouch for me was I accepted.

Most civilians believe that the experience of war makes a man braver. Why, after going through the horrors of war, how can anything else ever scare him? In a way this is correct, but in another way it's just the opposite. People who come through a war are also conditioned to be survivors, and are usually very cautious of every little thing.

Frankly, for a very long while after my return, I was scared and nervous all the time, and the things that scared me were things that civilians took for granted. For one thing, I'd developed a real "bunker mentality." I didn't like to be in buildings that were taller than one story, and preferred basements.

Large, open areas gave me the willies, especially when they were bordered by lines of trees or thick vegetation. I was much more afraid of thunderstorms than I should have been, and particularly of tornadoes. Sudden explosions, such as fireworks, sent me ducking for cover before I could stop myself, and even the occasional sound of approaching jets or helicopters affected me both physically and emotionally. I was a mess.

I was also very confused and lonely. In the Army, I'd always had built-in companionship and friends whether I'd wanted them or not. Now I had no friends and felt no desire to make any among the civilian population. I had nothing whatsoever in common with those people, nor they with me.

I had remained celibate since returning to the U.S. too, and not of my own choice. If I had trouble communicating with the average civilian male, it was twice as hard for me to do so with American women. I'd simply never learned how to play the game with them. I'd learned how to deal with the women in Asia, especially the professional types, and was very comfortable with them. But when I returned to the States, I was as ill at ease with my own countrywomen as a junior high school boy.

I became more and more reclusive, not wanting to venture

out among the civilians and have to deal with their mistrust and
fear of me. Mostly I sat in the apartment by myself, drinking
and trying to sort everything out. Every two weeks I got my hair
cut, keeping it the same length I'd worn it in the Army. I shined
my shoes every morning, and sent my dirty clothes out to be
done at a laundry . . . like a good soldier.

Several months passed that way, and suddenly it was spring.
I checked my quickly dwindling money supply and knew I'd
have to find some sort of job, even if it was just temporary. I first
checked on different police agencies, figuring police work was
the closest thing to what I already knew how to do.

The Houston police were recruiting like mad, but in those
days there was still a minimum height requirement of five feet
eight inches. I went down and tried anyway, thinking I could
stretch myself the extra inch if I stood straight.

"Five-seven and three quarters," the lady at the measuring
station told me. "Sorry, Mr. Wade, you're too short. Next!"

I found out I was tall enough to apply for the Border Patrol,
but I'd have to take the civil service test first and it wasn't being
given for six months. I sent in a request to take the test, and also
mailed off my résumé to the CIA, thinking maybe there was
something I could do for them on a short-term contract basis
in Laos.

In the meantime, I went downtown and talked to the operations manager at one of the large, international security companies. He was an old, gray, seedy character, full of cynicism after
years of involvement with that line of work. He'd retired from
the Army CID, and we hit it off right away.

"Let me tell you about the security guard industry, Wade," he
said, lighting one cigarette off another. "There's two kinds of
people who want to be security guards. There's young, cop
wanna-bes who like to carry around a chrome-plated pistol and
act important, and then there's old men who are looking to do as

little as they possibly can." He looked me in the eye. "Frankly, you don't fit in either category, and you'll probably hate the work, but we need people real bad, and if you want a minimum-wage, scuzzy job, we'll be glad to hire you on."

I told him I'd take it.

It was only the second job I'd ever had in my life. My first job, the Army, had lasted ten years. The manager who hired me had been right, I discovered, and I lasted two weeks before I quit.

I went around to a few other places, trying to get something better, and discovered that Granny was right. Good jobs didn't grow on trees—especially for the likes of someone with my background. . . .

"So, Mr. Wade," the snotty young punk of a personnel manager said, leaning back in his chair and giving me a knowing smile, "you say here on your application that you spent ten years in the Army."

"That's right," I told him.

"Now I wonder why someone would get out of the Army with all that time invested?" he said, giving me another one of those smug, all-knowing looks.

I wanted to jump across his desk and beat that snide expression off his sneering face, but instead I said, "Have you ever been in the military?"

"Well, ah, no," he answered, his eyes getting a little shifty, "I was going to college, and besides, I have flatfeet."

"If you'd ever been in the Army, then you'd probably understand why I got out with ten years served. Because you never experienced it, you'll never understand."

Of course, I didn't get *that* job.

The big problem was that I had no marketable civilian skills. Being in an elite combat unit such as Special Forces had given me a certain amount of status while I'd been in the Army, but it only made prospective civilian employers more suspicious and scared of me. It became obvious right away that the vets who were having the easiest time fitting back into civilian life were those who had done the civilian-related jobs while in the service. In other words, the goddamned REMFs!

One day, my mail contained two letters from the federal government. The first was from the Border Patrol, and told me that a one-year hiring freeze was in effect. The second was a photocopied form letter from the CIA, saying they couldn't use me.

I threw the letters in the trash, mixed myself a big drink, and right then and there decided to move to Rhodesia.

Actually, my plan was a little more complicated than that. First I would go to Paris and see about joining the Foreign Legion. If that didn't work out, *then* I'd go to Rhodesia. I thought that surely one place or the other would take me and put me back to work doing the only job I knew how to do.

I knew that I was risking the loss of my U.S. citizenship by taking either course of action, but by that time I just didn't care. America, and its people, had nothing to offer me. It was obvious that the war in Rhodesia would be lost in a year or so, and that I'd have to leave there too, but I figured I could drift down to South Africa and find something to do.

If I ended up in the Legion instead, that would mean a six- or seven-year enlistment. I'd heard they still had one parachute regiment left, and maybe I'd just stay with the unit until I retired, then live in France for the rest of my life. Any of the above possibilities seemed better than my current situation.

I was dead serious about all of that, and the very next day, after treating my hangover, I started getting things ready to go. My passport was still current, so there would be no problem there. I called a couple of airlines and found out the airfare from Houston to Paris and from Paris to South Africa. I talked to a couple of travel agencies about immunizations and so forth, and began trying to decide what to do about my bank account.

I was informed by the airlines that I needed to buy my ticket a week in advance, and looking at the calendar, I set my tentative departure date for two weeks hence, on the twenty-second of June 1971. Of course, I didn't tell my grandmother, aunt, or mother about any of my plans, knowing the reaction they would cause. I figured I'd get my mother off alone the day before I left and tell her—then run like hell.

With plans made, and my future all settled, I felt a whole lot better. I began a solitary going-away party, staying drunk as much of the time as possible and venturing out only when I had to replenish the liquor or food supply.

Then one day, only a week before I was due to leave for Paris, I checked the mail and found a letter from Bangkok. It was from Vicki, the girl I was still in love with, telling me she was on her way to live in London with a girlfriend. She said she'd be stopping in upstate New York to visit her grandmother before continuing on. "I'll only be there for a few days, but I wish you could come see me. I miss you dreadfully."

I decided that the Foreign Legion could do without me for a few more weeks, and bought a round-trip ticket to Albany.

Chapter 31

Vicki and her grandmother were at the airport to meet me, and Vicki looked better than ever. Vicki's grandmother, Grace, was a very straightforward, down-to-earth woman, and I liked her immediately. Grace lived in the country, on an old farm outside the small town of Ballston Spa, and we stopped at a motel on the way so I could get a room.

We had lunch, picnic style, out in the front yard of the farm-house, then Vicki and I wandered off around the fields to talk and get caught up on things.

"Are you anxious to get to London?" I asked her. "You've been talking about it a long time."

"I guess I am," she said. "Now that I'm finally out of Thai-land, though, there doesn't seem to be so much of a hurry. I was really just getting sick of Bangkok more than anything."

I asked her if she had a job lined up in England or anything, and she said she didn't. She said she was going to live with a British girl she'd met in Bangkok, and told me her name. "You re-member her, don't you?" she asked me, smiling wickedly. "She's the one you had that big fight with that time on Independence Day, remember?"

"Yeah," I said, "she's the one that kept referring to the United States as British colonies."

"That's her," Vicki said. "She still remembers you too."

"I can imagine," I said. "About all I can remember about her is that she was really pretty, in an English sort of way."

"Prettier than me?" Vicki challenged.

"No one's prettier than you," I told her. I meant it.

Vicki was supposed to leave in three days, but she extended her stay. I stayed too, and Grace let me move out of the motel and into a spare bedroom in her house so it wouldn't cost so much. Vicki's other set of grandparents lived seventy or eighty miles to the south, near Newburgh, and when they invited her down to visit them for a week, the London trip was put off again.

Vicki said I could come with her to meet this other group of family, and I did so, wanting to put off parting as long as pos-sible. Two days before Vicki was definitely due to leave, it suddenly dawned on me that I wouldn't be able to stand it if she did. It took me another day to get up the nerve, then I asked her to marry me, not really expecting her to accept.

"I thought you'd never ask," she said, kissing me. "But *you* have to be the one to tell my father, the colonel!"

"Good thing he's six thousand miles away," I said.

Chapter 32

Vicki said she wanted to get married in Houston, and a couple of days later we flew there, necking on the airplane like a couple of high school kids. The wedding wasn't scheduled for several weeks, and in an attempt to keep things proper, Vicki moved in with the women at my grandmother's house, while I maintained my bachelor quarters down the street.

The wedding was really nice, all things considered. It was a standard, classical, church affair, with Vicki outfitted in a thousand-dollar white dress and me in a rented tux. Vicki's mom flew all the way from Bangkok to attend, and my aunt had gone to a lot of trouble setting up a reception at their house. The thing is, neither Vicki nor I had any friends in Houston, so the ten or fifteen people who attended were mostly older friends of my grandmother and my aunt.

Vicki and I really didn't notice the weirdness of it, though, and after the reception we retired to my apartment down the street and began our honeymoon . . . which ended up lasting for several months.

I say it lasted for several months because neither of us was very interested in my getting a job. I still had some of my savings left, and Vicki had brought several thousand dollars of her own into the marriage. For many weeks it was strictly days of wine and roses, and I was about as happy as I'd ever been, I guess.

We even flew down to Guadalajara, Mexico, to visit my father for a couple of weeks. Dad had driven down there pulling a camper, and Vicki and I found him at the mobile home park he was living in. He was really surprised to see us as he hadn't maintained much contact with any of the family since the divorce, and the only address any of us had for him was a post office box number.

He was sitting out on his front yard, reading a Mexican newspaper, when Vicki and I drove up in a taxi. "How the hell did you find me?" he asked. I told him it had been easy. I'd simply told the taxi driver to take us to mobile home parks where Americans lived, and at the second one we checked, I'd spotted him sitting there.

There was a young Mexican woman puttering around in Dad's camper, and he introduced us to her as his cleaning lady. Her name was Maria, she was eighteen, and a year later—when Dad died—I found out that she was actually his wife.

My father was nice to us while we were there. That first night, he and I got horribly drunk together, drinking tequila at the Holiday Inn where Vicki and I were staying. We caused a big scene of some sort, and the hotel people told me the next day that my wife and I should find a different place to stay.

Dad fixed us up with an empty, furnished apartment that he somehow had acquired the use of, and Vicki and I stayed there for free the rest of our visit. We did the full tourist routine, with Dad taking us around as our guide. Toward the end of the two-week visit, Vicki began suffering bouts of morning sickness, which confirmed our suspicion that she was pregnant.

Dad drove us to the airport when it was time to leave, and seemed subdued when he shook my hand. He had a funny look when he told me good-bye, and I think he somehow knew this would be the last time we'd see each other.

Vicki was twenty-one when we married, and had grown up as an Army brat in Europe and Asia. She felt as confused and out of place in the U.S. as I did, and I suppose we made quite a pair. She had never learned to drive, and was used to having maids and servants around to do things. She was very insecure, and wanted me to stay at home all the time, which was fine with me.

When we got back from Mexico, we decided rather than go to work, I should go to college on the GI Bill, and we moved into a small, cheap apartment that was closer to the university. As Vicki's pregnancy progressed, I went through the nightmare hassle of getting registered. Then I began attending classes, and the nightmare got worse.

You'd have to understand the mood and spirit on college campuses in the early seventies to really know what this experience was like for me and other returning veterans. Not only the other students, but the majority of the faculty, despised us. I felt like a black man at a KKK rally.

Oddly enough, I discovered that during the ten years I'd been away from school, I'd somehow become a lot smarter. In high school I'd been a mediocre B student, and I now found that I could maintain a straight A average with little difficulty. This only made my younger, fellow students hate me more, of course.

Vicki made friends easily with other women around the neighborhood, but I made none. I'd stopped communicating with my mother, aunt, and grandmother, too, because they irritated me. The only person I had to talk to was Vicki, but for me that was enough.

Back then, there was still no way to tell for sure whether a fetus was male or female, and that added a bit of drama and suspense to the event of the birth. Also back then, men still were expected to stay in the maternity waiting room while the women gave birth. Vicki had a long labor, eventually requiring a cesarean. I flipped on the TV while I awaited word on the birth and caught the evening news.

There was a new Communist offensive in Vietnam, with many reported casualties. Four more U.S. congressmen had changed sides and were now calling for immediate withdrawal of all American aid to South Vietnam. Several Hollywood starlets had staged a benefit program, the proceeds earmarked to go to the Viet Cong. Students at a major university had taken over the dean's office and were filmed running through the streets waving Viet Cong flags while burning our own.

The doctor came out, smiling, so I knew everything had gone all right. "You have a nice, healthy son, Mr. Wade. He weighs seven and a half pounds. Your wife came through it just fine. Do you have a name picked out for him yet?"

"We're calling him Leigh," I told the doctor, "after his father."

It was June 14, Flag Day.

Chapter 33

The next nine years continued on about like the first one, and I won't bore you with all the details. I dropped out of school after a year, and we moved up to Oklahoma for a while. There was a string of terrible jobs, each one seeming worse than the last. I started, then dropped out of college again. Several times I tried to control my drinking but always began again after a few months.

Vicki and I watched the fall of Saigon on television, and I stayed drunk for a whole week afterward. As the goddamned NVA tanks rolled into South Vietnam, the U.S. cut off aid. I had to listen to people like Jane Fonda chortling such bits of wisdom as: "This is only an agrarian revolution playing itself out."

When my son was in the first grade, we left Oklahoma and moved back to Houston for a year and a half. Then, still looking for some place in America we could bear to live, we moved all the way to northern New York. A year later we were back in Houston.

Vicki had started working by then, because I couldn't get a job that paid more than minimum wage and then always quit after a few weeks. I must have had a hundred different jobs during that period, all menial and meaningless.

For the entire ten years I was out of the Army, I never made one friend. A few Vietnam veterans' groups were beginning to form by then, most of them self-help organizations called "rap-groups," and Vicki urged me to join one. I refused to have anything to do with them, though. For one thing, I considered the groups to be made up of sniveling whiners. For another, I didn't think there was anything wrong with me—at least, nothing caused by the war.

Vicki stuck with me through ten years of horrible life, which was much longer than most women would have. Finally, she could stand it no more and she left, taking my son with her.

That was the rock bottom for me, and I came about as close to committing suicide as I ever have. But as they say, once you hit bottom, there's no way left to go but back up, and that's what happened. I got a job doing hard manual labor, and quit drinking for a whole year. I paid off every debt I owed, and in 1981 rejoined the Army.

Going back in the Army was like returning home after a long, difficult journey. I immediately started making new friends again, and one of these friends introduced me to his sister, a vivacious woman named Pat. We were married a few months later, I adopted her young daughter, Sasha, and Pat was soon pregnant with my second son. We named him Thomas, after the brother who'd introduced us.

Unfortunately, that marriage also unraveled after five years, but I got through it all right. I guess practice makes perfect, or as Nietzsche said, "That which doesn't kill us, makes us stronger."

In 1987, I finally figured out that maybe I really did have a drinking problem, as people had been telling me for the last twenty years, and I volunteered to attend an alcohol abuse program. I was on recruiting duty at that time, stationed in the San Francisco Bay area, and spent six weeks at Oakland (aka Oak Knoll) Navy Hospital, learning how to stop drinking. The program was a success, I guess, because I've been sober now for over ten years.

When I finally retired from the Army in 1992, my youngest son came to live with me. He and I moved back to Tucson, where I'd been raised. We ended up living in a house that's only a block from the one I grew up in back in the fifties, and I felt like I'd come full circle in my life.

The other evening, as it was cooling off a little, I was outside wandering aimlessly around near the fence. The summer breeze brought the smell of burning charcoal and of my neighbor's freshly mown grass. Overhead, the sounds from the local news helicopter faded into the distance.

"What are you doing, Dad?" my son asked, startling me out of my reverie.

"I guess I'm checking the perimeter, son, before it gets dark."

"I don't get it," he told me.

"I'll explain it all to you someday," I said, then we went back in the house.

While my son played video games in his room, I sat in my chair, watching the evening shadows grow longer. I remembered back to those days of my youth, when I'd made the decision to stand with the South Vietnamese and fight a hopeless war. We lost, just as I suspected we would, but life goes on. As Edith Piaf sang in the song she dedicated to the Foreign Legion, *"Non, je ne regrette rien."*

Tucson
September 1997

Epilogue

Some Final Thoughts for Returning War Veterans

Like many others, I had a terrible time of it after I returned home after the Vietnam War. I left Vietnam for the last time in 1971, and it wasn't until 1987 that I began to fully recover. Today there are still Vietnam veterans living in our streets who never learned to cope with their condition, and they are now joined by veterans from the Gulf War who are also facing not the "horror of the war," but the "horror of returning home."

My publisher has given me this opportunity to air my opinions on this subject, and I hope the lessons I learned about "coming home" may be of help to others. Please remember that I am speaking only for myself, and do not represent any group, official or otherwise. Also be warned that what you are about to read may step on a few toes, but if the shoe fits . . .

The Experience of War Changes People

This is an inarguable truism. Throughout recorded history, societies have been waging war on each other, and after each war, the folks who stayed home have had to put up with the horde of returning veterans. In all cases the war veterans were very different people than the ones who originally left. That was true whether they were home from the Crusades or from the burning oil fields of Kuwait.

The folks who spend the war snugly at home always feel a certain amount of guilt when the young men, many permanently maimed or badly wounded, return. Any young men of warrior age who, for whatever reason, didn't go to war feel especially guilty.*

The society the veterans return to is anxious to put the war behind it and move on to new things. The veterans are a constant reminder of their guilt, however, and much of society tries to ignore them, or as in more modern times, they are "bought off" with government handouts such as the GI Bill, Veterans Rehabilitation programs, and so on. In a few cases, such as after the Vietnam War, the veterans are actually reviled by the very people who sent them to fight.

Just exactly how are war veterans different than they were before? One of the biggest changes is that most of them come home with a new philosophy of life. The way it happened in the Vietnam War is amusing because it is so ironic.

---

* Women being involved in war, and particularly in actual combat, is a new phenomenon and still quite rare. War always has been and always will be a man-thing.

Unlike some other wars—such as WWI, during which entire Ivy League classes gladly marched off to the trenches—Vietnam was fought mainly by young men from the blue collar and the professional military classes. The supposed "elite" of American youth were not interested in the war. Many of those noncombatants were dodging the draft by attending college, and the popular theme among hip, with-it kids at the time was the idea of dropping out of the hypocritical, materialistic society that Mommy and Daddy were trying to force them into. The young antiwar kids were into drugs, mystical experiences, alternate lifestyles, communal living, and anything else that might irritate Mom and Dad back in Westchester.

About the time the war in Vietnam ended, along with the draft, those "elite" young people lost interest in all of the antimaterialistic stuff and got down to the business of making lots of money. Many of them became so-called yuppies, and today are smug, fat, wealthy, and powerful members of that same system they once claimed to despise.

Now for the ironic part. Remember when I said that the experience of war changes a person's philosophy of life? Well, the philosophy that war veterans return with is the exact antimaterialistic one that their noncombatant counterparts in the sixties had been championing. The difference is that for the war veteran, the philosophy is real, not a game.

Many of the homeless Vietnam veterans you see roaming the streets today are doing this not because they can't find work, or are lazy, but just because they really know that the materialistic, money-grubbing, yuppie lifestyle is bullshit. For them the veil was torn away by observing and taking part in the life-and-death struggle which is combat, and those men will never fit in "normal" society again.

After the Vietnam War, the American people not only disliked war veterans, but were terrified of us. Part of that fear was fostered in the populace by antiwar—and anti-American—writers and producers of film and television. The myth of the drug-addicted, kill-crazy Viet vet was born there and repeated over and over again.

The story line of their version of the returning veteran went something like: although the vet in question was indeed a scary and dangerous person, it wasn't his fault. It was the fault of the military-industrial complex because it had drafted him against his will, sent him overseas, and turned the poor, innocent boy into the horrible creature who returned home.

I think the real reason the folks back home get edgy when the war veterans return is simply that they realize so many of us no longer buy into their system, the one which tells us that wealth and position equal human worth. Veterans all know that is absurd.

A person who has rich parents or graduated from Harvard, successfully dodged the draft, and is now an up-and-coming executive—or Senate leader, or President—is no better than the war veteran, who might be working for him as a janitor. To the veteran, the important questions involve things like how a man acts when the enemy rocket and mortars start screaming in, and whether or not he is willing to risk his life attempting to aid a fellow wounded soldier. *Those* are the kinds of things that determine human worth, not what type of car a person drives or the price he paid for his tie or the size of his stock portfolio.

How to Survive After a War

The longer the war and the more actual time in combat you have, the harder your reentry into the peacetime world will be. I'll list several coping strategies here, more or less in order from best to worst. Then I'll tell you the way I did it, which is definitely not the way to go.

Method 1. Stay in the military until you retire. This is the best solution, especially if the war was fairly long. The longer you are in the military, the harder the reentry into society will be; and the more time you've spent under fire, the harder it will be to readjust to being a peacetime civilian. Just about all the friends I had during the Vietnam War were professional soldiers, and most of them stayed in after the war until retirement. As far as I know, none of them had any real problems at all, and all of them had very successful careers. If you stay in the military, you stay with a support group, other men who understand you and what you've been through. Civilians just don't get it. They never will.

Method 2. Get out of the military and go home to whatever family you still have. Do not, however, sever your ties with old military friends. Join, and become active in, a veterans group. Join the local military reserve unit of whatever service you were with. Forget about the damned war the best you can, and get on with your life. If you think you may need professional counseling, do not be embarrassed: seek it out; these days there is plenty available, and much of it is free for veterans. I had several friends during the war who did get out of the military, and this was the route the successful ones took.

Method 3. Turn to religion and philosophy. This is one of the classical methods of coping with the situation. As I mentioned earlier, the experience of war tends to jolt people out of their robotic materialistic states and forces them to see that there is much more to the human condition than they once suspected. In times past, many great philosophers and religious leaders began life as soldiers. I know of at least one notorious case of religious conversion in the Special Forces community, and this old soldier is apparently quite happy with his born-again life.

Method 4. Get out of the military, cut all military ties, and try to forget completely about the war and anything remotely connected with it. Start life all over again. Refuse to talk about or think about the war. If asked, deny you were ever even in the military. Let your hair grow long. Move out to the woods and become a recluse. Claim to be a former hippie. I know several people who have taken that approach. Oddly enough, guys who fought with special units, especially units that get a lot of attention from war buffs, often take this route, simply because they are sick of talking and thinking about the war. I know several retired Special Forces soldiers with incredible war records who are currently living this life, and I guess it works for them.

Method 5. Get out of the military, turn against all your old friends, join the other side, and become a darling of the antiwar/antimilitary left. This approach works best if it's a long war and if it's still in progress when you make your switch. I know two men who left Special Forces during the Vietnam War and pulled this routine. The biggest benefit to doing this is that you will get lots of young, caring, college babes to crawl in bed with you to soothe your horrible, recurrent war nightmares (wink, nudge). Both the guys I know who did this also got their antiwar books published years before any of us other Vietnam War writers got in print.

And now, as promised, I'll tell you how I did it, which is the WRONG WAY.

Method 6. Get out of the service with no plan. Cut all ties with old military friends and with the military in general. Pretend you were never in the military, but never stop thinking about it. Brood about the course of the war. Brood about why you got out. Stay continually pissed off at the meaningless stupidity of American civilian society. Wallow in existential angst. Abuse the substance of your choice and brood some more.

If you have read my books, you will already know that alcohol was my substance of choice when it came time for me to chemically alter the ol' brain cells. Although drug abuse by soldiers during the Vietnam War got all the media hype and attention, drugs were never really a big problem. In Special Forces, I never knew of anyone doing drugs; drugs were something the counterculture hippies did, and we in Special Forces certainly didn't want to do anything those fools were involved in! The military's main problem has always been alcoholism.

In the next section I'll tell those of you who might be interested the story of how I quit drinking after being an enthusiastic boozer for more than thirty years. For those of you who aren't interested, well, go have a cold one.

How I Quit Drinking

Since the publication of my first book, *Tan Phu*, I've received many calls from old Army buddies. Most of them start off something like this: "Read your book, Wade. Hell, I thought you'd probably drunk yourself to death a long time ago. . . ." This is pretty embarrassing, of course, and I mention it only so you will get some idea of the kind of drinker I was. What I'm trying to say is, I was the real thing, and if a person with my long, infamous background of alcohol abuse can clean up his act, anyone can.

I started drinking when I was fifteen, and by the time I joined the Army three years later, I already had a reputation among the guys as a fellow who could hold his liquor. Social drinking has always been a big part of a professional soldier's life, and that is one of the reasons I liked the Army. I want to make it clear that the Army didn't corrupt me and turn me into an alcoholic. On the other hand, the way things used to be in the Army was certainly conducive to a drinking man's way of life.

Like most alcoholics, I never really thought I had a problem with drinking. However, as the years went by and I grew older, the drinking became less and less fun and more and more grim. The hangovers were getting really horrific. As someone once wrote of Hemingway, I had crossed that thin line that separates the world's great drinkers from the world's great drunks.

I was stationed out in California on recruiting duty when I started to realize something was wrong. I was under a lot of stress, working seventy-five hours a week in an attempt to make my quota of enlistments, and my marriage was starting to fall apart. When I finally went on sick call one morning, it didn't have anything to do with drinking. The reason I sought out medical help was that I realized I was experiencing a lot of short-term memory loss. Hell, I couldn't remember my own phone number or address.

I was living on a Navy base, so it was to a Navy medical facility that I went. The Navy doctors took my complaint seriously, and I soon found myself in their clutches. I went through probably half a million dollars' worth of medical tests, including CAT scans, blood work, brain-wave exams, and, toward the end of it all, I had a talk with a shrink.

The psychologist was a woman, and she had me fill out several mental health questionnaires. One of these was a test I had often seen in such publications as *Reader's Digest*. You've probably taken them yourself. "If you answer *yes* to two of the following twenty questions," the magazine articles say, "it indicates you may have a drinking problem and should seek help."

I was honest on the test and answered eighteen "yes" out of the twenty. It seemed like a joke to me. Hell, just goes to show how stupid these tests are, I thought, because I obviously don't have a drinking problem.

The shrink thought otherwise, and she told me that it was no laughing matter. She said there was a possibility that I was suffering from something known as Korsakoff's syndrome, which was an incurably fatal condition brought on by prolonged alcohol abuse. If I was indeed in the early stages of this condition, I didn't have long to live, she told me.

"But," she continued, "we won't know for sure until the results of all your tests come back. The symptoms you mentioned may be from a brain tumor, Alzheimer's, or even AIDS." She made an appointment for me with the head neurosurgeon at the Oakland Navy Hospital, and told me to report there in two weeks for the verdict. "In the meantime, Sergeant, it is imperative that you quit drinking alcohol immediately."

It wasn't so much the thought of dying but the part about becoming a vegetable that really scared me. I went home and told my wife I couldn't have the usual afternoon cocktails with her. "I may have to stop drinking for good," I said. She gave me a strange look.

The psychologist phoned my commander at the recruiting station and told him I was a confirmed, diagnosed, dyed-in-the-wool alkie. As was the usual procedure in such cases, I was immediately relieved of recruiting duty. This didn't particularly bother me, because I loathed the job anyway.

Two weeks later I reported to Oakland for my appointment with the neurosurgeon. I was scared as hell, having had two weeks to worry about what might be wrong with me. I was ushered into a small office and told to wait there for the doctor. It was quite a long wait because the hospital was understaffed and the doctors, especially those working with nerve and brain disorders, were very busy. The whole top floor of the hospital was nothing but AIDS patients, I'd been told, and many of them were in bad neurological shape.

The door opened and the doctor, who wore the rank of O-6, hurried in. This neurosurgeon was female, Chinese-American, and all business.

She glanced over at me where I sat sheepishly on the examining table, then picked up my medical records and quickly scanned through the reams of test results. She grunted and shook her head.

"Is it serious, Doctor?" I asked, fearing the worst.

She threw the records down and turned to go. "Only thing wrong with you, Sergeant, is you drink too much. Your brain is *pickled*!" She gave me one more disgusted look and hurried back to her more urgent patients.

"Then I guess this means that asking you out for a drink after work is a waste of time," I mumbled to the empty room after she left.

"Have you stopped drinking, Sergeant?" the shrink asked me the next day when I reported back to her.

"I've stopped," I told her, "but it hasn't been easy, and frankly I don't know how much longer it will last."

"I'll see about getting you into the alcohol rehab program here at the hospital," she said. "It's full all the time, but since you have mitigating physiological problems, you should get bumped to the top of the list." She leaned back in her chair and took off her glasses. "If you volunteer for the program, it will be better all around. Will you do that?"

"Sure," I said, not really knowing what I was getting into.

The shrink picked up her phone and made a call.

The Navy Alcohol and Drug Abuse Program (ADAP) was the first military program of its type. It was eventually copied by all the other services. This was also the program Betty Ford went through, and it is the basis for the ADAP named after her. The program consisted of an intensive six-week in-hospital phase followed by a year of follow-up visits.

Even though I had been advanced to the head of the waiting list, it took three weeks for me to get an open slot. During that three weeks I managed to stay sober, and at the "suggestion" of my psychologist, even forced myself to start sitting in on AA meetings. So when I checked into the hospital in September of '87, I was already ahead of the game.

My "class" had about thirty people in it, and we were broken down into six-person therapy groups. Because it was a Navy facility, most of the other attendees were Navy men and women. There were also a good many Marines and several Army personnel. As far as I remember, there weren't any Air Force people.

Until I started that program, I'd always felt Army guys were hard-charging, two-fisted drinkers. After a few days, however, I understood why the Navy was the first of the services to start an ADAP: the Navy had some hard-core, drinking dudes! Songs like "What Do You Do with a Drunken Sailor?" don't come out of thin air, you know.

One of the guys in my class was an E-6 who had about twenty-five years in Navy service and was almost as old as I was. He was not there because he wanted to be, but because he'd been ordered to the program by his command. Seven days before his report date, that ol' swabbie had started to drink, and he kept it up right until time to check in. They had to bring him to the hospital in an ambulance, and he spent the first week up in detox getting dried out enough to be able to figure out what was going on.

"Hell," he told me, "I figured if this was going to be my last chance to get drunk, then I might as well do it up right."

Every day, we spent our mornings in our small groups having therapy sessions. That involved sitting around in a circle with one of the staff as a facilitator, and talking about various things, such as why we drank, our past lives, what was bugging us, and all of that sort of thing. It wasn't a whole lot of fun, because every day one or two people would break down and start crying, and it was such an intense, emotion-charged atmosphere that sometimes the whole group would begin bawling and blubbering right along. There was a lot of hugging among group members, something that was encouraged by the facilitator.

We had one woman in our therapy group, who was the only civilian in our class. She was the wife of the E-6 swabbie I mentioned earlier and was a longtime drug abuser herself. One day she passed around photographs that showed her back when she was a hippie in the sixties, hanging out in San Francisco. Another time she went into a long story, saying how bad she felt about us poor guys who had been brutalized by the Vietnam War, and that it was no wonder to her so many of us were drunks and drug addicts . . . the usual line of crap.

"Look, goddamnit," I finally exploded, "it wasn't the fucking war that screwed me up, it was having to come back here and deal with stupid, ignorant bastards like you! The war was nothing compared to what it's been like since I came back to this god-awful place."

That started the poor woman crying, of course, and I immediately joined her. The other four guys in the group also broke down, and before it was over, we were all hugging and slobbering on each other. The facilitator was shaking his head approvingly.

In the afternoon we attended lectures on different topics concerning drug and alcohol abuse, and I discovered for the first time that drinking alcohol was very *unhealthy*. I found out that all those old wives' tales I'd heard all my life about how one drink of booze kills fifty billion brain cells were actually true! Alcohol is bad for every other cell in your body too, and if you keep it up long enough, eventually different organs are damaged—the liver, brain, and stomach being the usual ones—and you die. This information, coming as it did from medical professionals, had a very big impact on me, and I think it was one of the most beneficial parts of the program.

Every night after supper we got into Navy vans and attended local AA meetings. I am not a big fan of AA, even though it was an important part of the program. By luck, however, in that area of California there are some really cool AA chapters, with some very interesting and funny members.

We rotated to different chapters each night, but once a week we went to the meeting in Berkeley. That one was by far the best. The entertainment was so good—rivaling any comedy club—that the Berkeley meetings were always jammed. About half the people who attended the Berkeley meetings weren't even alcoholics, but people who had come just to see the show. There were actually several professional entertainers attending these meetings, whom I recognized from screen and television, but mostly the recovering drunks who got up to speak were simply amateurs—albeit usually witty, clever, and intelligent.

The attrition rate of the Navy ADAP was probably as high as that of their SEAL qualification course. After the first few weeks of very close supervision, we were allowed to go out on passes during the weekends to visit our families. Immediately upon return from these passes, there were mandatory urine and blood tests, and if the tests showed banned chemicals in your system, you were kicked out.

I got through the six weeks all right, and on the last day I went in to an interview with the head of the ADAP program, a psychiatrist. This guy was my age, held the rank of O-6, and like all the other staff personnel in the program, was a recovering substance abuser.

He looked at my medical history and told me he'd started drinking at an early age, just as I had. He stopped after a twenty-year go at it, and also suffered some short-term memory loss.

"Although some of the brain cells are actually killed and will never regenerate, most of them are simply damaged," he told me, drawing a sketch of one and showing me where the damage occurs. "They eventually grow back, but it takes a long time, something like ten years."

I nodded, and he went on.

"I need to warn you, Sergeant Wade, that you are in a dangerous position. You are lucky that you came in for medical treatment when you did and stopped drinking when you did, because once the alcohol starts actually having a measurable effect on one of the bodily organs, things go downhill very quickly."

I gulped and nodded again.

"If, say, after a year or so of sobriety, you begin to drink again, the degeneration will also pick up again, and because of the drying-out period, it will advance much faster than it would have had you continued on as you were. Within about six months you will be a helpless, mindless invalid, and a few months after that you'll die."

I thanked him and left the office. I never have figured out if he was just telling me that as a further inducement to stay sober or if it was true. I've never particularly wanted to put it to the test, however.

When I got home from my treatment, my wife told me that while I'd been gone she'd started an affair with some other guy. That put the finishing touches on our crumbling marriage. I was transferring to a new assignment in a few months, and she said she didn't want to go with me.

"I talked to my friend, the woman down the street," my wife told me. "She said her husband is an alcoholic, that he's been trying to quit for years, but never does. She said it's impossible to quit, and has never heard of anyone who has really done it."

Probably more than anything else, that little speech helped me make up my mind that I would never take another drink in my life.

They say that the first two years of abstinence are the hardest, and that if you can make it that long, things get easier. In my experience, that's how things worked out. I never suffered any of the normal withdrawal symptoms people talk about, nor did I ever have cravings for alcohol. My biggest problem was simply breaking habits of drinking that had been such a big part of my life for thirty years.

After a few months had passed, I started to become aware of the many benefits of staying sober. One of the first things to dawn on me was the fact that I suddenly had a tremendous amount of spare time—time that I had once devoted to drinking. I filled this time productively with physically active pursuits, which I also discovered were much easier to do without a hangover, and with reading.

For fear of getting in trouble, or simply of being frowned upon, I had become more and more reclusive in the latter days of my drinking career. Once sober, I realized I no longer had to schedule my life around my periods of drinking, and that I could go places anytime I felt like it. It was particularly nice being able to pass a police car without having to worry about getting stopped and possibly failing a Breathalyzer test.

Another big benefit of not drinking was that I magically had much more money in my pocket at the end of each month. I had been a drinker my entire working life, and the money required for booze had always come right off the top of my monthly budget. Hell, I was suddenly rolling in dough!

The Navy ADAP program required that I continue attending AA meetings for one year after I got out of the hospital, and I did so. As soon as the year was over, however, I stopped going. People who are big into AA will warn you that if you stop going to meetings, your chances of remaining sober are zero. However, this is not really the case. Once I stopped attending AA meetings and listening to a bunch of other whining, constantly relapsing, bellyaching drunks, it was actually *easier* for me. Each person is different, and each should search out his or her own methods to accomplish goals.

There were several activities, such as listening to and enjoying music, that I was in the habit of doing while drinking. Learning how to once again appreciate music while sober was one of my biggest challenges. It took me about a year before I could even stand music at all, because hearing it made me want to drink. When I finally was able to begin listening to it once more, the music no longer seemed to give me the same enjoyment it had while drunk. Slowly the appreciation came back, however, and in a short time I was able to get more enjoyment from it than I ever had before.

One morning about two years into my sobriety, I woke up with two realizations. In the first place, it dawned on me that I really and truly had beaten my alcoholism, which is something that very few people ever accomplish. Instead of feeling sorry for myself because I could no longer enjoy alcohol, I suddenly understood that I had done something to be proud of.

I also experienced a very subtle yet very important change of my own self-image. You might say I went through my own personal paradigm shift. The thought process that brought on this change went something like this: I had stopped smoking several years before I stopped drinking. When I did this, I didn't become a "recovering smoker," but simply a nonsmoker. When one walks into a restaurant, one is offered "smoking," or "nonsmoking." There is no third choice such as "no longer smoking, but still wishing I was, and God, ain't I pitiful?" So in my mind I became not a "recovering alcoholic," nor did I become an "exdrinker," but simply a "nondrinker," the same status I would have enjoyed had I never started in the first place. For some reason this made all the difference in the world, and after I experienced this enlightenment, I've always KNOWN with absolute certainty that I'll never have to drink again.

As the doctor promised, my brain cells apparently repaired themselves. Ten years have passed since I stopped drinking, and now I can usually remember my phone number and address when someone demands them. I'm healthy and in the best physical and emotional shape of my life, I guess, and because of this I'm able to handle the stress of single parenthood with no real problem.

Being sober has also allowed me to write three books about the Vietnam War. This accomplishment was very important to me, and I could never have done it as a drinking man.

"If you enjoyed getting shot at,
Tan Phu was a great place to be. . . ."

TAN PHU
Special Forces Team A-23 in Combat
by Leigh Wade

Vietnam, 1963. Leigh Wade was a radioman for Special
Forces Team A-23, a twelve-man unit sent to Tan Phu,
a hell on earth in the Mekong Delta where the VC had
the advantage of knowing the tangled terrain. In those
early days, Special Forces didn't have the "luxury" of
proper air, artillery, and logistical support, so patrols
moved through the black tropical night with the danger
of death lurking in every shadow. Wade left Vietnam
thinking the Americans would pull out within twelve
months, unaware that he would see five more years of
bloody combat. . . .

TAN PHU
Special Forces Team A-23 in Combat
By Leigh Wade

Published by Ivy Books.
Available in your local bookstore.

THE PROTECTED WILL NEVER KNOW

by Leigh Wade

Special Forces operator Leigh Wade outwitted death through five harrowing tours in Vietnam. In 1965, he volunteered for duty with the newly arrived 173rd Airborne and participated in the first battalion-size helicopter assault in Vietnam. In early 1966, after joining the highly classified all-volunteer C-5 unit, he engaged in unconventional warfare and clandestine ops in Cambodia.

Unlike many of his comrades, Wade lived to tell about what he saw. Captured in these pages are the combat, courage, and carnage of moments spent trapped precariously between life and death.

Published by Ivy Books.
Available in bookstores everywhere.

TEAM SERGEANT
A Special Forces NCO
at Lang Vei and Beyond

by Willaim T. Craig

The son of a career enlisted man, Bill Craig was a hard-bitten Korean War veteran and Special Forces brawler. Now here is his unvarnished account of a military career that catapulted him to team sergeant, the pinnacle of achievement for a Special Forces operator.

During Tet 1968, Craig's camp at Lang Vei was overrun by NVA, who parked a Soviet tank on his command bunker and dropped grenades down the air ducts. The riveting description of the breakout that followed and the raw courage of men fighting to save their comrades is an inspiration for anyone venturing into harm's way.

Published by Ivy Books.
Available in bookstores everywhere.

THE WAR IN I CORPS

by Richard A. Guidry

In 1967, one of the hottest areas in Vietnam was the so-called Demilitarized Zone in northern I Corps, where the NVA had abundant troops and could call up massive artillery firepower. For thirteen months, Richard Guidry, a young Marine from Texas, fought there as an infantryman in Bravo, 1/4, in some of the war's worst infantry combat.

In riveting, relentless, bloody detail, Guidry captures jungle, mountain, and grassland battles, where death could erupt in a second, your best friend could vanish without warning, and you could become just another loved one's memory.

Published by Ivy Books.
Available in your local bookstore.

FORCE RECON DIARY, 1969
by Bruce H. Norton

FORCE RECON DIARY, 1969 is the riveting, true-to-life account of survival, heroism, and death in the elite Marine 3rd Force Recon unit, one of only two Marine units to receive the Valorous Unit Citation during the Vietnam War. Doc Norton, a former 3rd Force Recon medic and retired Marine major, recounts his unit's experiences behind enemy lines during the tense patrols, sudden ambushes, and acts of supreme sacrifice that occurred as they gathered valuable information about NVA operations right from the source.

FORCE RECON DIARY, 1970
by Bruce H. Norton

Operating beyond the artillery fan of friendly forces, in the thick of a jungle war, the Marines of 1st and 3rd Force Recon companies understood that the only things keeping them alive in "Indian Country" were their own skills and courage and the loyalty they had to one another. Here is the continuing saga of life behind enemy lines by a former member of these fearless and peerless Force Recon companies.

Published by Ivy Books.
Available in bookstores everywhere.